PRAISE FOR
REIMAGINING SOCIAL SECURITY

"This book must be read by anyone interested in Social Security reform. It brings together experts from the US and abroad to examine successful Social Security reforms undertaken by other advanced countries. The examination provides a fresh perspective on how the US Social Security program can be fundamentally reformed. I finished the book with renewed optimism about the prospects for reform."
—John F. Cogan, Leonard and Shirley Ely Senior Fellow, Hoover Institution, and author, *The High Cost of Good Intentions*

"Social Security reform is neither a right- nor left-wing agenda. No program, however commendable, can command an ever-larger share of society's resources. While the book emphasizes benefits but not tax adjustments that may be necessary, I find particularly appealing how Boccia and Nachkebia illustrate how other countries—but not the US—adapt to uncertain demographic shifts in life expectancy and birth rates—a vital requirement for sustainable reform."
—Eugene Steuerle, Richard B. Fisher chair, Urban Institute

"Boccia and Nachkebia provide a welcome reality check to the Social Security policy discussion, accurately diagnosing not only our national pension system's problems but their causes. Though the picture is a daunting one, the reader is not left without answers, for not only do Boccia and Nachkebia provide their own well-considered recommendations, they also assemble the insights of other US Social Security experts as well as the best lessons from international experience. Readers of this volume will obtain a clearer sense of how Social Security reforms should be conceived and designed."
—Charles Blahous, J. Fish and Lillian F. Smith Chair, Mercatus Center, and former public trustee for Social Security and Medicare

"This book is a must-read for any policymakers who are concerned about the future of the Social Security program—and about the federal government's unsustainable finances more generally. The discussions are thoughtful and nuanced, drawing lessons from public pension systems in other countries. The authors make a compelling case for adopting a New Zealand–style flat Social Security benefit that focuses on keeping seniors out of poverty, while restoring the program to solvency and empowering all Americans to save for the future."

—Sita Nataraj Slavov, professor of public policy, Schar School of Policy and Government, George Mason University; and faculty research fellow, National Bureau of Economic Research

"Around the world, population aging has undermined financing for government pension programs. Household retirement savings have sometimes struggled to compensate. The challenges facing the Social Security program are not unique to the United States. They are worldwide challenges, and *Reimagining Social Security* has specific, actionable lessons for US policymakers on how to address them."

—Andrew G. Biggs, senior fellow, American Enterprise Institute

"America is in the Peak 65 Zone, a period where approximately 4.1 million Americans will turn age 65 every year between 2024 and 2027, or about 11,200 per day. Within the next decade, unless legislative action is taken, the Social Security retirement trust fund will become depleted, and retirees could face an automatic benefit reduction of between 20 and 25 percent. The nation faces a retirement challenge weighing the necessary tradeoffs required to support Social Security. Revenues into the program must be increased, or benefits reduced, or some combination of the two. There are no magic beans to solve Social Security's financial shortfall. But there are solutions. This book provides the public with the necessary information to be informed about the available policy solutions and policy tradeoffs required to put Social Security back into financial solvency for today's and tomorrow's retirees."

—Jason J. Fichtner, former chief economist, Social Security Administration

"This book, a conversation among policy experts, about the lessons learned from the creative Social Security reforms of other countries is a valuable contribution to the necessary discussion the American

public and policymakers must have on the overdue structural changes needed to our own Social Security system. Well organized with consistent metrics and comparisons, a particular benefit here is the wider perspective taken to include retirement policy more broadly."
—Mark J. Warshawsky, senior fellow and Wilson H. Taylor Chair in Health Care and Retirement Policy, American Enterprise Institute

"America's Social Security program has now gone more than four decades without reform. Boccia and Nachkebia perform a valuable service by detailing what we can learn from other countries' retirement systems. Several nations have demonstrated that it is possible to achieve lower rates of poverty among seniors with a better-targeted public pension system that does less to burden working adults."
—Christopher Pope, senior fellow, Manhattan Institute

"Social Security's growing deficits and impending insolvency threaten to upend the federal budget and the retirement of tens of millions of Americans. Yet most Americans and even many members of Congress do not fully grasp Social Security's financial challenges. Boccia and Nachkebia articulately define the funding challenge, explore reform options, and take us on a tour of successful reforms in other developed nations."
—Jessica Riedl, senior fellow, Manhattan Institute

"Good options must be on the shelf and ready to go when policymakers turn to solving problems. By comparing other countries' experiences to America's, *Reimagining Social Security* shows several ways to balance retirement security, prosperity, freedom, and modest taxpayer burdens. These lessons will help Congress succeed when the time comes."
—Kurt Couchman, senior fellow in fiscal policy, Americans for Prosperity

"This book shows that the US's looming Social Security crisis is not unique and that other countries were able to reform their retirement income systems while continuing to shield their elderly populations from poverty. If we adopted the reforms Boccia and Nachkebia advocate for in this book, we would not only avert a fiscal catastrophe but would have a retirement system that is more consistent with American values of individual choice and freedom."

—Alex Durante, senior economist, Tax Foundation

"The looming insolvency of the Social Security system has evolved from a long-term challenge to a near-term threat to the well-being of current and future retirees. Policymakers need look no further than *Reimagining Social Security* for a road map to reforming the nation's primary social insurance program. Boccia and Nachkebia offer solutions to this challenge that are grounded in a sweeping evaluation of international social insurance programs and can ensure Social Security remains a durable source of dignity and security for America's retirees."

—Gordon Gray, executive director, Pinpoint Policy Institute

"Social Security will be broke within a decade, before anyone of Generation X or younger receives a single full benefit. And politicians have no credible plan to fix it. The longer policymakers wait, the higher the costs will be of preserving Social Security. The good news is that common-sense changes like those discussed in *Reimagining Social Security* would not only preserve Social Security but also make it a stronger program for younger and future generations."

—Rachel Greszler, senior research fellow in workforce and public finance, Heritage Foundation, and visiting fellow in workforce, Economic Policy Innovation Center

"*Reimaging Social Security* demonstrates that while the United States has been slow to overhaul its insolvent Social Security program, it has the advantage of being able to learn from the reforms undertaken by nations facing similar demographic challenges. This book is an indispensable guide to how the United States can modernize its Social Security system to protect seniors without compromising the incentives for overall economic growth, especially by recognizing the importance of mobilizing often-overlooked private savings that benefit all without adding to the growing pressures on government debt."

—Philip Cross, senior fellow, Fraser Institute, and former chief economic analyst, Statistics Canada

"The US must have an evidence-led debate on every aspect of pensions, both public and private. It would be the first country in the world to do that. Whoever must make that decision should start with *Reimagining Social Security*. It illustrates, in detail, the different approaches adopted by selected developed countries to the universal issues. None has the answer for the US, but each has lessons for your policymakers. It's time to start that debate."
—Michael Littlewood, honorary academic, Retirement Policy and Research Centre, University of Auckland

"In aging societies, debates about retirement provisions are inevitable and difficult. Enriching them with insights from the international experience is always an eye-opener. A tremendously valuable book!"
—Martin Werding, member of the German Council of Economic Experts

"This book explains the mechanics of the US Social Security system and offers a set of potential reform options to restore fiscal stability in constructive ways. Because the format is interesting, accessible, and comprehensive, I expect this book to be useful to policymakers and researchers alike. I find the approach to be fresh and meaningful, and I offer my appreciation to the team who put this project together. Well done!"
—Frank Caliendo, professor and senior associate dean, Jon M. Huntsman School of Business, Utah State University

"Many thanks to the Cato Institute for fostering such an important global dialogue through its Social Security Symposium and the valuable publication that followed. It was a privilege for me to contribute Sweden's experience and perspectives and, perhaps even more importantly, to engage in an exchange of ideas with the distinguished experts present. Such exchanges are essential to enriching our collective understanding of how to effectively combine financial sustainability with benefit adequacy, as demonstrated by successful reforms. I firmly believe that this kind of collaboration is vital to shaping informed and hopeful policies for the future."
—Kristoffer Lundberg, acting head, Policy Analysis Unit, Swedish Ministry of Health and Social Affairs

REIMAGINING SOCIAL SECURITY

GLOBAL LESSONS
FOR RETIREMENT
POLICY CHANGES

REIMAGINING SOCIAL SECURITY

ROMINA BOCCIA
AND IVANE NACHKEBIA

All panel discussions are edited transcripts from the Cato Institute's event "Social Security Symposium: A Global Perspective," on May 9, 2024.

Copyright © 2025 by the Cato Institute.
All rights reserved.
Cato Institute is a registered trademark.

Hardcover ISBN: 978-1-964524-68-9
Ebook ISBN: 978-1-964524-69-6

Library of Congress Cataloging-in-Publication Data available.

Cover design by Derek Thornton, Notch Design.

Printed in the United States of America.

1000 Massachusetts Ave. NW
Washington, D.C. 20001
www.cato.org

CONTENTS

ABBREVIATIONS
xv

1. INTRODUCTION
1

2. OPENING REMARKS
Romina Boccia
29

3. OPENING REMARKS
Senator Bill Cassidy (R-LA)
31

PART ONE: **US SOCIAL SECURITY**

4. THE US RETIREMENT SYSTEM
37

5. PANEL DISCUSSION
US Social Security and OECD Retirement Systems: A Comparison
61

6. PANEL DISCUSSION
Securing the Future: Rethinking US Social Security
79

PART TWO: CANADA AND NEW ZEALAND

7. THE CANADIAN RETIREMENT SYSTEM
103

8. THE NEW ZEALAND RETIREMENT SYSTEM
123

9. PANEL DISCUSSION
Lessons from the Canadian and
New Zealand Pension Systems
141

PART THREE: GERMANY AND SWEDEN

10. THE GERMAN RETIREMENT SYSTEM
163

11. THE SWEDISH RETIREMENT SYSTEM
183

12. PANEL DISCUSSION
Lessons from the German and
Swedish Pension Systems
207

13. CONCLUSION
223

ACKNOWLEDGMENTS
231

APPENDIX
233

NOTES
239

ABOUT THE AUTHORS
262

ABBREVIATIONS

AIME	Average Indexed Monthly Earnings
ATP	*allmän tilläggspension*
CBO	Congressional Budget Office
C-CPI-U	Chained Consumer Price Index for All Urban Consumers
COLAs	cost-of-living adjustments
CPI	Consumer Price Index
CPI-W	Consumer Price Index for Urban Wage Earners and Clerical Workers
CPP	Canada Pension Plan
CPS	Current Population Survey
DB	defined benefit
DI	Disability Insurance
DIR	demographic impact ratio
EITC	Earned Income Tax Credit
EU	European Union
EU-SILC	EU statistics on income and living conditions
FBR	federal benefit rate
FPL	federal poverty level
FRA	full retirement age
GDP	gross domestic product
GIS	Guaranteed Income Supplement
GRV	Gesetzliche Rentenversicherung
IEA	Institute of Economic Affairs
IRAs	individual retirement accounts
MBM	Market Basket Measure
MSD	Ministry of Social Development

NDC	notional defined contribution
NEWS	National Experimental Well-Being Statistics
NIMs	non-income measures
NZS	New Zealand Superannuation
NZSF	New Zealand Superannuation Fund
OAS	Old Age Security
OASI	Old-Age and Survivors Insurance
OECD	Organisation for Economic Co-operation and Development
OPM	official poverty measure
PPP	purchasing power parity
QPP	Quebec Pension Plan
RET	retirement earnings test
RPP	Registered Pension Plan
RRSP	Registered Retirement Savings Plan
SEP	Simplified Employee Pension
SNAP	Supplemental Nutrition Assistance Program
SSA	Social Security Administration
SSI	Supplemental Security Income
START	Supplemental Transition Accounts for Retirement
TCJA	Tax Cuts and Jobs Act
TFSA	Tax-Free Savings Account
TTE	Taxed-Taxed-Exempt
UN	United Nations
USAs	universal savings accounts
VRS	voluntary replacement share
WHO	World Health Organization

1

INTRODUCTION

Amanda looked in the rearview mirror as she pulled out of the hospital parking lot, the setting sun casting a warm glow on the quiet streets. After a long day of seeing patients and filling out paperwork, she was eager to get home, her stomach growling. She looked forward to reading a few pages of *The Adventures of Pinocchio* to her kids as she tucked them into bed. It was a familiar routine—10-hour shifts followed by a quick dinner with her family, then collapsing on the couch once the house finally quieted down. But today, as she turned on the radio, something caught her attention.

NPR mentioned a report about Social Security and what would happen when the government can no longer pay full benefits. Experts invited on the program spoke of troubling projections: the trust fund was expected to run dry by 2033, and without reforms, benefits would be cut across the board. Amanda's grip tightened on the steering wheel. She'd heard these warnings before, but tonight it hit differently. She was 35—far from retirement, but not so far that she could ignore it.

As the report continued, Amanda's mind wandered. Her parents, comfortably retired, would be fine, but what about her? What about her kids? She knew that she paid for Social Security with every hard-earned paycheck, and that each payment reflected her hours upon hours of tending to patients in pain, administering IVs, and emptying bedpans. But what guarantee was there that the system would still be intact when she needed it? Rising debt, potential benefit cuts, and the burden of future taxes weighed heavily on her thoughts. She imagined a future where, despite all her hard work, her family might struggle in ways she never anticipated.

Pulling into her driveway, Amanda turned off the car and sat for a moment. She couldn't shake the feeling that the system was failing workers like her—people trying to build a secure future for their families while also meeting their day-to-day needs in an uncertain world.

* * *

Later that evening, after the kids were finally asleep, Amanda sat down with her husband, Dave, at the kitchen table. The house was quiet, save for the hum of the dishwasher. Dave was flipping through his phone, but Amanda's mind was elsewhere.

"I heard something on NPR today," she said, breaking the silence. Dave looked up, curious. "It was about Social Security. They were talking about how the trust fund might run out by 2033."

Dave raised an eyebrow. "Isn't that something they've been saying for years?"

"Yeah," Amanda sighed, "but it just feels . . . real now. I've been working for over a decade, we've been paying into the system all this time, but what if it's not there when we retire? I don't want to end up relying on something that might disappear."

Dave leaned back in his chair, thoughtful. "Your parents seem fine, though. They're retired and not worried about it."

"That's the thing," Amanda said, a hint of frustration in her voice. "They're set. They've already locked in their benefits. But for us? We're still paying in, every paycheck, and there's no guarantee it'll be there for us when we need it. I looked into it, and if Congress doesn't act, benefits will automatically get cut by 20 or 25 percent. That's huge."

Dave nodded, but Amanda could tell he wasn't as rattled as she was. "We're saving, though. We've got retirement accounts."

"I know," Amanda replied, "but what if higher taxes kick in because they have to cover Social Security's shortfall? That's going to hit our take-home pay. Or what if the economy slows down because the government is borrowing more and more to cover the gap? I feel like we're the ones who are going to get squeezed, Dave. Our generation. And it's not like we can just stop paying into Social Security—we're stuck with it."

Dave set his phone down, sensing the depth of Amanda's concern. "So, what do you think we should do?"

Amanda shrugged, feeling the weight of the uncertainty. "I don't know. It feels like we're paying into this system that was designed for a completely different world. I mean, it was set up 90 years ago, and the way things are going now, it just doesn't add up anymore. People are living longer, fewer workers are supporting more retirees, and the debt is skyrocketing."

She paused, her voice quieter. "It's like we're caught in the middle. We're working hard, raising kids, paying taxes, saving for the future . . . but what if that future isn't as secure as we think? It just feels like a broken promise."

Dave reached across the table and took her hand. "We'll figure it out," he said, offering comfort, though Amanda could tell the uncertainty had started to weigh on him too.

"I hope so," she said softly, staring at the pile of bills on the counter. "I just hope we're not the ones left picking up the pieces."

* * *

Amanda's story is far from unique. Like millions of workers in their 30s and 40s, she is navigating a system designed 90 years ago, one that often feels out of step with the realities of today's economy. While policymakers work to safeguard the benefits of current retirees—those already secure in their retirement plans—the long-term challenges for younger workers are often overlooked.

As Social Security's debt burden continues to grow, the cost of maintaining the program threatens to limit opportunities for Amanda's generation and the ones to follow. Higher taxes, reduced benefits, and an uncertain economic future loom large if no reforms are made. Amanda's fear that her payroll taxes may not result in the promised security reflects the cognitive dissonance shared by many: workers are paying into a system they increasingly worry won't support them when the time comes.

This book aims to explore this dilemma. While protecting today's retirees is crucial, real reform must consider the well-being of current and future workers. Social Security reform cannot simply be about patching up an aging system—it needs to reflect the financial realities and changing demographics of the modern workforce.

By drawing on lessons from other developed countries such as Canada, Germany, New Zealand, and Sweden, this book provides a fresh perspective on how the United States can restructure Social Security to protect seniors from poverty in old age and preserve economic opportunities for younger workers, ensuring that Amanda's story—and the stories of millions like her—don't end with broken dreams.

Reform shouldn't just aim to sustain government-provided benefits, but to build a stronger, more flexible approach that enables workers to own and control more of their personal retirement savings while ensuring that the US budget is sustainable for generations to come.

Social Security at a crossroads

The consistent long-term increase in life expectancy is one of humanity's most remarkable achievements. Between 1900 and 2023, global average life expectancy has more than doubled, from 32 years to 73 years.[1] This progress has been fueled by human ingenuity and innovation.

However, this impressive trend has been accompanied by decreasing fertility rates—the projected average number of children born to a woman—dropping from nearly 5 in 1950 to 2.3 in 2023.[2] These demographic developments have resulted in a higher proportion of older individuals in nearly every country.[3] According to the United Nations, by 2050, the number of individuals aged 65 and older will be twice that of children under 5 and roughly equal to the number of children under 12.[4] The World Health Organization also predicts that the proportion of the global population over 60 will double from 2015 to 2050.[5]

These developments have led to large increases in the old-age dependency ratio, the number of individuals aged 65 and over (seniors) per 100 individuals aged 20 to 64 (working-age people), negatively affecting the finances of public pensions that run on a pay-as-you-go model. Under this system, taxes paid by current workers are dedicated to covering the benefits of current retirees. As the number of seniors and the ratio of seniors to workers both increase, pension expenditures rise, adding to the burdens on the working population. In fact, the Organisation for Economic Co-operation and Development (OECD) identifies population aging as the primary factor straining public pension systems, leading to reforms among many member nations.[6]

According to the OECD, the average old-age dependency ratio more than doubled from 13.8 seniors per 100 workers in 1952 to 31.3 in 2022.[7] This trend will continue, with projections indicating that the ratio will reach 53.8 by 2052 and 66.1 by 2082. The United States is no outlier, with its old-age dependency ratio roughly doubling between 1952 and 2022, from 14.9 to 29.4, and projected to reach 43.4 by 2052 and 57.7 by 2082.

While the US old-age dependency ratio is lower than the OECD average and is projected to remain so, population aging has nevertheless affected Social Security, the largest component of public old-age provisions in the United States. Beyond demographic challenges, structural elements within Social Security (such as the benefit calculation formula) have made the program's finances increasingly unsustainable over the years. The Social Security Board of Trustees has been warning about the program's unsustainable trajectory since 1984.[8] Yet the last time major changes were adopted was in 1983, in response to an impending benefit cut scheduled into law as the trust fund was running short at the time.[9]

Now Social Security is projected to become insolvent in less than a decade. Based on available revenues, it will be unable to pay scheduled benefits to retirees.[10] By 2033, when Social Security's trust fund becomes depleted, total benefit payments for all retirees, regardless of their income or assets, could be cut by 21 percent.[11]

The fact that Social Security has covered its benefit obligations so far, or will continue to do so until 2033, does not mean the program has been financially sound. Since 2010, the program's revenues—collected from workers' payroll taxes and the taxation of benefits—have been consistently lower than the program's costs, resulting in cash-flow shortfalls.

To cover Social Security's funding shortfalls, the Department of the Treasury has been borrowing money to make benefit payments—based on the balance recorded in the program's trust fund. This can be confusing because the trust fund is often described as holding "asset reserves," which may suggest it has real savings set aside. In reality, when Social Security was running surpluses, instead of saving those funds, the government immediately spent the money. In return, it credited the Social Security trust fund with special-issue bonds—essentially IOUs—promising to compensate the program when needed. Since the program began running cash-flow shortfalls in 2010, the government has been borrowing to honor those IOUs. As a result, between 2010 and 2023, the US government borrowed US$1.08 trillion.[12] The government will borrow an additional US$4.1 trillion between 2024 and 2033, including interest costs, until the IOUs in the trust fund are exhausted, leading to possible benefit cuts, if current law holds.[13]

As the Social Security trust fund is becoming depleted, the political opportunity for meaningful reform is growing. In May 2024, the Cato Institute organized the half-day conference, Social Security Symposium: A Global Perspective, to bring attention to the urgent need for policy action. The symposium panel discussions were dedicated to analyzing Social Security's challenges and potential solutions, informed by how the retirement systems of Canada, Germany, New Zealand, and Sweden have dealt with similar political and demographic challenges. This book features transcripts of the conversations held at the symposium to capture those insights for posterity and to allow readers to draw their own conclusions. These discussions provided valuable insights, identifying potential ways to not only stabilize Social Security's finances but also to modernize the program and expand private retirement options for younger workers.

- On the first panel, Andrew G. Biggs (American Enterprise Institute) and Romina Boccia (Cato Institute) compared the US Social Security system with other OECD retirement systems, with Veronique de Rugy (Mercatus Center) moderating the discussion.
- On the second panel, Philip Cross (Canada, Fraser Institute) and Michael Littlewood (New Zealand, University of Auckland) focused on the pension systems of Canada and New Zealand, highlighting key lessons that could inform US reforms. This panel was moderated by Chris Edwards (Cato Institute).
- On the third panel, Kristoffer Lundberg (Sweden, Swedish Ministry of Health and Social Affairs) and Martin Werding (Germany, Ruhr University Bochum) provided insights from Sweden and Germany, sharing how these countries are dealing with demographic and economic pressures, with Romina Boccia as moderator.
- On the fourth and final panel, Jason Fichtner (Bipartisan Policy Center) and Rachel Greszler (Heritage Foundation) examined ways to secure Social Security's future and improve the system, with Andrew Moylan (Arnold Ventures) serving as moderator.

The diverse perspectives and experiences shared at the symposium offer valuable lessons for US legislators and their staff, the White House, academics, and think tanks.

This chapter introduces these lessons, drawing insights from Canada, Germany, New Zealand, and Sweden, which have proactively reformed their retirement systems to confront challenges similar to those the United States is facing now. It also highlights certain negative aspects of international reforms and elements of these countries' retirement systems that should be avoided when considering changes to Social Security or the broader US retirement system.

The subsequent chapters begin with a discussion of the US retirement system, identifying the causes of Social Security's challenges and potential reform options. This is followed by a detailed overview of the retirement systems of Canada, New Zealand, Germany, and Sweden, identifying the most relevant takeaways and additional reform options for the United States, as the US government faces challenges similar to the ones these countries have already met.

To evaluate the other countries' systems and their relevance to US reform, we use metrics, such as replacement rates, the old-age dependency ratio, and pension spending as a share of gross domestic product (GDP). We have also introduced a new measure, the demographic impact ratio (DIR), which combines a country's pension spending as a percentage of GDP with its old-age dependency ratio. The DIR shows how pension spending is affected by an aging population, which in turn allows us to see which countries face greater demographic pressures on their pension systems even if their raw pension spending numbers are similar. We further rely on the World Bank pension pillar framework to compare individual system components and the role they play in the retirement of our comparison countries' residents.

Our goal in hosting the symposium and in publishing this book is to promote reforms to the US Social Security system that enhance long-term fiscal sustainability while respecting individual freedom, reducing the burden on current and future workers, and ensuring a fair and efficient system that meets the needs of vulnerable retirees without compromising economic growth.

Key frameworks and metrics for evaluating retirement systems

The term "retirement system" encompasses more than just government-provided old-age benefits. Developed economies, including the OECD member nations,[14] aim to alleviate old-age poverty and support their populations in accumulating retirement wealth through a combination of mandatory and voluntary sources of retirement income. Therefore, while this book primarily focuses on Social Security, it provides a comprehensive overview of the US and international retirement frameworks, evaluating their mandatory and voluntary components. This approach allows us to identify potential improvements in the overall US retirement system beyond Social Security.

To compare retirement systems across countries effectively, the book uses the World Bank's five-pillar model, which (confusingly) starts with zero. This structured framework—summarized in Box 1.1—provides a clear understanding of a nation's retirement system and the role of its various components or pillars.

Box 1.1: The World Bank pension pillar framework

- **Zero pillar:** The primary objective of this pillar is to provide minimum anti-poverty protection to seniors. Usually financed from general revenues, zero-pillar programs provide a flat benefit to all recipients who meet certain eligibility criteria, such as age and residency requirements. The benefit can be either universal, available to all seniors irrespective of their income or assets, or means-tested, where the flat rate decreases or is fully clawed back as income or assets increase. The benefit may also be subject to income taxes.
- **First pillar:** This pillar refers to mandatory "social insurance" schemes, where benefits depend on an individual's lifetime earnings and years of paying dedicated taxes. These schemes typically operate on a pay-as-you-go basis, with current workers' taxes funding current retirees' benefits. This structure makes the schemes vulnerable to demographic pressures, as a lower worker-to-beneficiary ratio weakens the program's financial stability. While first-pillar pensions also contribute to old-age poverty protection, their primary objective is to replace retirees' preretirement income to maintain their standard of living in their senior years.
- **Second pillar:** This pillar includes mandatory private savings schemes, where benefits are strongly linked to individuals' contributions. Contributions are invested in private savings accounts and are not used to pay benefits to other retirees. The investments are typically managed by third parties, usually selected from government-approved

entities. Benefits depend on contributions made and investment returns. While specific design features vary by country, the primary objective of second-pillar schemes is to supplement other public pension sources and provide additional retirement income.
- **Third pillar:** This pillar includes voluntary savings by individuals that can take the form of occupational or personal retirement plans. Governments often offer tax advantages to encourage participation in these schemes. Third-pillar plans give individuals more freedom in their consumption and saving decisions, allowing them to save for retirement at their discretion.
- **Fourth pillar:** This pillar encompasses various other sources of retirement support, such as family assistance to the elderly, other social programs (e.g., health care, housing), and individual financial and nonfinancial assets (e.g., corporate stock ownership, homeownership).

Source: Robert Holzmann, Richard Paul Hinz, and Mark Dorfman, "Pension Systems and Reform Conceptual Framework," SP Discussion Paper no. 0824, World Bank, June 2008.

To evaluate the effectiveness of the retirement systems discussed in the country chapters, we use a variety of metrics, most of which are drawn from the OECD's biennial *Pensions at a Glance 2023* report, which also provides the necessary data.[15] Additional metrics have been included to provide a more comprehensive assessment of each retirement system. To convert local currencies to US dollars for consistent cross-country comparisons, we used purchasing power parity (PPP) data from the OECD, International Monetary Fund (IMF), or World Bank, depending on data availability. These sources were accessed between July 1 and August 31, 2024. Each country chapter summarizes the country's system according to the World Bank's pillars and the following metrics, and compares it to the US retirement system:

- **Old-age dependency ratio:** This metric measures the number of individuals aged 65 and over (typically retirees) per 100 individuals aged 20 to 64 (typically workers). This metric is crucial for assessing demographic pressures on pension systems, particularly those operating on a pay-as-you-go basis. An increase in the ratio—indicating a higher proportion of retirees (who receive benefits) to workers (who pay for the benefits)—negatively affects the system's sustainability. Life expectancy, fertility rates, and migration rates influence the ratio.
- **Replacement rate:** This metric measures the ratio of retirement benefits to an individual's lifetime earnings, showing how income from public or voluntary retirement plans compares to earnings during working years. The OECD calculates this rate for full-career workers who enter the labor force at age 22 and work until the normal retirement age, using projected benefits under current laws. While the OECD offers replacement rate figures for low, average, and high lifetime earners, we primarily highlight those for average earners, presenting information for other income levels where necessary. Notably, the OECD provides replacement rates of voluntary plans only from countries with high coverage, including four of the five countries studied in this volume—Canada, Germany, New Zealand, and the United States.
- **Voluntary replacement share:** This measure is calculated by dividing the replacement rate provided by voluntary retirement plans by the total replacement rate of a country's retirement system, which includes all sources of retirement income (both public and private, mandatory and voluntary). Except for Sweden, the countries in our case study all have high coverage of voluntary plans, so this metric provides a meaningful way to understand the role of voluntary plans in maintaining a retiree's standard of living. This metric is particularly relevant for assessing the third pillar of a retirement system, voluntary savings.

- **Participation rate in voluntary retirement plans:** This metric measures the percentage of the working-age population that participates in voluntary retirement plans. Unless otherwise noted, the data are sourced from OECD's *Pensions at a Glance 2023* report, which presents participation rates for occupational and personal plans as separate categories. This metric is useful for evaluating the third pillar of a retirement system, as it highlights the extent to which individuals engage in voluntary savings to support their retirement income.
- **Voluntary retirement assets as a share of GDP:** The OECD provides data on voluntary retirement assets as a share of GDP, offering insights into the level of retirement savings accumulated through voluntary plans, including employer-sponsored and personal plans. This metric is useful for assessing a retirement system's third pillar of voluntary savings, providing additional information about the level of individual autonomy in retirement planning.
- **Total spending on public pensions as a share of GDP:** This metric indicates how much of a country's economic output is dedicated to supporting retirees. While the OECD provides these figures for its member nations, it often includes programs that provide benefits to retirees but are not strictly old-age pension programs, which are the focus of this book. For example, in addition to Social Security spending, the US pension expenditures figure presented by the OECD includes civil servant pensions, veterans' pensions, and the Railroad Retirement program. Because of this, the chapters on international systems present both the OECD data and the expenditures for the old-age programs relevant to this book, comparing them to Social Security spending. Furthermore, the chapters also include per-person spending, calculated by dividing the total pension figure by the country's population and adjusting for purchasing power parity, offering insights into the burden on individuals.

- **Demographic impact ratio:** This metric provides additional insights into the pressure that an aging population places on a public pension system. The DIR is calculated by multiplying a country's pension spending as a percentage of GDP by its old-age dependency ratio. This adjustment allows for a more accurate comparison between countries by factoring in the influence of aging populations on pension systems. A higher DIR indicates that a pension system is under greater strain because there is a larger senior population consuming a fixed percentage of national output. For example, two countries may spend a similar percentage of their GDP on pensions, but if one has a significantly older population and consequently higher DIR, it indicates that the country with the higher DIR is experiencing more demographic pressure, which may not be evident in its raw pension spending total.
- **Poverty rate among seniors:** Alleviating old-age poverty is a core objective of the public part of a country's retirement system. As such, the poverty rate among seniors is a key metric when evaluating the effectiveness of public pension programs. While the OECD provides data on old-age income poverty, it relies on a relative income measure, which can lead to misleading results. Specifically, the OECD considers an individual to be living in poverty if his or her income is below 50 percent of the median equivalized household income in a country.[16] However, falling below this threshold does not always imply living in poverty, especially in wealthier countries with higher median incomes. The OECD poverty figures do not say much about the share of the population truly living in poverty (meaning lack of access to basic needs such as food, clothing, and shelter). Rather, these figures are more indicative of income inequality.

  A better approach would involve country-specific income poverty thresholds or universal measures that are not affected by country-specific circumstances. For this reason, in addition to the OECD senior poverty data, this book includes poverty figures from other sources, such as national statistical offices or government ministries. That said, caution is necessary when comparing these figures to US senior poverty data, as countries use different methodologies to define and measure poverty.

In addition, official measures reported by the US Census Bureau tend to overstate senior poverty levels because the underlying data understate seniors' incomes.[17] Specifically, the Census Bureau's poverty rates are calculated based on the Current Population Survey, which fails to account for most of the income seniors derive from private retirement plans such as 401(k)s and individual retirement accounts (IRAs). Recognizing this problem, the Census Bureau released the National Experimental Well-Being Statistics (NEWS), which revised the Census Bureau's 2018 poverty estimate. The result was a significant decrease in estimated senior poverty, from the initial 9.75 percent to 5.73 percent.[18] While the Census Bureau has not yet adjusted senior poverty figures for other years, we can assume they are lower than previously reported.

- **Homeownership rate among seniors:** This metric reflects the percentage of seniors who own their homes. It is a key indicator we use to assess the fourth pillar of other sources of retirement income support.
- **Median senior net worth:** This metric reflects the median value of seniors' total assets—both financial and nonfinancial—after subtracting liabilities. It provides insight into seniors' overall financial security.

These metrics also help evaluate how a country's retirement system compares with one that has minimal government involvement and that emphasizes individual responsibility and personal savings over state income support.

A fully libertarian system would leave individuals entirely responsible for their retirement savings, with voluntary charity, mutual aid societies, family, friends, and other community support—not compulsory government redistribution—as the safety net for poor seniors. A more politically realistic goal would be to limit government provision to only a basic pension benefit that is focused on alleviating poverty in old age. Instead of generous taxpayer-provided benefits, such a system would rely more heavily on private savings, allowing competition to drive innovation and efficiency in private retirement products, including investment accounts and private insurance options. Regulations would be limited to ensuring transparency and protecting against fraud, while individuals would have the freedom to choose how to save and invest for their retirement as they deem best. This approach would aim to increase personal choice and substantially reduce government intervention, moving policy more toward core libertarian principles of self-reliance and economic freedom.

International lessons and reform options for Social Security in the United States

Other developed countries' experiences with retirement system reforms offer important lessons for US policymakers looking for practical and effective strategies to strengthen Social Security and the broader US retirement system. A clear trend emerges when analyzing the approaches of countries such as Canada, Germany, New Zealand, and Sweden: these nations have proactively addressed the challenges of demographic shifts and economic pressures. Moreover, they have embraced bold, transformative reforms to enhance the sustainability, fairness, and efficiency of their retirement systems—providing valuable blueprints for potential policy innovation by US policymakers.

The last major Social Security reform in the United States occurred in 1983. Since that time, by contrast, the countries profiled in this volume have implemented substantial changes to their retirement systems.

For example, Sweden in 1994 partially privatized its public pensions by introducing the Premium Pension, which directs a portion of workers' contributions into private accounts and allows individuals to choose how their funds are invested. Then, in 2022, the Swedish

Parliament passed a reform that will link pension eligibility ages to average life expectancy, starting in 2026.[19]

Canada in 1998 improved the financial outlook of the Canada Pension Plan (CPP) and in 2009 introduced Tax-Free Savings Accounts (TFSAs), flexible savings vehicles that allow Canadians to save for retirement and other goals without restrictions typically found in traditional retirement accounts.[20]

In 2004, Germany, recognizing the pressures of an aging population on its earnings-related scheme, implemented an automatic stabilizer that inversely linked benefit growth to adverse demographics.[21]

Finally, in 2007 New Zealand introduced KiwiSaver, a voluntary saving scheme with automatic enrollment and flexibility to opt out, with the goal of increasing retirement savings.[22]

This proactive approach to reforming both public pensions and private retirement savings is in stark contrast with Congress's inactivity. With Social Security's insolvency date on the horizon, the window for substantial, forward-looking changes is narrowing. However, policymakers still have a wide range of options before them. They should explore these possibilities—including a more fundamental transformation of Social Security rather than mere tweaking around the edges—with an open mind.

By drawing lessons from the following international examples, US policymakers can ensure the long-term sustainability of Social Security without introducing additional tax burdens or increasing the federal debt. By adopting more transformative changes, Congress can modernize the system to better enable younger workers to own and control more of their own retirement assets, while protecting seniors from old-age poverty.

The following is a summary of key reforms, inspired by international practices that US legislators should consider.

- **Raising the Social Security eligibility age:** As noted, demographic shifts are putting significant strain on pension systems, especially those operating on a pay-as-you-go basis, where current workers pay for the benefits of current retirees. Put simply, when there are fewer workers to support each retiree, the financial burden on the working population increases significantly.

An effective way to address this challenge is to raise the retirement age. Doing so can alleviate the pressure on younger workers and distribute the impact of an aging population across generations.

In 2007, Germany passed legislation to gradually raise the eligibility age for its Statutory Pension Insurance from 65 to 67, starting in 2012, with full implementation due in 2031.[23]

Similarly, Sweden increased the earliest age to receive its earnings-related Income Pension from 61 to 62 in 2020.[24] In 2023, this threshold was further increased from 62 to 63, with another increase to 64 scheduled in 2026. The eligibility age for the basic Guarantee Pension was increased from 65 to 66 in 2023 and will further increase to 67 in 2026. Starting in 2026, both of these thresholds will be indexed to average life expectancy at 65, a measure aimed at mitigating the effects of projected increases in Sweden's old-age dependency ratio.[25] Notably, 25 percent of OECD nations have adopted such a link.[26]

Congress, like the German Bundestag and the Swedish Riksdag, should be more proactive in addressing its country's demographic challenges and their impact on Social Security. Since the introduction of Social Security, the average life expectancy at birth has increased by nearly 16 years.[27] Furthermore, between 1935 and 2022, life expectancy at 65 increased from 12 years to 17.5 years for men and from 14 years to 20.2 years for women.[28] On the other hand, the fertility rate has substantially declined, reaching its record low in 2022.[29] Meanwhile, Social Security's full retirement age has only been raised by two years, a change that was phased in so slowly that it took nearly 40 years to fully implement.[30]

The aging of the US population has been a primary factor driving the increases in Social Security costs.[31] To mitigate these effects, Congress should raise the early and full retirement ages further and index all eligibility thresholds to rise with increases in longevity. Phasing in a gradual increase by three years each, from 62 to 65 and from 67 to 70, respectively, would be an appropriate target, followed by continued automatic adjustments based on increases in life expectancy.

The Congressional Budget Office (CBO) estimates that raising the full retirement age from 67 to 70 for workers born in 1981 or later would reduce the program's costs by $95 billion from 2025 to 2034 and eliminate 33 percent of the program's 75-year actuarial deficit.[32] This reform would improve both the program's finances and its intergenerational fairness, easing the burden on younger workers, who fund the benefits of often wealthier retirees. Moreover, it may encourage longer labor force participation and thereby boost economic growth.

- **Transitioning Social Security to a flat-benefit structure:** Social Security is an earnings-related program that primarily focuses on replacing lifetime income, rather than on alleviating senior poverty. This structure results in lower benefits for those with low lifetime earnings—who are most vulnerable to old-age poverty—while higher earners receive relatively high benefits compared to retirees in other developed countries. For example, in 2024, the maximum annual benefit a retiree could receive was about US$60,000, four times the senior poverty threshold.[33]

  One alternative to an earnings-related structure is a flat-benefit system, which provides anti-poverty benefits to all eligible seniors regardless of their individual earnings history. By concentrating on poverty elimination, such a system would be more effective at reducing old-age poverty and less expensive, depending on its features, such as the level of benefits provided.

  An example of a flat-benefit pension is the New Zealand Superannuation (NZS), which offers basic benefits to all retirees who meet the residency requirements. While the

NZS replacement rate for low-income retirees is higher than the OECD average and what US Social Security provides, the replacement rate for higher earners is significantly lower than the OECD average and Social Security.[34] This structure has resulted in low poverty rates among seniors in New Zealand, along with relatively low program costs.

In 2021, the New Zealand Ministry of Social Development conducted a study that adapted the European Union's material and social deprivation index for New Zealand. This index measures deprivation based on the inability to afford basic necessities, such as adequate home heating or a balanced diet. The study found that about 4 percent of New Zealand seniors experienced material and social deprivation in 2018.[35] When compared with 27 European Union countries, along with Norway and Iceland, only 7 countries had lower rates than New Zealand.[36] Notably, New Zealand's senior material deprivation rate was lower than that of some wealthier countries, such as Germany, France, and the Netherlands. (The United States was not included in this study, so we cannot make direct comparisons in that regard.)

New Zealand's pension expenditures, at 4.9 percent of GDP, were significantly lower than both the OECD average and total US pension spending of 7.1 percent of GDP.[37] However, this US figure includes the costs of civil servants' pensions, veterans' benefits, and the Supplemental Security Income program. When comparing share of GDP, NZS's was slightly lower than Social Security's, at 4.9 percent and 5 percent, respectively, in 2023.[38] However, part of this difference can be attributed to the higher US old-age dependency ratio.[39]

Canada's and Sweden's retirement systems also feature basic pensions with wide coverage, although these programs complement their earnings-related schemes.

Canada's Old Age Security and Guaranteed Income Supplement programs have proven effective at reducing old-age poverty while costing only 2.59 percent of Canadian

GDP in 2023.[40] Comparisons with the United States are more relevant in this context since Canada uses a similar poverty calculation methodology. However, there are important differences between the two methodologies, meaning these comparisons should be made with caution. According to the Census Bureau's NEWS, the more accurate estimate of the US senior poverty rate in 2018 is 5.73 percent.[41] In comparison, Canada's old-age poverty was slightly lower at 6 percent that year.[42]

Sweden's Guarantee Pension, along with other means-tested benefits, achieved the lowest rate of material and social deprivation in the EU at just 1.9 percent in 2023, while costing less than 1 percent of Swedish GDP.[43]

A more libertarian retirement system would favor Swedish-like means-tested benefits, which are less costly because they are provided only to those in poverty. However, such systems tend to discourage saving and investment and are prone to individuals gaming the system. For example, individuals might reduce reported assets or transfer them to family members in order to qualify for means-tested benefits. If Congress were to transition Social Security to a universal flat-benefit system like NZS, it would still be less expensive than the current system, depending on the level of benefits provided. The new system might provide prorated flat benefits to all seniors based on their number of years worked. Eligibility might require at least 10 years of work, with full benefits after 35 years, regardless of annual earnings.

Under these eligibility criteria, CBO estimates that replacing the current benefit structure with a uniform Social Security benefit set at 150 percent of the federal poverty level would fully eliminate the program's 75-year deficit and result in an actuarial surplus.[44] If Congress is unwilling to implement such a fundamental change, it should at least consider reducing benefits for wealthier retirees.

- **Implementing an automatic balancing mechanism into Social Security:** Political considerations have led US politicians to delay implementing Social Security reforms that, while improving the program's finances, would be politically unpopular. For example, raising the Social Security eligibility age is a prudent step, but fear of backlash from voters discourages many lawmakers from even discussing such a reform. To date, the politically safer option has been to delay addressing Social Security's problems. Yet this procrastination has only worsened the program's financial outlook, setting the stage for imposing higher costs on younger generations by exempting previous generations from sharing those costs.

  A potential solution to mitigate the effects of this political timidity is to introduce an automatic balancing mechanism into Social Security. Such a mechanism would adjust system parameters to ensure the program is balanced in the long term, avoiding indiscriminate benefit cuts or ill-advised payroll tax increases at the time of the trust fund's exhaustion. Earnings-related schemes in Canada, Germany, and Sweden all feature automatic stabilizers.

  For example, if the Chief Actuary of Canada determines that the Canada Pension Plan is unsustainable over 75 years, federal and provincial financial ministers are required to devise a plan to fix the program's finances. If they fail to act, an automatic stabilizer is triggered, freezing benefit growth and increasing CPP taxes automatically.[45] This mechanism has helped maintain the CPP's long-term sustainability.

  Germany adopted an automatic balancing mechanism for its Statutory Pension Insurance program in 2004.[46] Known as the sustainability factor, it is inversely linked to the ratio of retirees to workers paying taxes into the system. If the ratio increases, annual benefit increases are reduced. Additionally, if the system's finances are deemed unsustainable, the Statutory Pension Insurance tax rate rises to help restore balance.[47] This tax increase, in turn, slows benefit growth, as the benefit adjustment formula factors in changes in the tax rate. In other words, as pension taxes go up, the growth in benefits slows down to distribute the financial burdens of demographic changes between workers (who pay higher taxes) and retirees (who receive slower benefit increases).

Similarly, in 2001 Sweden introduced an automatic balancing mechanism to address demographic trends that threatened to strain the Income Pension's finances.[48] If the program's liabilities exceed its assets, the mechanism is activated and slows the rate of growth in pension balances (which determine future payouts) and benefits, ensuring the system always remains balanced. For example, in the aftermath of the Great Recession, the mechanism was triggered to stabilize the system by slowing the growth of both notional balances and benefits. Between 2010 and 2017, this slowdown mitigated the impact of the 2008 financial crisis on the system's finances.[49]

If Congress remains unwilling to enact fundamental changes to Social Security's structure, it should, at a minimum, implement an automatic balancing mechanism into the system. Such a mechanism should align the program's costs with its revenues, by slowing the growth in benefits and adjusting the program to reflect changing demographic realities. However, Congress should not increase taxes on workers to fund the cost of rising benefits, which would reduce workers' disposable income and further displace private savings.

Importantly, such a mechanism could also encourage timely action by policymakers, as its activation would result in changes that would directly and immediately affect voters, encouraging more regular debate of available policy solutions. The prospect of automatic adjustments could motivate politicians to take preventive measures to avoid more unpopular changes, thus eliminating delays that worsen the program's financial outlook and reduce the number of available policy options that can be applied across generations. Even if politicians remain reluctant to act, the system would self-correct.

- **Establishing universal savings accounts (USAs):** The US retirement system's third pillar, which includes voluntary retirement savings, is stronger than those in most other OECD countries. More than half of American workers participate in private retirement plans, and voluntary savings represent an important source of US seniors' retirement income.[50] Yet there is room for improvement.

    To increase personal savings, including among workers who are not contributing to currently available retirement accounts, Congress should consider introducing USAs. These accounts would function similarly to existing retirement accounts such as IRAs, but without the same restrictions. Specifically, a Roth-style USA would allow individuals to contribute after-tax earnings that would grow tax-free, and withdrawals would also be tax-exempt. Individuals would not be restricted from accessing their funds until age 59½, as is the case under current retirement account rules, and so would have the freedom to use their savings at any time and for any purpose. This flexibility is particularly important for low-income and younger workers, who are often reluctant to lock away their funds until retirement.

    Canada introduced such accounts, called Tax-Free Savings Accounts, in 2009, and they have gained widespread popularity.[51] Notably, TFSA adoption rates among younger and low-income Canadians are higher than adoption rates for traditional retirement accounts.[52] Following Canada's example, Congress should consider establishing USAs to boost personal savings especially among low-income and younger workers. Making it easy for workers to save in these accounts automatically, similarly to how workers save in 401(k)s through automatic payroll tax deductions, would further facilitate participation across a broader section of the US population.

Avoid higher taxes and excessive benefits

It is important to recognize that some of these countries' reforms are less favorable and should not be adopted in the United States. For example, the 1990s Canadian CPP reforms sharply increased the CPP tax.[53] While a sharp payroll tax increase could cover Social Security's long-term actuarial deficit, it is one of the least desirable ways to address the program's financial problems.[54] If the required payroll tax increase was implemented immediately, payroll taxes would need to increase from 12.4 percent to 16.7 percent. This would raise the annual payroll tax burden for a median earner with US$60,000 in annual income by US$2,600, bringing that individual's total payroll tax burden to more than US$10,000 per year.[55] Burdening American workers with a steep tax hike to finance the benefits of significantly wealthier retirees is economically damaging and unfair, especially when there are better options to address the program's financial challenges.[56]

Canada has also expanded the CPP, beginning in 2019, by gradually raising the tax rate from 9.9 to 11.9 percent by 2023,[57] and introducing an additional 8 percent tax on higher earners, on earnings that fall within a specific range.[58] The stated objective of these significant tax hikes was to increase CPP benefits. However, various fiscal experts have criticized the CPP expansion, arguing that it unnecessarily raised the tax burden on workers, as Canadian seniors have sufficient retirement income without an expanded benefit.[59] Congress should resist similar calls to expand Social Security, such as a bill proposed by Sens. Bernie Sanders (I-VT) and Elizabeth Warren (D-MA) that would increase program benefits and saddle the economy with a US$33.8 trillion tax hike.[60] If US policymakers want to enhance retirement income, they should pursue policies that encourage more personal savings, rather than introduce detrimental multitrillion taxes on workers, investors, and small businesses.

Moreover, in some respects, Social Security and the US retirement system outperform the public pensions and the broader retirement systems of the other countries discussed in this book, and these advantages should be maintained. For example, the German Statutory Pension Insurance tax of 18.6 percent is higher than the Social Security payroll tax and the OECD average.[61] Additionally, the government's role in retirement is significantly larger in Germany than in the United States. Government-provided benefits made up 68 percent of total senior income in Germany, compared with 39 percent in the United States.[62] This highlights the stronger role of voluntary retirement savings in the United States, a strength that should be preserved, as it secures Americans' freedom to save and invest as they deem best for themselves.

A similar pattern can be seen when comparing the Swedish and American retirement systems. In Sweden, individuals have very limited autonomy in retirement planning, with most workers required to participate in two government-run programs, alongside occupational pensions established through collective agreements. As a result, only 5 percent of total retirement income in Sweden comes from voluntary savings.[63] Furthermore, 71 percent of all senior income comes from government-provided benefits, compared with 39 percent in the United States.[64] Greater individual autonomy in retirement planning is a positive feature of the US retirement system that should be safeguarded and ideally enhanced. US policymakers should resist any push toward a system with more compulsion and government involvement.

Apart from the potential reforms drawn from the experiences of Canada, Germany, New Zealand, and Sweden, members of Congress should also consider the following:

- **Indexing initial benefits to prices instead of wages:** Initial Social Security benefits grow with wages to account for improvements in the economy and standard of living. However, wages tend to grow faster than prices, so this approach often results in adjustments that far exceed the increases needed to preserve purchasing power. In addition, wage indexing leads to inconsistencies, where workers with similar career histories receive significantly different benefits in real terms, depending on when they retire.[65]

    Switching to indexing initial benefits to prices would remove these disparities while avoiding a significant drop in the standard of living of seniors upon retirement, compared to their preretirement years. Importantly, this shift would significantly improve the program's financial outlook, closing about 85 percent of Social Security's long-term funding gap.[66] Limiting this change to the highest 70 percent of earners would close 47 percent of the program's funding gap.

- **Adopting a more accurate inflation adjustment measure:** Every year, Social Security benefits are adjusted through cost-of-living adjustments (COLAs) to ensure that the purchasing power of seniors' benefits does not erode over time because of inflation. However, the Social Security Administration (SSA) currently uses an outdated measure called the Consumer Price Index for Urban Wage Earners and Clerical Workers (CPI-W), which reflects the purchasing behavior of only 3 in 10 Americans.[67] In addition, the CPI-W does not account for the substitution effect, whereby consumers opt for cheaper alternatives when the price of a certain good rises. Thus, it covers a too-small subset of workers and does not reflect real-world consumer decisions.

    The Chained Consumer Price Index for All Urban Consumers (C-CPI-U) is a more accurate measure because it covers a larger subset of workers and better accounts for real-world consumer behavior. Specifically, it considers the spending patterns of 8 out of 10 Americans and factors in the substitution effect.[68] Adopting the C-CPI-U measure would adjust seniors' benefits for inflation more accurately and result in savings in Social Security's long-term costs. According to the CBO, if implemented in 2026, switching to the chained CPI would save Social Security US$204 billion by 2034.[69]

- **Reducing benefits for wealthier beneficiaries:** By discontinuing COLAs at the top end, this change avoids benefit cuts for current retirees and reduces real benefits for higher earners.[70] In addition, Congress should consider adjusting the Social Security benefit formula to reduce benefits based on higher lifetime earnings.[71]

Congress has a range of policy options to significantly improve Social Security. The time to act is now, as delaying necessary reforms reduces the number of effective measures and deepens the program's financial challenges. US lawmakers must overcome political concerns about Social Security reform if they wish to prevent the looming across-the-board benefit cuts that would harm vulnerable seniors, without relying on further borrowing or imposing vastly larger tax burdens on younger workers.

This chapter began with the story of Amanda, a 35-year-old nurse grappling with the unsettling uncertainty of what Social Security might look like when she retires and how her taxes and economic opportunities might change as the government tries to address the program's financing challenges. Through Amanda's personal reflections and conversations with her husband, we explore the concerns shared by many middle-aged workers—fears about rising debt, potential benefit cuts, and the sustainability of a system designed for a different era.

Structural challenges facing Social Security, including the impact of demographic shifts such as increasing life expectancy and the growing old-age dependency ratio, significantly affect the US financial outlook. Social Security's projections of insolvency by 2033 are well known. Less well known are the borrowing mechanisms currently used to cover shortfalls, which will add more than US$4 trillion to the public debt if Congress waits until the last minute to make changes.[72]

While it is essential to make financial tweaks to avoid indiscriminate benefit cuts, higher debt, and taxes, Congress should also consider a more fundamental restructuring of Social Security, focusing program benefits on seniors who need financial support in old age the most while enabling younger workers to accumulate and control more of their personal retirement savings in ways they deem best. As the robustness of the private voluntary retirement savings system illustrates, Americans are capable of saving for their own needs. Congress can enable even more workers to save by introducing more flexible accounts such as USAs and reducing workers' tax burden.

2

OPENING REMARKS: ROMINA BOCCIA

Good morning, distinguished guests here in our auditorium and online.

It is my pleasure to welcome you to the inaugural Cato Social Security Symposium.

My name is Romina Boccia, and I'm the director of Federal Budget and Entitlement Policy here at the Cato Institute.

Today, we're gathered to deliberate on one of the most pressing issues of this decade: reforming Social Security.

As the program's trustees reminded us earlier this week, legislative inaction will trigger a severe benefit cut by 2033.

Our discussions today are informed by a global perspective. And while we will explore a variety of proposals, please don't take any comments from our speakers or moderators as specific policy endorsements.

Cato is excited to share with you that we're in the process of building our own in-house Social Security model, which we will leverage over the coming years to propose and score a comprehensive Social Security reform plan.

The discussions today and over the coming months will inform our policy considerations and will be captured in a book for posterity. More on that soon.

We're privileged to have with us today, Sen. Bill Cassidy, who has advanced a commendable bipartisan approach to addressing the challenges facing Social Security.

His collaboration with Sen. Angus King has been pivotal in bringing this issue to the forefront of our national discourse.

Senator Cassidy's initiative, the *Bill on the Hill* video series, has been instrumental in raising public awareness about the potential benefit cuts that Social Security beneficiaries might face.

And last, his inquiries to US Treasury Secretary Janet Yellen and his appeals to President Biden underscore the senator's dedication to finding sustainable solutions for America's retirement system across party lines.

Here at the Cato Institute, our mission is to originate, disseminate, and advance solutions based on the principles of individual liberty, limited government, free markets, and peace.

Today's symposium aligns with that commitment by seeking to foster Social Security solutions that enable an American society that is freer, happier, and more prosperous.

Please join me in extending a warm welcome to Senator Cassidy.

3

OPENING REMARKS: SENATOR BILL CASSIDY (R-LA)

I was just at breakfast with a gentleman from the EU [European Union], and we talked about many things. He asked, "But what about your debt?" The Europeans are concerned about our debt. The Global South cannot borrow money because our interest rates are absorbing capital worldwide, making it more difficult for the Global South to develop. Social Security and other entitlements are a major part of this problem. These issues are so important that we've got to do something. While solutions like cutting benefits or raising taxes exist, both are politically nonstarters.

We tried to look at the fundamentals and come up with a different approach to address this and other issues. In five minutes, I'll explain our idea.

First, let's talk about what actuaries say. The Social Security trust fund will be insolvent in nine years. There are excess dollars paid in some years, which go into the trust fund. Ideally, this trust fund should have been invested in high-yield assets, but it was put into Treasuries and cash instead. They bought a lot of Treasuries at 1, 2, 4, and 5 percent interest rates, and now we're in a high-inflation environment. In this environment, the 1 percent Treasury is losing value. That Trust

Fund is like the Silicon Valley Bank of pension funds, with a maturity risk all related to interest rates. So we've missed this investment opportunity.

We have a "big idea," recognizing that the investment strategy of the trust fund has not really contributed. In fact, it's been negative for the financial health of Social Security. Instead, we propose setting up a separate investment fund. We will fund it with $1.5 trillion over five years. This money could be borrowed or raised by selling government assets. For example, President Trump suggested developing more oil and gas resources to help Social Security. Frankly, that could fund this over 10 years. You put that $1.5 trillion in, and you allow it to grow.

Using the Rule of 72, the amount doubles every 72 months or so. If you don't touch it and reinvest all the dividends, it grows significantly, looking like a martini glass. Around year 60, it blossoms out, addressing 70 percent of the unfunded accrued liability plus the borrowing cost.

This approach is incredibly powerful. Another problem with our current law is that when the Social Security trust fund becomes insolvent, benefits are automatically cut to match income. This would result in a 21 percent cut in benefits, doubling the rate of elderly poverty. Another part of our proposal is to repeal that portion of the law and borrow money in the interim. So when I say the "big idea" offsets 70 percent, it is offsetting the unfunded accrued liability and the borrowing costs required to fund that.

Some might say, "Oh, you should just cut benefits or raise taxes." Politically, that will never work. Our solution might not be perfect, but it's like foreign policy: you're choosing the least bad option. I once told this to a former high-ranking Democratic official who was nitpicking our proposal. He had an epiphany and said: "You're right. One side doesn't want to raise taxes. Neither side does. One side doesn't want to cut benefits, and neither side does." So the only way to meet our obligations is by another mechanism.

Let me finish with this. Every other funded pension fund around the world uses this strategy. Eight pension funds in Canada were failing about 20 years ago. Now, they are all in good financial health because they adopted this investment strategy, principally investing in the United States with about a 10.5 percent rate of return. The federal government has done this with the railroad retirement pension fund. Under George W. Bush, due to more retirees and fewer workers, they invested proceeds in the market. Now the railroad retirement pension fund is in good shape.

The Norwegians do this. Globally, everyone else does it except the Social Security retirement system. But we're not going to do this with the trust fund itself. Instead, we'll set up a parallel fund.

Thank you for considering this issue. You will hear from other speakers today who may have heard about our proposal. Some will be critical, and some will be laudatory. But I conclude by saying this is the least bad option. If we're going to do something, it has to be something that can pass the United States Congress and be signed into law.

At one point, we had seven Democrats and seven Republicans, as well as House members from both parties, willing to support our proposal. Then President Biden, in his State of the Union address (after we had briefed the White House on four different occasions), attacked Republicans on Social Security. Afterward, one of my Democratic colleagues said: "The deal's off. He's running for reelection on Social Security." We need more responsibility than that. This conference is about creating an atmosphere of responsibility, which is expected rather than avoided.

Thank you.

PART ONE
US Social Security

4

THE UNITED STATES RETIREMENT SYSTEM

In August 1935, amid the most severe economic crisis in US history, the federal government established Social Security. Congress designed the program to provide anti-poverty protection for seniors. It was not designed as a welfare program. Instead, it relies on the "social insurance" model, a pension scheme in which workers pay into the system via payroll taxes and receive earnings-related benefits in retirement. This model was first introduced in Germany by Chancellor Otto von Bismarck in 1889.[1]

Social Security was originally intended to be a modest income support program, providing benefits to individuals who lived more than three years beyond the average age of life expectancy.[2] When President Franklin D. Roosevelt signed the Social Security Act in 1935, he remarked:

> We can never insure one hundred percent of the population against one hundred percent of the hazards and vicissitudes of life, but we have tried to frame a law which will give some measure of protection to the average citizen and to his family against the loss of a job and against poverty-ridden old age.[3]

Today, the program's annual benefits, which can exceed US$60,000 for an individual, far exceed the modest "measure of protection" FDR envisioned.[4]

Initially, Social Security provided old-age pensions only to retired workers. In 1939, Congress amended the program to extend benefits to dependents and survivors.[5] Despite the program's expansion, the Social Security Board, in a report sent to President Roosevelt recommending these changes, remained cautious about the program's costs and, like Roosevelt, viewed Social Security as a modest income support program. The report stated:

> It is impossible under any social insurance system to provide ideal security for every individual. The practical objective is to pay benefits that provide a minimum degree of social security—as a basis upon which the worker, through his own efforts, will have a better chance to provide adequately for his individual security.[6]

Social Security was further expanded 17 years later, when President Eisenhower signed the 1956 Amendments to the Social Security Act, introducing the Disability Insurance program.[7] Today, 90 years after its launch, Social Security is the largest federal program, with expenditures on its Old-Age and Survivors Insurance (OASI) and Disability Insurance (DI) programs totaling US$1.35 trillion, or 5 percent of US gross domestic product (GDP).[8]

Importantly, Social Security has been running cash-flow deficits since 2010, which has led the program to tap into its trust fund reserves to pay out full benefits. These reserves exist only on paper and serve primarily as accounting entries that track how much of Social Security's historical surpluses the federal government has spent. In reality, nothing has been saved for the program over time, and the Department of the Treasury borrowed about US$1.08 trillion to cover the program's funding shortfalls from 2010 to 2023.[9] The program will add more than US$4 trillion to federal deficits until 2033. At that point, Social Security will exhaust its trust fund reserves—or, more accurately, the government's authority to borrow further to pay promised Social Security benefits will expire.[10] That could lead to a 21 percent benefit cut for all beneficiaries, regardless of their income or need.[11]

Congress has less than a decade to address Social Security's funding shortfall before automatic benefit cuts take effect. Congress should focus on securing anti-poverty protections for low-income seniors while reducing benefits for wealthy retirees. Such measures would uphold the program's original intent—avoiding poverty among seniors—while addressing the unsustainability of the current system without imposing excess tax burdens on younger workers.

When Social Security was introduced in 1935, its minimum eligibility age of 65 was three years above average life expectancy at the time.[12] Since then, average life expectancy has increased by 16 years, while the program's full retirement age (FRA) has increased by only 2 years. Meanwhile, fertility rates have substantially declined during this period.[13]

Social Security is a pay-as-you-go system in which younger workers fund the benefits of current retirees. Demographic changes, including an aging society and declining birth rates, put significant strain on the system's finances—unfairly burdening younger generations who face higher taxes to finance benefits that often support wealthier retirees.[14] It's the Robin Hood principle in reverse, with the federal government taking funds from relatively poorer workers to give them to relatively wealthier retirees.

To begin to address the problem, Congress should raise the early and full retirement ages by three years, from 62 to 65 and from 67 to 70, respectively. These changes would improve the program's finances and enhance intergenerational fairness. Individuals who are unable to work until age 65 due to severely disabling conditions would still be able to apply for Social Security disability benefits.

Initial Social Security benefits are rising too quickly because they are tied to wage growth instead of to price changes. Wages tend to grow faster than prices, leading to benefits that outpace inflation and exceed what most retirees contributed through payroll taxes. For example, someone retiring in 2020 who received US$37,333 in annual benefits would receive over US$7,500 more than a retiree with the same work history who started collecting in 1995 (adjusted to 2020 dollars). The 1995 retiree's benefit increased from US$17,688 to US$29,785 over 25 years due to inflation adjustments, while the 2020 retiree starts with a significantly higher amount due to wage indexing. This creates a growing gap between the taxes that workers pay and the benefits they receive, a problem worsened by the declining ratio of workers to retirees. If initial benefits were indexed to prices instead of wages, benefits would grow in line with inflation. That would help bring benefits closer in line with what retirees have paid into the system and would close about 85 percent of Social Security's long-term funding shortfall.[15]

Moreover, Social Security beneficiaries receive outdated annual inflation adjustments that do not accurately reflect the actual impact of cost-of-living increases. The Social Security Administration (SSA) currently relies on an outdated measure to adjust benefits to inflation, which reflects the spending patterns of only a small segment of Americans and fails to account for changes in consumer behavior when prices rise.[16] Adopting a more accurate inflation measure would generate substantial savings over time while protecting the purchasing power of seniors' benefits.[17] Congress should adopt the Chained Consumer Price Index for All Urban Consumers (C-CPI-U) to more accurately tie Social Security benefit adjustments to actual changes in the price level and their impact on purchasing power.

Beyond these changes, Congress should consider a more fundamental reform of the Social Security system. Social Security should primarily focus on keeping seniors out of poverty. The current earnings-related structure provides the highest benefits to higher earners who are capable of saving for their own retirement. Social Security could transition to a prorated flat-benefit structure that prioritizes reducing old-age poverty. A new flat benefit would require at least 10 years of qualifying earnings with the full benefit payable after 35 years, regardless of the size of individual lifetime earnings. This system would continue to distinguish Social Security from means-tested old-age welfare, such as the Supplemental Security Income (SSI) program, while prioritizing government benefits for lower-earning workers who have less capacity to save. In addition, Congress should reduce payroll taxes in line with lower benefit costs to enable workers to save more on their own.

Such a targeted approach would be less expensive and more effective at combating old-age poverty, aligning the Social Security program more closely with its original goal of protecting the most vulnerable seniors from privation.[18] If Congress is unwilling to adopt such a fundamental change in Social Security's structure, it should, at a minimum, consider reducing benefits for wealthier retirees.

Policymakers should also consider strengthening voluntary retirement accounts, another crucial component of the US retirement system. Existing retirement accounts such as 401(k)s and individual retirement accounts (IRAs) represent an important source of income for many seniors, with a significant portion of American workers participating in these plans.[19] However, participation in private plans could be further increased if Congress were to establish universal savings accounts (USAs). These accounts would offer the same tax advantages as current retirement accounts at lower contribution levels but without withdrawal restrictions. International experience suggests that USAs could be particularly appealing to low-income and younger Americans, who are generally reluctant to lock away their funds until the age of 59½.[20]

The current American retirement system is far from the libertarian model. That model would leave individuals fully responsible for their own retirement savings, with no forced redistribution, relying on voluntary charity, mutual aid societies, and other community initiatives to support poor seniors. Nor is the system close to a slimmed-down approach that would provide only a basic pension benefit focused on reducing old-age poverty, while leaving income replacement and consumption smoothing decisions up to individuals. Instead, it relies on an earnings-related structure that replaces the preretirement income of medium and high earners, leading to unsustainable expenditures that significantly contribute to the country's fiscal challenges. The program's financial burden could be reduced within the existing structure by adopting reforms to lower its long-term costs. The ultimate realistic policy goal should be to transform Social Security into a more targeted benefit scheme focused on poverty prevention while reducing the program's costs. Additionally, lower-income and younger Americans could be encouraged to save more by the introduction of flexible savings accounts such as USAs.

Overview of the US retirement system

The US retirement system includes all of the World Bank pension framework's pillars except the second—mandatory private pensions.

Supplemental Security Income represents the zero pillar of the system. However, it is not a senior-only benefit, and it is also available for disabled and blind individuals. As of 2024, SSI covered only 4 percent of individuals aged 65 and over, with its total expenditures amounting to 0.24 percent of GDP.[21] Notably, its maximum benefit, which decreases with the recipient's other income, is lower than the senior poverty threshold.[22]

Social Security is the primary government retirement program in the United States, and it is the US system's first pillar. It is an earnings-related, pay-as-you-go scheme consisting of two programs: Old-Age and Survivors Insurance and Disability Insurance. Benefits are calculated through a progressive formula that replaces a higher share of pre-retirement earnings for lower-income retirees.[23] As of 2024, the Social Security payroll tax of 12.4 percent was only applied to earnings up to US$168,600, which also limits the program's benefits.[24] The current full retirement age ranges between 66 and 67, depending on the birth cohort. Early retirement at age 62 reduces benefits, while late retirement up to age 70 leads to increased benefits.[25]

Social Security is the largest government program, accounting for 5 percent of US GDP.[26] Notably, it has been running cash-flow deficits for the past 15 years, meaning its sole sources of revenue—payroll tax revenues and the taxation of benefits—have been insufficient to cover expenditures.[27] For instance, in 2023, payroll taxes and the taxation of benefits covered approximately 90 percent of the program's total expenditures, with the remaining gap filled by redeeming trust fund reserves, which is essentially borrowing from the public.[28] Unless Congress intervenes, Social Security will continue operating with cash-flow deficits, contributing US$4.1 trillion to federal deficits until its insolvency in 2033, triggering benefit cuts.[29] The program's deteriorating finances are strongly related to the aging of the American population, with the old-age dependency ratio, which has been steadily rising, projected to increase further from 29.4 in 2022 to 57.7 by 2082.[30] Additionally, the program provides overly generous benefits for the highest earners, with the maximum benefit exceeding US$60,000 annually, four times the poverty threshold.[31]

The third pillar of the US retirement system, which comprises private retirement plans such as 401(k)s and IRAs, is stronger than that of most other OECD countries, with plan assets reaching US$35 trillion, or 137.5 percent of GDP in 2022.[32] Contributions to these plans are tax-advantaged, where investment gains are always tax-free, and either contributions or withdrawals are tax-free, depending on whether the account is traditional or Roth-style. Contributions to both 401(k)s and IRAs are limited to certain thresholds, and early withdrawals before the age of 59½ are subject to a 10 percent penalty.[33] As of 2023, 56 percent of American workers participated in employer-sponsored plans such as 401(k)s, while 25.3 percent of households owned IRAs as of 2019.[34] Combined with Social Security, these voluntary plans achieve a 73.2 percent replacement rate for an average worker, which is significantly higher than the OECD average of 55.3 percent.[35]

The fourth pillar of the US retirement system is also strong, with 76.1 percent of seniors aged 65–74 and 81 percent of those 75 and older owning their homes.[36] In 2022, roughly 31 percent of the average American senior's income came from sources other than government-provided benefits and private savings in retirement accounts.[37]

Zero pillar

The US retirement system does not include a basic benefit program exclusively for seniors. However, SSI, a means-tested flat benefit provided for blind and disabled individuals, also covers people aged 65 and older with little or no income. The program's primary objective is to provide a guaranteed basic income for its beneficiaries to help them afford basics such as food and shelter.

To qualify for SSI, individuals must meet both categorical and financial criteria. In addition to blindness, disability, or being 65 or older (the categorical requirements), applicants must have resources below a specific threshold—US$2,000 for individuals and US$3,000 for couples. These resources include cash or liquid assets that can easily be converted to cash, such as stocks, bonds, and savings accounts, but do not include an individual's primary residence. Notably, these resource thresholds are not adjusted for inflation.[38]

The maximum SSI benefit, known as the federal benefit rate (FBR), was US$943 per month for an individual in 2024, which is about 18.4 percent of the average US wage and is lower than the poverty threshold for individuals aged 65 and over.[39] The FBR is adjusted annually for inflation. However, an eligible individual's "countable income," which includes earnings from work and nonwork income such as Social Security, is subtracted dollar for dollar from the maximum benefit to determine one's monthly payment. In February 2024, the average SSI payment for a senior was US$575.

The Social Security Administration manages the SSI program. However, the program is not part of Social Security and is financed from general revenues, with its total expenditures for all beneficiaries (not just seniors) amounting to US$64.6 billion, or 0.24 percent of GDP in fiscal year 2023.[40] Despite being independent from Social Security, one of the goals of the SSI program is to supplement Social Security income for seniors. However, in 2024, SSI covered only 2.4 million, or 4 percent, of the American senior population (individuals over the age of 65).[41] By the end of 2022, 57 percent of senior SSI beneficiaries were also receiving Social Security.

First pillar

Social Security is the first pillar and the central component of the US retirement system, providing old-age, survivor, and disability benefits. It is an earnings-related scheme in which individuals pay 12.4 percent of their wages in payroll taxes. This tax is divided equally between employees and employers, while the self-employed pay the full 12.4 percent. The payroll tax is allocated between two programs:

10.6 percent funds the OASI, and the remaining 1.8 percent goes to the DI program. Unless stated otherwise, the term "Social Security" refers to the OASI program for the remainder of this chapter.

Earnings subject to payroll taxes are capped at US$168,600 as of 2024.[42] This threshold is designed to avoid indefinitely increasing high benefits while maintaining a link between individual earnings and benefits, as benefits are related to the taxes paid by workers. According to 2022 OECD data, this threshold stood at 227 percent of the average gross wage in the United States. Among the 36 OECD member nations with earnings-related pension schemes, 8 have no such cap, while 12 set a lower limit.[43]

To become eligible for Social Security benefits, an individual must pay into the system for at least 40 quarters (10 years), earning at least US$1,730 per quarter (2024 threshold).[44] Full benefits are accessible once an individual reaches the full retirement age, which varies between 66 and 67 based on a retiree's birth year. For those born in 1960 or after, the FRA starts from the age of 67. All retirees can opt to start receiving benefits from the age of 62 or delay their retirement up to the age of 70, with early retirement reducing and delayed retirement increasing monthly benefits.[45]

Since Social Security's inception in 1935, the FRA has increased by only two years despite significant changes in life expectancy and fertility rates.[46] When the program began, the average life expectancy was 61.7, more than three years lower than the original FRA of 65.[47] Since then, life expectancy has increased by almost 16 years to 77.5, while the FRA has increased by only two years.[48]

Meanwhile, the fertility rate has significantly decreased over the years, dropping to its historic low in 2022.[49] As a result of these dynamics, the US old-age dependency ratio, defined as the number of individuals aged 65 and over per 100 individuals aged between 20 and 64, has substantially increased over time. As noted, this ratio, which was 29.4 in 2022, is expected to rise to 57.7 by 2082, although it will remain lower than the OECD average.[50]

The development of this trend is critical for Social Security, as the program is a pay-as-you-go scheme. In such schemes, payroll taxes collected from current workers fund the benefits of current retirees

FIGURE 4.1

Senior Americans are the wealthiest age group
Median net worth by age group, thousands, 2022

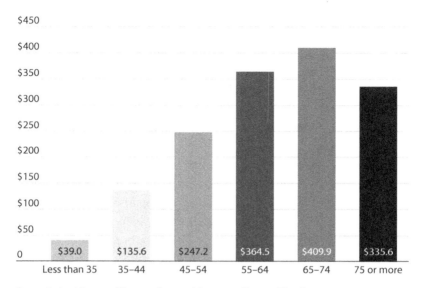

Source: Federal Reserve, "The 2022 Survey of Consumer Finances," October 18, 2023.

rather than being saved in either individual or government accounts. In other words, workers' payroll taxes are not set aside to fund their own retirement, with the Supreme Court ruling that individuals do not have a property right to their Social Security payments.[51] Notably, seniors receiving benefits are wealthier than the younger workers who pay for them. As shown in Figure 4.1, Americans aged 65 to 74 have the highest median net worth among all age groups.[52]

Social Security is an intergenerational income transfer program, where younger generations pay for the benefits of wealthier seniors. That means that the rising old-age dependency ratio puts an enormous strain on the program's sustainability. To address this challenge, Congress should raise the early and full eligibility ages for Social Security—from 62 to 65 and from 67 to 70, respectively—and index these thresholds to rise with life expectancy. The Congressional Budget Office (CBO) estimates that gradually raising the FRA from 67 to 70—increasing it by two months per birth year for workers born between 1964 and

1981—while keeping the early retirement threshold at 62 would reduce the program's unsustainable spending by US$95 billion between 2026 and 2034 (the program's financial challenges are discussed in more detail later in this chapter).[53] This change would also address 33 percent of the program's long-term funding shortfall.

Exacerbating the fact that workers' payroll tax payments are not locked away for their own retirement, the method used to calculate benefits further loosens the link between individual benefits and work histories. When a person retires, the SSA identifies their 35 highest-earning years. These earnings are then indexed to wage growth to ensure that past wages are adjusted to reflect today's economic conditions. The SSA then calculates the average of the 35-year earnings, a figure called Average Indexed Monthly Earnings (AIME), which serves as the basis for determining initial benefits. The benefit calculation formula is progressive, so it replaces a higher portion of AIME for lower earners.[54] As a result, Social Security's replacement rate of preretirement earnings for an average worker is 39.1 percent. The program replaces 49.4 percent of preretirement earnings for low earners (those with earnings at half the average) and 27.8 percent for high earners (those earning twice the average).[55]

In 2025, an individual's primary insurance amount, or initial benefit at full retirement age, is calculated as the sum of

- 90% of the first US$1,226 of AIME
- 32% of AIME between US$1,226 and US$7,391
- 15% of AIME above US$7,391

In addition to the progressivity of the benefit formula, wage indexing of initial benefits further weakens the link between working histories and benefits. As mentioned, the SSA indexes lifetime earnings to wage growth to account for improvements in the standard of living over a worker's career. However, this process is performed regardless of whether an individual's wages actually kept pace with the growth in average wages, giving all workers a benefit boost based on overall improvements in the economy unrelated to their earnings.

As noted, because of wage indexing, an individual applying for Social Security in 2020 would receive a maximum of US$37,333 in benefits— US$7,548 more than someone with the same earnings history who

FIGURE 4.2

New Social Security benefits grow by $7,500 more than inflation over 25 years

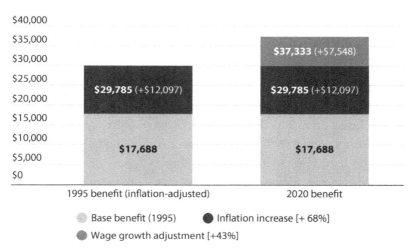

Source: Social Security Administration, "2023 OASDI Trustees Report: 2022 Annual Statistical Supplement."

Note: The 1995 maximum initial annual benefit is adjusted for 25 years of inflation to 2020. The illustrative 2020 maximum initial annual benefit is adjusted for 25 years of wage growth, since 1995.

applied in 1995 (receiving $29,785 in 2020 instead). As Figure 4.2 illustrates, this US$7,548 discrepancy arises from wage indexing, which causes Social Security benefits to grow much faster than inflation, exceeding what is necessary to maintain purchasing power over time.

Social Security should revise the initial benefit formula to adjust along with increases in prices rather than wages. Such a change would protect retirees from inflation while significantly improving the program's financial health. According to the SSA, implementing this reform in 2031 would close 85 percent of the 75-year actuarial deficit of Social Security.[56] If this change applied to only the highest 70 percent of earners—so that initial benefits for workers with AIME equal to the taxable maximum grow with prices instead of wages—it would reduce the program's 75-year actuarial deficit by 47 percent (individuals in the top 70 percent but below the very top would experience a blend of price and wage indexing).

After calculating the initial benefit of a retiree, this amount is regularly adjusted for inflation through cost-of-living adjustments (COLAs). However, the SSA currently relies on an outdated measure for these adjustments—the Consumer Price Index for Urban Wage Earners and Clerical Workers (CPI-W), which covers the purchasing behavior of about 3 in 10 Americans. Furthermore, this measure does not account for changes in consumer behavior in response to price increases, known as the substitution effect. Put simply, the CPI-W does not account for the fact that when a price of a certain good increases, consumers buy more of its cheaper alternative. A better inflation measure is the C-CPI-U, which represents the spending patterns of 8 out of 10 US individuals and accounts for the substitution effect.[57]

As illustrated in Figure 4.3, using the flawed CPI-W measure instead of the C-CPI-U results in a faster increase in Social Security benefits. To ensure a more accurate inflation adjustment, Congress should index Social Security benefits to the C-CPI-U. This change would both protect retirees' benefits against increases in the cost of living and

FIGURE 4.3

Social Security's average monthly benefit is rising faster under outdated measure, $

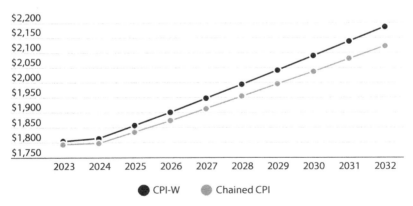

Source: US Bureau of Labor Statistics, "Consumer Price Index: Urban Wage Earners and Clerical Workers (Current Series)"; "Consumer Price Index: All Urban Consumers (Chained CPI)"; and "Social Security Administration, Monthly Statistical Snapshot (January 2022)."

Note: CPI-W = Consumer Price Index for Urban Wage Earners and Clerical Workers; Chained CPI = Chained Consumer Price Index.

improve the financial sustainability of the system. According to the CBO, this switch would reduce Social Security's costs by US$204 billion by 2034, if implemented in 2026.[58]

The earnings-related structure of Social Security, combined with indexing initial benefits to wage growth and adjusting them using a measure that overstates cost-of-living increases, results in excessively high benefits that are especially pronounced for the highest earners. According to the SSA, an individual retiring at age 70 who consistently earned the maximum taxable amount throughout their career would receive US$5,108 monthly from Social Security, or about US$61,000 annually in 2025.[59] This amount far exceeds what is necessary to prevent old-age poverty. The maximum Social Security benefit is four times the poverty threshold for individuals over 65, as determined by the US Census Bureau.[60] Moreover, according to the Internal Revenue Service, in

FIGURE 4.4
The largest share of Social Security payments goes to individuals with adjusted gross income over $100,000
Distribution of Social Security payments by income range, tax year 2021

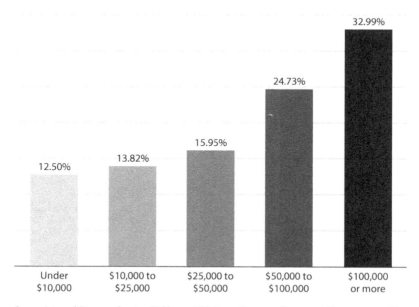

Source: Internal Revenue Service, "Table 1.4. All Returns: Sources of Income, Adjustments, and Tax Items, by Size of Adjusted Gross Income, Tax Year 2021 (Filing Year 2022)"

2021, the largest share of Social Security payments went to individuals with an adjusted gross income of more than US$100,000 (Figure 4.4).

The combination of Social Security's benefit structure and the country's aging population has transformed Social Security from a modest old-age support program into the largest federal government program—one that redistributes income from working Americans to mostly wealthier retirees. In 2023, Social Security expenditures, including OASI and DI programs, amounted to US$1.35 trillion, or 5 percent of GDP, which amounts to roughly US$4,021 per person.[61] Spending on the OASI program alone reached US$1.2 trillion, or 4.4 percent of GDP, in the same year.[62]

Importantly, Social Security has been running cash-flow deficits since 2010. That means that its only sources of revenue—payroll taxes from workers and taxation of the benefits of retirees whose incomes exceed certain thresholds—are falling short of covering the program's total costs. This deficit is bridged with borrowing based on the program's trust fund balance.[63]

It is crucial to recognize that the trust fund reserves exist only on the SSA's ledgers and do not comprise real assets. Previously, when Social Security revenues exceeded the program's costs, the resulting surpluses were recorded in the trust fund. However, those surpluses were not set aside to cover future cash-flow shortfalls, defined as the program's costs exceeding its revenues (payroll taxes and the taxation of benefits). Instead, Congress immediately used the surpluses for other non-pension-related expenditures. In response, the Treasury issued special-issue bonds to Social Security as compensation for the spent surpluses. These bonds are essentially IOUs from the Treasury, promising to repay Social Security when the funds are needed. The Treasury has no money except what it collects in revenues from taxes or receives from bondholders when selling US Treasury bonds, and the United States is already running vast deficits. That means that every additional dollar needed to cover the Social Security financing gap adds directly to the publicly held debt.

Between 2010 and 2023, the Treasury borrowed US$1.08 trillion to cover Social Security benefits in excess of revenues (Figure 4.5).[64] For example, in 2023, payroll taxes and the taxation of benefits covered

FIGURE 4.5

The US government borrowed $1.08 trillion to cover Social Security deficits
Income sources for the OASI program costs, billions $

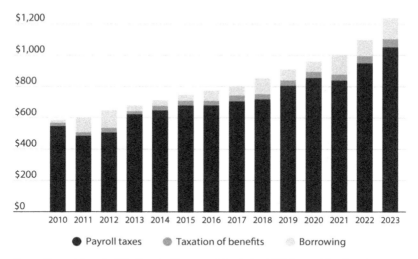

● Payroll taxes   ● Taxation of benefits   ● Borrowing

Source: "Annual Report of the Board of Trustees of the Federal Old-Age and Survivors Insurance and Federal Disability Insurance Trust Funds," 2010 to 2023, Social Security Administration.

Note: OASI = Old-Age and Survivors Insurance.

89.3 percent of the OASI program's costs, with the deficit of 10.7 percent, or US$133 billion, funded through the issuance of new debt.[65]

As illustrated in Figure 4.6, this situation will be exacerbated over time, with Social Security projected to contribute about US$4.1 trillion to the federal government's deficits between 2024 and 2033, including the interest costs associated with said borrowing.[66] In 2033, the trust fund reserves will be depleted. Social Security will no longer have the authority to call on the Treasury to borrow on its behalf, leading to the program's insolvency. This could result in 21 percent benefit cuts for all beneficiaries if current law holds.[67]

According to a 2024 CBO report, to eliminate the combined OASI and DI programs' 75-year actuarial deficit—defined as the programs' future projected costs exceeding its revenues plus trust fund "reserves"—payroll tax rates would need to immediately increase from 12.4 percent to 16.7 percent. In other words, after Social Security spends all dedicated revenues (plus the interest earned on surplus revenues that the

FIGURE 4.6

Social Security adds $4.1 trillion in deficits over the next 10 years
Projected federal and Social Security deficits from 2024 to 2033, billions $

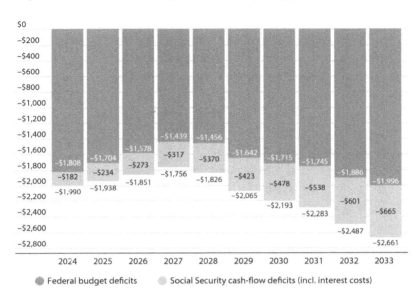

Source: Congressional Budget Office, "An Update to the Budget and Economic Outlook: 2024 to 2034," June 18, 2024.

Note: Social Security refers exclusively to the Old-Age and Survivors Insurance Trust Fund.

Treasury borrowed from the program between 1983 and 2010), it will still run a massive 75-year deficit to the tune of US$25 trillion in net present value terms.[68] The payroll tax increase to cover that shortfall would equate to roughly US$2,600 for a median earner, for a total payroll tax burden exceeding US$10,000 per year.[69]

One proposed solution to strengthen Social Security's finances is to eliminate the payroll tax cap (US$168,600 in 2024), thereby taxing all earned income. However, had this change been enacted in 2024, it would have covered only half of the program's long-term funding shortfall, and the system would have returned to running deficits in 2029, just five years later. Even if uncapping the payroll tax was not accompanied by corresponding increases in benefits for higher earners, the system would still continue running deficits by 2029.[70] In addition, eliminating the tax cap would effectively impose a 12.4 percent marginal tax increase on higher earners, pushing their tax rates to economically harmful levels. For instance, a 2018 study found that a 1 percent increase in the marginal tax rate for those in the 90th percentile reduces the number of inventions and patents by 1.8 percent.[71]

However, as outlined in this chapter, Social Security's financial sustainability could be significantly improved without resorting to steep tax hikes that further burden American workers. Measures such as raising retirement ages to better align with increases in life expectancy, switching from wage indexing to price indexing for initial benefits, and adopting a more accurate inflation adjustment formula could greatly strengthen the program's finances.

A more structural reform would involve reducing excessive benefits for higher earners and focusing on those with low earnings. This could be achieved by making the current progressive benefit formula even more progressive. For example, the CBO estimates that reducing average annual benefits by 10 percent for middle earners and 26 percent for the highest earners would eliminate 42 percent of the program's long-term funding shortfalls and save about US$200 billion over the next decade.[72]

Congress should also consider discontinuing COLAs for higher earners, which would ensure that current retirees are not affected by benefit cuts, while it gradually reduced real benefits for higher earners. The SSA estimates that adopting the C-CPI-U for COLAs for individuals below specified income thresholds—US$110,800 for single filers and US$221,500 for joint filers—starting in 2026 and eliminating COLAs for filers above those thresholds would reduce Social Security's long-term actuarial deficit by 37 percent.[73]

An even more targeted alternative would transform Social Security from its expensive earnings-related structure to a flat-benefit system. Instead of focusing on income replacement, this scheme would aim to prevent old-age poverty by providing a flat benefit to all eligible retirees.

The CBO estimates that replacing Social Security's current benefit structure with a uniform flat benefit for all newly eligible beneficiaries at full retirement age would eliminate the program's 75-year deficit and result in an actuarial surplus. If enacted in 2026, this reform would save

US$283 billion with the uniform benefit set at 150 percent of the federal poverty level (FPL), or US$607 billion with the benefit set at 125 percent of FPL, by 2034. It would also bring Social Security's cost down to 4.4 percent (150 percent FPL) or 3.8 percent GDP (125 percent FPL) by 2054, compared with 5.9 percent GDP under current law. The reform also would increase average annual benefits for the lowest earners born between 1970 and 1979 by 52 percent (150 percent FPL) or 27 percent (125 percent FPL), while reducing benefits for medium earners by 21 percent (150 percent FPL) or 34 percent (125 percent FPL) and for the highest earners by 46 percent (150 percent FPL) or 55 percent (125 FPL). The current eligibility requirement of at least 10 years of work would remain unchanged under either benefit level.[74]

Based on the Census Bureau's official poverty measure (OPM), 9.7 percent of American seniors lived in poverty in 2023.[75] However, this measure inflates the actual senior poverty figure, as the Current Population Survey (CPS)—which it is based on—does not account for most of the income the elderly receive from their private retirement accounts such as 401(k)s.[76] The Census Bureau, acknowledging this issue, released the National Experimental Well-Being Statistics (NEWS), which relies on more comprehensive income data to produce more accurate estimates.[77] The 2025 NEWS report compares the 2018 CPS-based figures with its own estimates for the same year. While the OPM indicated a 9.75 percent senior poverty rate in 2018, the NEWS estimate was substantially lower, at 5.73 percent.[78] Although there are no NEWS adjustments for years after 2018, the 2023 poverty figure of 9.7 percent should be looked at with caution, as it likely overestimates senior poverty.

In addition, about 3 percent of American seniors receive no Social Security benefits at all because of insufficient earnings, and this group experiences higher poverty rates than other beneficiaries.[79] Some experts have suggested that all older Americans should be eligible for a new flat Social Security benefit regardless of their earnings history.[80] This would ensure that people in this vulnerable group also receive basic anti-poverty benefits, which would lead to lower senior poverty rates. On the flip side, this would pay benefits to recent immigrants or those with very limited work histories, thereby expanding Social

Security beyond its current target group of workers with a minimum of 10 years of sufficient earnings.

Third pillar

The US retirement system stands out among developed nations with a robust third pillar, which includes voluntary retirement savings. According to the OECD, assets held in voluntary plans in the United States reached US$35 trillion in 2022, or 137.5 percent of US GDP. This makes the United States one of only seven OECD nations—alongside Australia, Canada, Denmark, Iceland, the Netherlands, and Switzerland—where private retirement assets exceed the size of the country's GDP.[81] Importantly, the United States and Canada are the only OECD countries where these private retirement plans are larger than GDP despite the plans being noncompulsory.[82]

Notably, while Social Security provides a 39.1 percent replacement rate for an average earner, which is below the OECD average, the total US retirement system, including voluntary retirement savings, achieves a 73.2 percent replacement rate, well above the OECD average of 55.3 percent.[83] In fact, the 34.1 replacement rate of US voluntary retirement savings is the highest among the OECD nations. The US voluntary replacement share—the ratio of the replacement rate provided by voluntary plans to the total retirement system's replacement rate—stands at 0.47.[84]

The United States encourages private retirement savings through various tax-advantaged special-purpose savings accounts, including employer-sponsored 401(k) accounts and IRAs.

A 401(k) plan allows employees to allocate a portion of their wages to an individual account within an employer-provided plan.[85] These contributions can be invested in various assets, such as stocks, bonds, or mutual funds. Many employers also offer matching contributions as part of their benefit packages. As of 2024, employee contributions cannot exceed US$23,000, while combined employee and employer contributions are capped at US$69,000.[86]

Contributions to traditional 401(k) plans are tax-deferred, meaning they are not included in the taxable income of the employee or employer at the time of contribution. Additionally, investment gains on these contributions are exempted from capital gains and dividend taxes. However, withdrawals from these plans are taxed as ordinary income.[87] Thus, traditional 401(k)s are taxed under the Exempt-Exempt-Taxed (EET) regime.

Apart from contribution limits, withdrawals made before the age of 59½ are generally subject to a 10 percent penalty. Exceptions to this penalty include cases of disability or death, where the funds are transferred to participants' survivors.[88] Some plans also allow for temporary borrowing from these funds for major purchases such as a home, which must be repaid to avoid a future penalty. Furthermore, individuals are required to begin withdrawing their accumulated savings by age 72, or by age 73 if they turn 72 after December 31, 2022.[89]

Employees can choose to designate a portion of their 401(k) distributions as Roth contributions, which changes the tax treatment of these funds. Specifically, Roth 401(k) contributions are taxed as part of an employee's income, meaning taxes are paid up front. The investment gains remain untaxed, and withdrawals during retirement are also tax-free (the Taxed-Exempt-Exempt regime). However, if an individual withdraws funds before age 59½, the 10 percent penalty will apply to the portion that represents investment gains (the contributions portion is tax-free because the contributions are already taxed).[90]

Workers can also save for their retirement through IRAs. These personal savings plans have the same withdrawal age limitations as 401(k)s, and they are taxed similarly, depending on whether they are traditional or Roth IRAs. However, the contribution limits for IRAs are lower, capped at US$7,000, or US$8,000 for workers aged 50 and older as of 2024.[91] Additionally, IRAs can be funded through rollovers, which involve transferring assets from another retirement plan such as a 401(k) to an IRA. Unlike contributions, rollovers are not subject to contribution limits.[92]

As of 2019, 25.3 percent of American households owned an IRA, while 56 percent of American workers participated in employer-sponsored plans such as 401(k)s.[93] These figures are significantly higher than the average participation in voluntary retirement plans among OECD nations.[94]

While the US retirement system's third pillar is strong, representing an important source of income for many American seniors, it could be further strengthened by the introduction of USAs. Those accounts would operate as personal Roth-style retirement accounts, where individuals would deposit after-tax contributions that grow tax-free, with withdrawals being tax-free as well.

Unlike existing retirement accounts such as 401(k)s and IRAs, withdrawals from USAs would not be restricted until age 59½, which would allow individuals to access their funds at any time for any purpose. The current age limitations and penalties primarily discourage lower earners and younger workers, who are less inclined to lock away their savings until retirement because of the potential for financial emergencies or the desire to invest in their education, start a business, or use those funds for other reasons.

Canada's experience with similar accounts, known as Tax-Free Savings Accounts (TFSAs), which were introduced in 2009, demonstrates that these accounts are more appealing to lower earners and younger workers than traditional retirement plans. Among low-income Canadians, 15 percent owned a TFSA, while only 3 percent contributed to private retirement plans in 2015. In 2022, 51 percent of Canadians aged 18 to 34 owned a TFSA, compared with 38 percent who owned a retirement plan.[95] Congress should establish USAs to encourage more Americans to save for their retirement while having access to their savings for immediate needs.[96]

Fourth pillar

The fourth pillar of the US retirement system comprises assets and income from sources other than Social Security, public pensions, and retirement accounts.

According to the 2022 Survey of Consumer Finances, homeownership is high among American seniors, with 76.1 percent of individuals aged 65 to 74 and 81 percent of those aged 75 and over owning their primary residences. Additionally, 19 percent of seniors aged 65 to 75 and 15.5 percent of those aged 75 and over, respectively, owned a nonresidential property. Furthermore, around 20 percent of both age groups reported holding stocks outside of retirement accounts. The median net worth of American seniors aged 65 to 74 group was US$410,000, while for those aged 75 and over, it was US$336,000.[97]

Social Security and private retirement plans are the main income sources, making up 66 percent of an average retiree's total income. For income sources other than pensions and retirement plans, 23 percent of total senior income comes from wages and salaries, 8 percent from returns on personal assets, and the rest from other government benefits. Additionally, 88 percent of Americans aged 60 and over reported having some form of retirement savings, including savings in non-retirement accounts.[98]

Summary

The primary component of the US retirement system is the earnings-related Social Security program. This system provides substantial benefits to high earners instead of focusing on supporting the most vulnerable seniors. The program's benefit structure, coupled with the increasing old-age dependency ratio, has made Social Security's finances increasingly unsustainable, with the program projected to reach insolvency by 2033. Moreover, the program's trust fund does not hold any real assets, which means that Social Security will add more than US$5 trillion to the federal debt to cover promised benefits before the projected insolvency date.

To better align Social Security's benefits and income streams and to enhance private ownership of retirement savings, Social Security should transition from its earnings-related structure to a flat, anti-poverty benefit model. This approach would focus benefits on the lowest earners while reducing them for higher earners. Such a change would restore the program's original objective of providing a safety net for those in poverty. Furthermore, transitioning to a flat-benefit system could reduce costs, thus avoiding higher taxes, and their negative consequences, for younger workers.

While this fundamental transformation should be the primary goalpost, Social Security could also be improved within its existing structure through more marginal reforms that reduce costs, avoiding tax increases or adding to the already unsustainable debt.

First, to address the challenges posed by an aging population, both the early and full retirement age thresholds should be raised by three years and indexed to life expectancy. This change would be both financially responsible and intergenerationally fair, easing the burden on younger workers who currently fund the benefits of often-wealthier retirees.

Second, to curb unsustainable growth in benefits, Social Security should switch from wage indexing to price indexing for initial benefits. Even if this change affected only the highest earners, the program's finances would still be substantially improved. Furthermore, the program should adopt a more accurate inflation adjustment measure that better reflects increases in the cost of living. Congress should also consider ending COLAs for the highest-earning beneficiaries.

These reforms would eliminate the need for drastic and economically harmful tax increases on American workers or increased borrowing that could drive the United States into a debt crisis. Congress should not remove the payroll tax cap. Doing so would be ineffective for three reasons. First, this change would cover only half of the program's long-term shortfalls. Second, surplus funds would likely be spent on other government programs or tax cuts, as has been the case in the past. Third, it would impose higher tax burdens, thus reducing growth by stifling innovation.

The US retirement system's third pillar, which includes voluntary retirement savings, is one of the strongest among OECD nations, playing a crucial role in total income replacement for American workers. However, this pillar could be further enhanced by universal savings accounts that do not have the restrictions governing existing tax-advantaged accounts such as 401(k)s and IRAs. Withdrawals from USAs would be permitted at any time for any purpose, eliminating disincentives to save for lower-income and younger workers.

5

PANEL DISCUSSION: US SOCIAL SECURITY AND OECD RETIREMENT SYSTEMS: A COMPARISON

PANELISTS

- **Andrew Biggs,** Senior Fellow, American Enterprise Institute, former principal deputy commissioner of the Social Security Administration, and former associate director of the White House National Economic Council
- **Romina Boccia,** Director of Budget and Entitlement Policy, Cato Institute
- Moderated by **Veronique de Rugy,** George Gibbs Chair in Political Economy and Senior Research Fellow, Mercatus Center at George Mason University

KEY HIGHLIGHTS

- **Romina Boccia:** "The [Social Security] program is actually called Old-Age and Survivors Insurance, separate from Disability Insurance. The key question is, 'What are we insuring against?'"

- **Andrew Biggs:** "[The United Kingdom, Canada, Australia, and New Zealand] are, by and large, similar to the US in our general philosophy. However, . . . [t]**heir old-age programs are much more focused on reducing poverty in old age.** . . . We have no minimum benefit, and 20 percent of seniors receive Social Security benefits below the poverty line. At the same time, this earnings-based system means **we're paying, by international standards, extremely high benefits to high earners. This requires higher taxes than necessary to provide benefits that these high earners don't really need.**"
- **Andrew Biggs:** "If we can encourage people to have longer work lives, that increases the number of workers and helps your finances. The problem with the Social Security program is that the benefit formula penalizes work past retirement. If you claim benefits later, say you'll retire at 62, but don't claim benefits until 65, there is an actuarial adjustment. But if instead of retiring, I keep working from 62 to 63 to 64, and so on, most people receive almost no additional benefits for their additional time. . . . **That is why I've argued for lowering the payroll tax rate on Social Security at those ages, which some other countries do to encourage people to work longer.**"
- **Andrew Biggs:** "Social Security should support those who can't or wouldn't save on their own. But for higher earners, Social Security and private savings are close substitutes. **I don't see why you would want to provide excessive benefits through a tax-and-transfer scheme that reduces labor supply and savings compared to voluntary savings, where people contribute and build capital.**"
- **Romina Boccia:** "If you've been paying attention to efforts to either undermine or promote ESG [environmental, social, and governance] efforts, there's been a lot of pressure on public pensions to divest from certain funds, whether it's oil and gas or whatever is politically unpopular. **If the US

federal government becomes a major shareholder in the stock market, that will almost certainly create distortions."

- **Romina Boccia:** "I support a flat benefit so people know what to expect from Social Security and can plan accordingly. Very few people understand how much they can expect from Social Security. **By flat benefits, I mean a universal or means-tested amount that everyone who's eligible receives, tied to a percentage of the average wage in the country or based on the prevalent measure of poverty.** This predictability helps people determine how much they need to supplement their retirement savings. The current benefit formula is highly complicated."

Transcripts have been edited for style and clarity.

Veronique de Rugy: The theme of this panel is "US Social Security and the OECD Retirement System: A Comparison." Andrew, I'm going to turn to you first and ask you to please set the stage for the situation of our Social Security system and give us a few points on how you would define the system since we're going to be talking about global comparisons.

Andrew Biggs: Sure. The phrase "social security" in other countries often refers to a broader social welfare system. Here in the US, it refers to the Old-Age and Survivors Insurance and the Disability Insurance Trust Funds, which provide retirement, survivor, and disability benefits to eligible workers and their families. When we talk about Social Security, the focus is mostly on the retirement program, which is the largest component of the Social Security system.

That program is essentially a pay-as-you-go system, which taxes workers 12.4 percent on wages, split evenly between the worker and their employer. This money goes into the Social Security program, and the vast majority of it is immediately used to pay benefits. Benefits are based on a complex formula that replaces some portion of preretirement earnings. The key issue is that a pay-as-you-go program's math is simple but depends crucially on the level of promised benefits and the ratio of workers to beneficiaries.

If more people are paying in and fewer are collecting, as was the case in the past, the program is very affordable. But as the demographics shift from five workers per retiree to three—and by the 2030s, a little over two—the burden of funding those benefits is divided among fewer workers, causing costs to rise.

As Senator Cassidy was saying, beginning in about 10 years, the Social Security trust funds will run out. At that point, the law dictates that the system be balanced by reducing benefits. Essentially, benefits will be cut across the board for all beneficiaries—new and old, retirees, survivors, and the disabled. That is the default position of the program. The question is how to address this more rationally, not just to make Social Security solvent but to make it work better for the people of this country.

Veronique de Rugy: So in this context, what is your idea or your theory about the role of government in addressing that need? Or what should the government's role be in retirement security, if any?

Andrew Biggs: That's a great question because the role of government, as we know, is a philosophical question. As I said to Veronique in the green room this morning, I don't care what France does. This may be a little bit insulting, but the point here is that it's coming from a different philosophical viewpoint about the relative roles of government, households, and the private sector.

What I think is more interesting, when I consider the US Social Security program and retirement income provision in general in an international context, is how US Social Security compares to what goes on in other Anglo countries like the UK, Canada, Australia, and New Zealand. These countries are, by and large, similar to the US in our general philosophy. However, the interesting thing is that these Anglo countries do things differently than we do in the US. Their old-age programs are much more focused on reducing poverty in old age. They provide a stronger safety net than we do here in the US. At the same time, they provide much less generous benefits for middle- and high-income retirees.

Just an example: if you look at the maximum benefit for Social Security this year for a single person, it would be about $48,000. That is two to three times more generous than what you receive in Canada, the UK, Australia, or New Zealand. We have a system that is really not as good at preventing poverty in old age as other countries, which is, to me, clearly a role of government.

Veronique de Rugy: Is it because it's a universal system that benefits everyone?

Andrew Biggs: The reason for it in the US is that Social Security is an earnings-based system. That model was adopted for a political reason. When Social Security was introduced, there was a belief that a program overly generous to low-income people and not providing much to higher-income people would not be politically viable. So they created an earnings-based program: the more you pay in, the more you get out. It's progressive, but it's based on your earnings and contributions.

The problem with this, from a social insurance perspective for the elderly, is that if you didn't earn much during your working career, you won't receive a high benefit in retirement. We have no minimum benefit, and 20 percent of seniors receive Social Security benefits below the poverty line. At the same time, this earnings-based system means we're paying, by international standards, extremely high benefits to high earners. This requires higher taxes than necessary to provide benefits that these high earners don't really need. The higher tax is discouraging labor supply, and the higher benefits are discouraging savings. Much of what happens with middle- and high-income seniors stems from political economy arguments, which make little sense from a policy standpoint.

Veronique de Rugy: If I understand you correctly, you think the role of government in the context of Social Security and retirement is to ensure retirement security for lower-income people? And we don't do very well on that front?

Andrew Biggs: Precisely. Government has a place, but government needs to know its place. Government is good at redistributing to people. It should do that. But it is not good at prefunding pensions. Around the world, governments are very poor at actually funding their pension systems. Leave that to households and the private sector that have done an extremely good job in the US.

Veronique de Rugy: One of the many ideas that have been floated to fix Social Security—at least on the finance side—is to encourage labor participation for seniors, which would increase the tax base effectively. So first, what do you think of this idea? And which steps should be taken if this is something that should be done? I assume you believe that solving this problem is not a one-step process. It's going to require a lot of things. But if this is part of the steps that need to be taken, how do we do that?

Andrew Biggs: Sure. As I said before, with a pay-as-you-go program like Social Security, the number of workers paying in matters crucially. If we can encourage people to have longer work lives, that increases the number of workers and helps your finances. The problem with the Social Security program is that the benefit formula penalizes work past retirement. If you claim benefits later, say you'll retire at 62, but don't claim benefits until 65, there is an actuarial adjustment. But if instead of retiring, I keep working from 62 to 63 to 64, and so on, most people receive almost no additional benefits for their additional time.

Veronique de Rugy: The tax penalty is also quite heavy, right?

Andrew Biggs: That's a claiming decision. But let me just focus on the contribution side here, that you're paying 12 percent of your earnings into the program. If you're receiving a benefit back from that, if you say, "OK, I'm paying 12 percent in, but I'm earning benefits," then the disincentive effects of the tax are not so bad. You see it as a contribution, not as a tax. But for people who are 62 years old or in that age range, almost all of that 12.4 percent tax is essentially a pure tax. You don't get anything back for it. That would discourage work in any context. But these are people who precisely have the ability to do something else. They can retire. So these are the people who are most sensitive to tax rates. That is why I've argued for lowering the payroll tax rate on Social Security at those ages, which some other countries do to encourage people to work longer. That will cost Social Security some money, but they will also continue to pay federal income taxes, Medicare payroll taxes, and state income taxes. The work has been done, and it finds that's roughly revenue neutral, believe it or not. But it encourages more work, raises your economy, and increases those people's retirement security. So I think that's one facet of what we can do, not just to help Social Security but also to improve retirement security overall.

Veronique de Rugy: How does this compare to raising the retirement age?

Andrew Biggs: This year, the retirement age turns 67. If you raise the retirement age by a year, all that means is it's essentially a 7 percent across-the-board benefit cut, regardless of when you retire. When we talk about the Social Security retirement age, it's not the first age at which you can retire. It is simply a calibrated point in the benefit formula. If we set the retirement age later, it simply means you're going to receive lower benefits at any age at which you retire. Now, when I've outlined plans for Social Security, I have not included an increase in the retirement age because I think if you do other policies, you don't have to do it. At the same time, I will be surprised if an eventual fix doesn't include it, because it is a way of reducing benefits. It is a way of encouraging people to work longer. In general, Congress is so uncreative in their solutions for Social Security that they're going to have to fall back on things like raising the retirement age and reducing the cost-of-living adjustments because they leave so many other options off the table.

Veronique de Rugy: And finally, how does this compare to raising taxes, which is on the table, even though apparently no one wants it?

Andrew Biggs: Nobody wants to raise Social Security taxes. I mean, most of the proposals from congressional Democrats on Social Security would be the largest peacetime tax increases in history. These tax increases, particularly on high earners, would essentially raise the top rate on earned income by 12 percentage points.

At the same time, when congressional Democrats had the chance to push these plans forward early in the Biden administration, they didn't because they understood that it was unpopular. Again, think about the level of benefits we are paying to middle- and high-income retirees: If you had two middle earners retiring today, they would receive close to $60,000 in combined benefits before they touched a penny of their own savings. That's three times the poverty line they would be at before using any of their savings.

As I said before, if you raise taxes to pay higher benefits, the tax side discourages labor supply because people view the Social Security tax as a tax rather than a contribution. And paying higher benefits displaces retirement savings. And I think the evidence on that side is pretty clear. If you think about the strength of your economy, it depends on the amount of labor and capital. Raising taxes on Social Security is going to discourage both of those sides. I will not be shocked in any way if an eventual fix includes a tax increase. But I think it should be done less rather than more.

Veronique de Rugy: So let's take a global perspective. What are other OECD [Organisation for Economic Co-operation and Development] member countries doing to address the aging population?

Andrew Biggs: I think mostly in terms of other Anglo countries because I think the values and the political-economic systems are similar to ours. All of them focus their resources much more on low earners and much less on high earners. I mean, there is a difference between what you have in the United States, but you have a political difference as well. The US political system is one of divided power between the House of Representatives and the Senate. And in the Senate, you need 60 votes out of 100 to pass, and then it has to be signed by the president. Then, the way we are, it probably ends up in the Supreme Court. It is very, very hard to enact serious legislation here in the US. These other Anglo countries have parliamentary systems. It is much, much easier for them to do that.

One result of that is that other countries have tended to be much more proactive in addressing their pension problems and examining the finances of their systems, looking to improve retirement savings on the household side. We have done nothing on Social Security for 40 years, despite knowing throughout that period that the system faced a long-term gap.

I mean, I worked in the [George W.] Bush White House in 2005, where we controlled the White House and both houses of Congress and didn't come close to enacting reform. If it's difficult to do that, the temptation is always to kick the can down the road and say: "I'm not going to handle that. I'll do something else and just ignore it."

I remember when I was working in this building at Cato, we looked at a 75-year funding gap for Social Security, and it was around $3 trillion. We said, "Oh, that's so much money." Today, it's $22 trillion. Most of that is simply because we failed to address the problem.

Veronique de Rugy: When I worked here, during the war in Iraq, there was a request for supplemental funding of $87 billion for the war, which seems so small compared to whatever they are asking each time anyone coughs anywhere in the world. And I remember being on TV saying: "You don't understand. We have to prune the budget now because in 25 years, the Social Security trust fund. . . ." I mean, we've been saying the same thing for a while, and now it does really feel close. But I've heard that President Bush actually said, and I think he wrote it in his book, that if he had tackled immigration first, he would have been able to do immigration and Social Security.

Andrew Biggs: It's possible. I know in his book, he expressed regret over the failure to enact Social Security reform. When I look back at that, I think he should have prioritized Social Security reform before implementing a tax cut because reforming Social Security requires funding. Using available resources for this would have been more beneficial.

I also believe the framing was overly technical. I think you have to speak to people in plain English and talk about policy goals, such as preventing poverty, that people can understand. At the time, working on the National Economic Council, I had people from Capitol Hill calling and saying, "We have no idea what you're talking about." While the issue has technical aspects, the goals are simple: guaranteeing no one retires into poverty and ensuring middle- and upper-income people save more for retirement, facilitating that process. Actuarial formulas are not easily understood, but these goals are. One of the lessons from the Bush reform, which you can now see, is you don't get these chances very often. I mean, that's almost 20 years ago. And since then, you now have some discussions on the Hill, but if an effort fails, that really does scare people off. Therefore, correctly framing it is crucial.

Veronique de Rugy: I have a last question before I turn to Romina. Which country's retirement system do you find most compelling?

Andrew Biggs: I'll hedge and give you two examples: New Zealand and Australia. Both have good systems but approach them differently. Both countries offer a flat dollar benefit to all retirees, which ensures poverty protection but is less generous to the middle and top earners. The way they differ illustrates some core policy problems or decisions to make.

The New Zealand benefit is not means-tested, meaning everybody gets it, but it's subject to taxation. It means that household retirement savings can essentially be voluntary. They have supplementary accounts with automatic enrollment, but participation isn't mandatory. Australia, on the other hand, has a means-tested benefit, making it cheaper as benefits reduce with additional retirement savings. However, in that case, retirement savings on top of the government benefit can't be voluntary because you'll have a moral hazard problem. You'll be playing one benefit against the other. So Australia requires compulsory workplace retirement plans with employer contributions.

New Zealand says, "Well, our government benefit is going to be a bit more expensive, but then you don't have to have compulsion over privacy." It's not immediately clear which is superior, but both offer valuable insights into different policy approaches.

Veronique de Rugy: Romina, you organized this event. Can you explain why it's important to have a global perspective on retirement issues?

Romina Boccia: There's a sense in the United States, and I think it's very much deserved, that we are a unique and exceptional country. But there are also many similarities in policy goals that other countries have for their public pension programs. It's particularly informative that many OECD countries have much older populations than the United States has today. So it is a good idea to see what other countries have done, which have faced similar challenges as we have with an aging population and declining fertility rates. We can look at examples of how other countries have handled those challenges. It gives us case studies for which policy reforms ended up working as intended and which ended up backfiring.

There's this misconception that the US is less generous than European countries in providing benefits, which isn't true. As Andrew pointed out, the United States has some of the highest benefits for the highest-income earners. For example, in the UK, the maximum benefit for a two-earner couple is about $35,000 a year, which aligns more with bringing people above the poverty level but not paying them excessive benefits to a degree that undermines their incentives to work and save. Whereas in the United States, a two-earner, high-earning couple could collect almost $120,000 a year. I find that very excessive.

Some countries also use marginal triggers to match revenues with outflows, depending on their system's funding. Prefunded systems, like Australia's, allow for diversification of population risk and investment in global markets, tapping into the growth and innovation of other countries to help finance retirement benefits.

US lawmakers should consider more transformative changes than minor tweaks seen in past reforms, especially as Social Security turns 90. Structural changes should focus on [President Franklin Delano] Roosevelt's original promise of protecting against poverty in old age.

I want to make a small correction. The program is actually called Old-Age and Survivors Insurance, separate from Disability Insurance.

The key question is, "What are we insuring against?" If it's poverty, the US system exceeds that.

Veronique de Rugy: The World Bank offers a framework for retirement income systems. Can you briefly describe the four pillars of this framework?

Romina Boccia: The World Bank's framework has five pillars, starting with a zero pillar, which is the anti-poverty benefit. In the US, this would be the Supplemental Security Income program.

The first pillar is the government scheme, similar to Social Security in the United States. It's mandatory and funded by taxes, ensuring everyone receives something. This is where the government goes beyond poverty protection and says: "We know best when you need to retire, and we don't trust you to make your own consumption-smoothing decisions over your lifetime. So we are going to force you to have a certain amount of income." This might have made sense in the past. However, with financial sector innovations, it's now easier for people to save for their retirement.

Features like auto-enrollment in private-sector plans, target-date retirement funds, and low-cost index funds enable people to save automatically without needing financial expertise. Many end up with significant retirement savings.

Voluntary saving is considered the third pillar by the World Bank. However, their structure shows a bias toward the government. The second pillar would be mandatory savings or occupational schemes, like Australia's superannuation fund.

The fourth pillar includes any other assets for retirement, such as reverse mortgages, rental income, or family support. So zero is the anti-poverty benefit; the first pillar is the mandatory government scheme; the second pillar is mandatory savings or occupational schemes; the third pillar is voluntary retirement savings like 401(k)s; and the fourth pillar includes any other assets.

I'd love to ask Andrew to briefly talk about the way the United States handles the third pillar. From my reading of the OECD *Pensions at a*

Glance report, the US has an extensive third pillar of voluntary savings, more so than most OECD nations.

Andrew Biggs: Yes, that's an interesting angle. If you compare the US to other developed countries, our Social Security benefits don't seem as generous, partly due to measurement issues. However, private retirement savings in the US are exceptionally high. Retirement plan assets in the US are roughly twice the OECD average.

A few years ago, riots in France over raising the retirement age highlighted that part of the problem was that they delayed changes too long. But another aspect of the problem was that retirement savings in France were around 12 percent of GDP. If you look at retirement savings in the US, they're equal to 125 percent of GDP or thereabouts. For French seniors, this was a critical issue due to their limited retirement savings. In contrast, US households have significantly increased their savings outside of Social Security.

From the time of traditional defined-benefit pensions, which never covered more than 40 percent of private-sector workers, we switched to defined-contribution plans. Now, 70 percent of employees in the private sector are offered a plan at work. Contributions have increased, and assets have increased in every age, income, educational, and racial category. Retirement savings are at record levels across the board. Retirement incomes are at record levels, and poverty in old age is at record lows.

What this highlights is that while the Social Security side has been neglected for 40 years and the unfunded liabilities have gotten bigger, households have increased their savings dramatically. They are not just saving more; they are working later in life and claiming Social Security later in life. This brings up a key political economy question. If you look around the world or the United States, not just at Social Security but also at state and local government pensions, the government plans are always underfunded. It's just as certain as day follows night: politicians promise things without paying for them.

Behavioral economics suggests people often don't make the right decisions when it comes to saving. I grant a lot of that is correct. But at the end of the day, If I don't save enough for retirement, I am the person who suffers from that. So the incentives say I should save, and, by and large, Americans do save.

The real retirement crisis, to foreshadow my upcoming book, is on the government side. I'm not saying this as an anti-government person. I'm just saying if you look at the numbers, it's all on the government side. So we have a success story in household retirement savings alongside very poor stewardship of the federal government's largest program.

I understand Senator Cassidy's point that we don't want to raise taxes or cut benefits, but guess what? Those are your choices. And you know, I don't like the law of gravity, but I still have to obey it. Similarly, Social Security finances are such that you either need more money going in or less money coming out.

Veronique de Rugy: While you were discussing private savings, I wondered: What does the literature say about Social Security's impact on savings and labor?

Andrew Biggs: On the savings part, an influential article by Harvard economist Marty Feldstein in the 70s argued that Social Security displaces private savings. And in a sense, that's obvious. At the low end, a lot of low earners will not save for retirement for various reasons. For middle and high earners, Social Security should theoretically act as a substitute for private savings. This idea was controversial for a while, but over the past 20 years, studies examining changes in household savings in response to social security reforms in other countries support this view. Unfortunately, because we have not reformed Social Security in the US, it's hard to get those clean experiments, but there have been studies done in other countries, and they confirm that low earners don't take social security into account. High earners, middle earners, educated people, and financially literate people do. If you look at the accrued Social Security benefits, which are benefits people have earned but have not been paid out yet, that is somewhere north of $40 trillion. Let's assume half of that would have otherwise been saved by people if Social Security didn't exist. That's an extra $20 trillion of national savings, which is not a small amount.

Social Security should support those who can't or wouldn't save on their own. But for higher earners, Social Security and private savings are close substitutes. I don't see why you would want to provide excessive benefits through a tax-and-transfer scheme that reduces labor supply and savings compared to voluntary savings, where people contribute and build capital.

This relates to the effects of Social Security on labor supply. Again, we don't have clean experiments, but for those close to retirement, the incremental gains from working and contributing to Social Security are minimal compared to simply claiming benefits. So particularly around retirement age, Social Security likely reduces labor supply—not as severely as in some other countries, but I think Social Security could do a better job.

Romina Boccia: I'd love to bring a political economy angle to this. In theory, Social Security benefits are partially prefunded. Until 2010, the program collected more in payroll taxes than was needed for benefits, accumulating a roughly $3 trillion trust fund. This trust fund has been used since 2010 to fund benefits in excess of payroll taxes and is projected to run out by 2033. However, the trust fund is really an accounting mechanism; there are no real assets. It's quite a misnomer to call it a trust fund. It's more accurate to call it an accounting ledger, tracking what was allocated for Social Security.

In reality, those payroll taxes went into the Treasury as part of general revenues and funded various government expenditures, such as emergency spending, economic stimulus during the Great Recession, war efforts, and new programs like Medicare Part D.

The political economy aspect is that surplus Social Security funds, redirected to other programs, likely fueled government growth because taxes didn't need to be raised as much. This enabled the creation of new benefit programs, which are rarely repealed. In the history of the federal government, you'd be hard-pressed to find an example where a benefit program has ever been repealed.

So we're facing this double whammy now. We were trying to prepare for baby boomers by prefunding benefits, but because those taxes weren't set aside, they likely fueled the growth in government. Now, we have a bigger government to sustain with a very low tax base. The United States likes to spend like a European country but taxes at a much lower rate. At the same time, we're experiencing the baby boomers' entering Social Security in large numbers, causing a shortfall in the program.

The broader federal budget issue is that we fueled government growth without adequate funding provisions, affecting both Social Security and the general budget.

Veronique de Rugy: What do you think about countries like Australia and New Zealand, which invest their reserve funds in assets beyond government debt securities, including private equity and non-US bonds?

Romina Boccia: In theory, setting aside revenues and investing them in the market is appealing. We know that if the economy grows, it can generate returns to fund benefits. But in practice, if you've been paying attention to efforts to either undermine or promote ESG [environmental, social, and governance] efforts, there's been a lot of pressure on public pensions to divest from certain funds, whether it's oil and gas or whatever is politically unpopular. If the US federal government becomes a major shareholder in the stock market, that will almost certainly create distortions. I don't think we want politicians to throw their weight around when it comes to the capitalist engine of this country, which produces growth, innovation, and increases in living standards—all the things that make America a global leader.

While it has worked in some countries, considering the existing political polarization, I would be extremely concerned with the government playing such a large role in deciding how capital is allocated toward the private sector.

Andrew Biggs: There's another point related to your previous comment. From the 1980s until about 2010, Social Security was running surpluses. Those surpluses were credited to the Social Security trust funds but were spent. They were invested in nontradable intergovernmental securities, meaning the federal government could borrow from Social Security surpluses in ways that didn't increase the unified budget surplus or the publicly held national debt. This accounting setup encouraged the government to borrow, tax less, or spend more than it otherwise would have.

Investing those funds outside the federal process, in corporate bonds or other securities, would have provided real assets to help pay Social Security benefits and avoided accounting problems. That is something meaningful, but it doesn't fix Social Security on paper. Private investment for Social Security aims to leverage the risk premium of stocks over bonds. However, if it's not a good idea for an individual preparing for retirement to borrow to invest in the stock market (and it's not), then it's not a good idea for the federal government either. But at the federal level, you can plan these things out a bit more.

For example, Social Security cost 4 percent of GDP in 2000, 5 percent today, and will be 6 percent in the future. Paying full promised benefits means allocating a larger GDP share for benefits, regardless of the funding source. You could get it through a payroll tax by having the government buy stocks. Through income taxes, you're purchasing assets, which will come out of the economy. Unless you're making a real investment in the economy, future GDP isn't going to be any bigger by simply borrowing on one side to invest in the other. It doesn't change the size of the economic pie in the future or the share allocated to seniors. The economic burden on working-age people remains unchanged. It's purely a financing play.

On the other hand, if you scale down benefits over time for middle- and upper-income people, they will likely work longer and save more, which increases the size of the economic pie. This macro-level effect is worth considering.

I understand the political considerations. For instance, Bill Clinton proposed investing part of the budget surpluses in the stock market. In retrospect, I might have supported that despite the risks, as it would have set aside some of the surpluses that were ultimately not preserved.

It's not optimal, but purely a financing play like borrowing to invest doesn't seem beneficial.

Veronique de Rugy: Let me quickly ask, should we means-test Social Security? And if we do, should we adopt a flat-rate income support similar to other countries?

Andrew Biggs: First, I think we will likely end up doing some means-testing or increasing means-testing for Social Security simply because we'll be desperate for money. Second, I am OK with means-testing Social Security if we strongly facilitate or require that people save for retirement on top of it. Without mandatory retirement savings, people will play strategy games with their finances.

Romina Boccia: We already have a progressive benefit structure, where lower earners get a higher return on their Social Security taxes, and higher earners get a lower return. There's also income tax that applies to up to 85 percent of Social Security benefits, depending on non–Social Security income. This was adopted in 1983, the last time the trust fund was running out.

I support a flat benefit so people know what to expect from Social Security and can plan accordingly. Very few people understand how much they can expect from Social Security. By flat benefits, I mean a universal or means-tested amount that everyone who's eligible receives, tied to a percentage of the average wage in the country or based on the prevalent measure of poverty. This predictability helps people determine how much they need to supplement their retirement savings. The current benefit formula is highly complicated.

We likely will see more means-testing, and we should consider lifetime earnings to be more economically efficient with fewer distortions. A blunt means test based on assets and income can create gaming scenarios. Looking at lifetime earnings, there will be very few people who will work less during their lifetimes just to collect higher benefits.

6

PANEL DISCUSSION: SECURING THE FUTURE: RETHINKING US SOCIAL SECURITY

PANELISTS

- **Jason Fichtner,** Chief Economist, Bipartisan Policy Center
- **Rachel Greszler,** Senior Research Fellow, Workforce and Public Finance, Roe Institute at the Heritage Foundation
- Moderated by **Andrew Moylan,** Vice President of Public Finance, Arnold Ventures

KEY HIGHLIGHTS

- **Jason Fichtner:** "We have 4.1 million Americans turning 65 every year until 2027, and by 2030, all baby boomers will be 65 or older. To keep them in the workforce, we could consider exempting them from paying payroll taxes, at least for Social Security, once they reach 65. You cannot be eligible for Disability Insurance once you hit your full retirement age. So why are you still paying the Disability Insurance

taxes? ... **Apart from reducing payroll tax rates, we could also eliminate the retirement earnings test, which confuses people who see it as a tax rather than a test.** These changes could help older workers stay in the labor force."
- **Rachel Greszler:** "If we consider Social Security's goal of preventing or reducing poverty in old age, it doesn't make sense for the program to pay three times higher benefits to those with the highest incomes compared to the lowest earners. Gradually shifting to a system that credits work regardless of earnings could be more effective. **Instead of replacing a portion of income, it should focus on providing a base level of support, particularly since high earners can and do save more independently.**"
- **Rachel Greszler:** "I'm all for a more progressive benefit structure, and **a flat benefit would be significantly more progressive.** It would increase the benefits for about a third of workers. I think that is important because Social Security is not keeping everybody out of poverty."
- **Jason Fichtner:** "We need to facilitate personal savings and convert defined-contribution assets into reliable income streams for retirement. If they're getting 40 to 50 percent income from their defined-contribution plan and personal savings, they might not need 40 percent from Social Security. You could lower the replacement rate and still have them be well-off in retirement. We need to think about this holistically as a retirement ecosystem and where income is coming from."

Transcripts have been edited for style and clarity.

Andrew Moylan: First, just to set the table before we jump into the conversation, let's recap some numbers that are worth referencing. According to the recent trustees report, the OASI [Old-Age and Survivors Insurance] Trust Fund will be depleted in the year 2033, which is not far off and falls within the political lifetimes of most current members of Congress. Without reform, the program's shortfall would necessitate a 21 percent across-the-board benefit cut or a 27 percent increase in the payroll tax—a little over three percentage points. In present value terms, this is a $24 trillion shortfall, presenting a significant challenge that US politicians have largely avoided. It has been more than 40 years since the last major reform to Social Security, making this an opportune time for action. The best time to address this issue was years ago; the second-best time is today.

Let me start with a question for both of you, beginning with Rachel. Given that any reform to Social Security is politically difficult and likely unpopular, what is your perspective on how lawmakers should approach this issue? What messaging should they use, and what policy implications arise from this difficulty?

Rachel Greszler: It is difficult because Social Security has expanded so far beyond its original scope. I think that transformative change is required, which is challenging. But I would start by going back to what was Social Security's original purpose. It was a Depression-era program for people who had lost their life savings. It was designed to protect seniors from living in poverty. Also, its purpose was to prevent younger workers and people raising families from having to finance poverty among older generations. Ironically, it was intended as a forced savings program but has become an intergenerational transfer program, burdening current workers to finance retirees.

Additionally, Social Security was supposed to be one of three pillars, starting as a 2 percent tax with a promise never to exceed 6 percent. Today, it takes 12.4 percent, and the CBO [Congressional Budget Office] says it needs to take 17.5 percent to maintain current benefits. We need to understand what the program was, see how it has deviated, and recognize the current realities. If we can agree on the program's current state, we will better evaluate reform proposals.

Andrew Moylan: Jason, what are your thoughts on that? It's a difficult political nut to crack, but you are nothing but a nutcracker.

Jason Fichtner: I think Rachel is right about emphasizing the original intent of Social Security as an old-age insurance program. It's important to discuss retirement and survivors separately from disability. However, Americans lead busy lives with different attention spans, making it difficult to explain programmatic details. For politicians and the media, we need to start with the stark reality that the trust funds will be depleted. That does not mean Social Security is going bankrupt. It will be there in some fashion for you. But there is no such thing as a free lunch, and waiting has a cost as well.

You mentioned that there could be a 20 percent benefit cut if we do nothing. Well, that's today. If we wait until 2033 when the OASI Trust Fund is depleted, that 20 percent cut becomes 24 or 25 percent. It's hard to imagine Congress allowing a 25 percent benefit reduction, but that is what current law would require. I think we need to be honest with the American people that they cannot just say, "Congress will raise taxes" or "Congress will do something to fill the hole." We don't know what's going to happen. We face market risk, inflation risk, sequence-of-return risk, and now political risk. Who's going to be in Congress in 2033? Who's going to be in the White House? Are they going to negotiate? Are they not? I don't know. But the cost of delaying is significant. We need to tell people that if we do nothing, benefits could get cut, and that's the default. Getting anything done on a bipartisan basis will require revenue increases and changes to benefits.

Andrew Moylan: Let's stick with you for a moment, Jason. You've written about encouraging higher labor force participation among people over 55. There have been some discouraging trends in that regard. What do you see as the benefits of increased participation, and what role, if any, should Congress have in directly encouraging this among older Americans?

Jason Fichtner: Work provides financial benefits, giving individuals more income to spend. For the economy, it keeps people in the labor force, boosting productivity and raising tax revenues for the government. So from fiscal and financial standpoints, it's a good thing. There are also mental health benefits from working for those who can work. We need to reduce barriers to continued employment without forcing anyone to work. One way Congress could help, as Andrew Biggs mentioned this morning, is by addressing the negative return on Social Security contributions and payroll taxes for those in their 60s.

We have 4.1 million Americans turning 65 every year until 2027, and by 2030, all baby boomers will be 65 or older. To keep them in the workforce, we could consider exempting them from paying payroll taxes, at least for Social Security, once they reach 65. You cannot be eligible for Disability Insurance once you hit your full retirement age. So why are you still paying the Disability Insurance taxes?

When thinking about Social Security reforms, we need to consider the three-legged stool: Social Security, defined-contribution plans, and individual savings. All three have to contribute to your income in retirement. That third stool, which could be individual savings, could also be work. How do we help people work in senior years? Apart from reducing payroll tax rates, we could also eliminate the retirement earnings test, which confuses people who see it as a tax rather than a test. These changes could help older workers stay in the labor force.

Rachel Greszler: A lot of my work focuses on the workforce and the labor market. I think there are positive trends here in terms of independent work, an option for people to work in a way that allows them to be their boss. This can be particularly helpful for older Americans ready to leave traditional nine-to-five jobs. They can work for themselves in a way that accommodates their lifestyle changes, whether that's working remotely or fewer hours. Congress could remove barriers, especially recent ones that discourage this type of work.

Andrew Moylan: Rachel, part of your prior work has been on the notion of shifting Social Security to a flat benefit structure. Can you expand on what appeals to you about that model and what the transition challenges might be?

Rachel Greszler: If we consider Social Security's goal of preventing or reducing poverty in old age, it doesn't make sense for the program to pay three times higher benefits to those with the highest incomes compared to the lowest earners. Gradually shifting to a system that credits work regardless of earnings could be more effective. Instead of replacing a portion of income, it should focus on providing a base level of support, particularly since high earners can and do save more independently.

Social Security has three bend points in its formula. We could gradually reduce the bend point for upper earnings while increasing benefits for lower earners. Over 20 or 30 years, younger workers would adjust, and the system would credit years worked rather than income levels. It's more of a contributory program in terms of the number of years you've worked.

Andrew Moylan: Let's discuss two major opposing views on Social Security reform. On the left, Bernie Sanders proposes a different vision compared to Senator Cassidy's. Jason, what are the highlights of the Cassidy proposal, and what are its challenges?

Jason Fichtner: First, individuals, policymakers, and researchers should create a safe space for members of Congress to talk about Social Security reform. That's important because not many politicians are willing to do so. Senator Cassidy deserves credit for initiating this conversation.

So what's the trust fund? It currently invests in special-issue Treasuries—essentially an accounting gimmick. In some ways, it has already been spent, but it is owed back to Social Security, which is a liability for taxpayers.

In a regular pension plan, investments would be diversified: bonds, Treasuries, equities, and maybe real estate. Why should we not think about Social Security's trust fund in the same context? Had we done this in 1983, despite the market crash in 2008 and COVID-19, we would be better off today. However, implementing this now is challenging due to the imminent trust fund depletion. Financing is a major concern.

Additionally, some people are concerned about the government's investing in the market. I remind you that we have the Thrift Savings Plan for government employees. They do a nice job walling off the political interference, but with Social Security, we're talking about a larger amount of money. While the idea of market investment has merits, there are significant challenges, such as political meddling and ensuring the funds aren't diverted for other uses.

The concern many people express is how to finance this. In 1983, payroll taxes created a surplus, which was added to the trust fund.

Now, we don't have surplus funds. You could sell the trust fund, but it's not going to be enough. We're facing a $22 trillion to $23 trillion shortfall on a net present value basis. That's the money you would need to put in the bank, earning a government return to cover the shortfall for the next 75 years. Discounting this back to a market rate equates to about $2 trillion to $2.5 trillion. The question is, can we borrow $2.5 trillion today and invest it in the market? That's what it would take to make this work, but borrowing that amount might not be feasible anymore.

However, if we do nothing and reach 2033, we'll face an annual gap of about $400 billion. Given Congress's current tendency to avoid raising taxes or implementing benefit cuts, they might opt to borrow the money instead. The real question is whether the market would support that decision when the time comes.

Andrew Moylan: Jason has created a safe space to discuss the Cassidy proposal. Rachel, what are your thoughts on the borrowing and investing component? While not entirely new, it is a fresh legislative approach.

Rachel Greszler: Borrowing and investing are essentially a form of arbitrage, hoping for higher returns. In today's environment with higher interest rates, the real return is just the market rate minus what you pay on Treasury. We're hoping the markets perform well, but borrowing to get out of debt hasn't worked well in places like Puerto Rico or Detroit. If borrowing doesn't make sense for the federal debt, it likely doesn't for Social Security.

However, I would like to recognize the benefits of investing. But instead of the government borrowing, we could allow individuals to own a portion of what they're paying. State and local pensions in the US benefit from positive returns but still face massive shortfalls due to the tendency to increase benefits. Usually, government ownership does not avoid these pitfalls.

Jason Fichtner: Rachel gave me a good segue to talk about individual accounts. When Senator Cassidy proposed this idea, interest rates were at 0 to 1 percent, making the potential equity premium attractive. Now, with higher borrowing costs, it's riskier. That's not a good investment strategy.

But we are talking about rethinking Social Security. I think we should rethink what the trust fund is if we're going to maintain it. Should it hold Treasuries, corporate market securities, or a diversified portfolio for better long-term returns?

Regarding private accounts, political feasibility is a concern. In a paper with Gary Koenig from AARP and William Gale from Brookings, we proposed START [Supplemental Transition Accounts for Retirement] accounts. This idea involved a two percentage point payroll tax increase, split between employer and employee, going into individual savings accounts. These accounts would be used to delay Social Security claims, providing higher, inflation-protected monthly benefits late. So if someone went into Social Security at 62 and said, "I want to get my benefit," they'd say "Great, you've got a START account value of $100,000. We're going to take your age 62 benefit and pay you today." When that START account was zero, you would put in the Social Security program at the delayed age, which would give you a higher monthly benefit. This would be a way to keep the current system in some fashion, have private accounts, access the market, and facilitate late claiming, all of which would help Social Security and help individuals' retirement security overall.

Andrew Moylan: Let's continue discussing private accounts. Has the political window for this closed, if it was ever open? During the first Bush administration, there was a significant push for private accounts in Social Security, but it wasn't successful. Rachel, what's your assessment? Jason mentioned a hybrid idea, but is there still political support for private accounts?

Rachel Greszler: I'd like to be optimistic and say it is possible. As we get closer to Social Security's becoming insolvent or even facing a broader fiscal crisis, the likelihood of raising taxes decreases, potentially opening the door for shifting toward savings increases that are privately owned. This shift is necessary because Social Security has grown significantly since its inception. Initially, it started with a 2 percent tax, never expected to exceed 6 percent. Today, it's at 12.4 percent, and it needs to be 17.5 percent to maintain current benefits.

Currently, workers' paychecks fund Social Security, which provides a benefit that replaces roughly 40 percent of income. To maintain this benefit, workers would need to contribute 17.5 percent of their paychecks. In contrast, financial advisers recommend saving 10 to 15 percent to replace at least 75 percent of income. Social Security doesn't offer a good deal because contributions are not positively invested. We need a system that enables some form of savings.

My proposal addresses Social Security solvency separately, adding an optional component for wealth building by redirecting part of the taxes into personal savings accounts. But I think the other reason we need private accounts is the ownership component. Social Security was intended to ensure against outliving savings, but life expectancy has increased unevenly across different groups. Unfortunately, two of my colleagues at the Heritage Foundation have passed away within the past couple of years in their late 50s. They paid into the system for decades, and they had families. One was not legally married, and in both cases, they got little or nothing out of it.

Lower-income Americans tend to have lower life expectancies. One out of four African American men will die between the ages of 45 and 64 when they have paid in all that time, getting nothing out in return. Even the lowest-income earners could accumulate significant retirement savings if they invested what Social Security requires, creating wealth they can pass on to their heirs. This is why private savings accounts should be a part of future reforms.

Jason Fichtner: Rachel raises important points about replacement rates. I also want to go back to the three-legged stool because it's an important metaphor we should be using in these conversations.

Social Security was designed to replace about 40 percent of the average worker's income, with lower earners getting higher replacement rates. Financial advisers suggest retirees should replace 70 to 80 percent of their income. With Social Security providing 30 to 40 percent, there's a gap to fill.

Historically, defined-benefit pension plans filled this gap, but these have largely transitioned to defined-contribution plans, placing more responsibility on individuals. We need to facilitate personal savings and convert defined-contribution assets into reliable income streams for retirement.

If they're getting 40 to 50 percent income from their defined-contribution plan and personal savings, they might not need 40 percent from Social Security. You could lower the replacement rate and still have them be well-off in retirement. We need to think about this holistically as a retirement ecosystem and where income is coming from.

Andrew Moylan: Rachel and Jason, reflecting on the three-legged stool metaphor, can you share your perspectives on non-Social Security elements? As Jason points out, while discussing Social Security's solvency, it's important to consider retirement security holistically. What role do you think employer-sponsored plans and private savings play in retirement security outside of Social Security?

Rachel Greszler: I think that's a huge role, and we have seen great success from the 401(k) system in the US. Overall, older Americans are doing better today than any previous generation. It often gets mismeasured and wrongly reported. These misconceptions are based on survey data designed to capture only defined benefits, regular pensions, and Social Security. There was a study comparing income under this survey versus the IRS tax data that shows your actual income. It showed that women had 45 percent higher retirement income. It is because of these private savings like 401(k)s, which don't provide a monthly benefit but can be drawn upon as needed. People usually withdraw a few times a year. There has been tremendous growth in these savings, and there are new features making it simpler for Americans to save. And simplicity is huge.

On the employer-sponsored side, automatic enrollment and auto-escalation of contributions help. Default life-cycle plans adjust risk over time, starting with riskier portfolios that offer higher returns early in one's career and shifting to more conservative investments later. These employer-sponsored plans are making significant progress. Universal savings accounts can also be beneficial. For people who bounce from one employer to another or who have lower income and feel like, "I don't think I can put this money away now, what if my car breaks down next week?," these accounts would allow flexible savings for any purpose.

Andrew Moylan: On the three-legged stool topic, I'd like to ask about the political implications for Social Security stemming from other battles. My boss, John Arnold, made himself public enemy number one among public employee unions for many years because of his efforts to support reforms for public employee pensions at the state and local levels. Jason, do you think there are lessons we can draw politically from how these state-level issues played out?

Jason Fichtner: One lesson is understanding the moral hazard problem in public finance and public choice issues in state and local pension plans and Social Security. When people think the cost of something is free, they ask for more of it. For instance, state and local pension plans often promised higher benefits without sufficient funding, leading to underfunded pensions and financial crises.

For Social Security, the focus should be on making it financially stable for the long term. Rachel mentioned the 12.4 percent Social Security payroll tax, but when you include Medicare, it's 15.3 percent. Let's leave Medicare reform out for a moment but something's got to be done on the Medicare side too. If taxes are the only solution, by 2033, we could see payroll taxes increasing by four percentage points. Now, we're close to a 20 percent payroll tax rate without considering Medicare. That makes the cost of labor very expensive.

I think we need to look at different sources of revenue for Social Security. I know people aren't happy with this. I know [Charles] Blahous would get mad at me. Andrew [Biggs] might as well. But the point is that we rely too much on the payroll tax. We could really be harming workers. We need to find a different revenue source that might make up that difference as part of the overall package of options to consider.

Andrew Moylan: Let's return to specifics on revenue and benefits shortly. But, Rachel, I wanted to ask you what we might be able to learn from state pension fights. Do you think it will take a crisis to achieve necessary reforms, similar to some state and local pension systems, or can we address it sooner? Can state-level experiences inform federal Social Security reform?

Rachel Greszler: We've known for decades that Social Security is becoming insolvent. I would argue, from having been up on the Hill for a while, it's even more difficult to talk about reform now. While it should happen soon, logically, I'm not optimistic. Social Security is relatively straightforward compared to state and local pensions, which are massively underfunded—by about $7 trillion. Some states have implemented positive reforms by shifting from defined-benefit plans to defined-contribution plans. However, many still face crises within the next couple of decades, which will affect taxpayers. Some of these states have constitutionally protected pensions, forcing them to raise taxes on workers who are already struggling to save. This raises the question, are we protecting generous public service retirement benefits at the expense of ordinary Americans trying to save for themselves?

Jason Fichtner: Or they raise property taxes, making it more expensive to live there, and people start moving out. We already see people moving in response to various tax increases.

Andrew Moylan: Let's talk about the tax side of things. Even today, with the current rate structure before any expirations of TCJA (Tax Cuts and Jobs Act) components next year, when you add it all up—federal, Medicare, state, and local income taxes—rates are above

50 percent. One of the things you often hear in the context of Social Security is that if we just eliminated the cap, you could solve this problem, which is not precisely true. It solves about half the problem, and it does so at the cost of a very steep tax hike that would put our top rates north of 65 percent in some places, which is not just high by US standards but by virtually anybody's standards. Rachel, why don't you talk me through your thoughts on the revenue side? In conversations we've had previously, you've noted that one of the big components we need to keep in mind is not killing the golden goose, which is economic growth. Tax increases are going to be a hindrance to that. So what are your thoughts about the revenue side, and what's your guidance to lawmakers?

Rachel Greszler: Well, there's only so much revenue that can be raised, especially with massive federal deficits and significant shortfalls in Social Security and Medicare. But let's focus on Social Security. You can look at the proposals to significantly increase taxes, whether to keep the program solvent or to keep it solvent and increase benefits, versus a more targeted approach, similar to shifting to a flat benefit and making other common-sense reforms. Penn Wharton has a budget model that shows that raising taxes could reduce GDP by six to seven percentage points over 30 years, which is about a $1.75 trillion difference. We talk about trillions a lot, which doesn't mean much to the average person. But that translates to having $5,000 more for every household every year in America.

It is really important to have a Social Security program that will help grow the economy. The $22.6 trillion shortfall means every household pays $172,000. But if you reform the system in a way that boosts the economy, that $172,000 could be reduced in the long run.

Andrew Moylan: Economic growth papers over a lot of the hardest challenges. Jason, how do we achieve this while addressing Social Security's revenue needs?

Jason Fichtner: You mentioned raising the taxable maximum, which right now is $168,600. That goes up every year when there's a cost-of-living increase. I'm not saying I support this proposal, but removing the tax cap during the [George W.] Bush or Obama administrations, back when I was a deputy commissioner of Social Security, would have solved the 75-year solvency. Now, as Andrew said, it addresses about half the problem.

As for taxes, I can see the rhetoric right now: the left might say, "For four cents on the dollar, we can save Social Security," while the right could say, "For a 33 percent tax increase."

We need to be creative. Think about this as a cafeteria menu of options for revenue and spending. For example, President Biden doesn't want to tax anyone making under $400,000. Whether that's a good or bad policy, the math makes it more challenging. But imagine you want to do something above $400,000. You don't have to tax at 12.4 percent. Why not 2 or 3?

Rachel mentioned the insurance value of Social Security and what we're trying to achieve with the program. What is the goal? We're trying to eliminate poverty. However, the maximum benefit for an individual on Social Security is $4,873. Let's round up to $5,000 per month or $60,000 a year. I think that keeps you out of poverty. These beneficiaries also have 401(k)s and other savings. We can see where we can make some changes. We could increase the lower benefits and lower those at the top. It doesn't need to be flat, but it would be a bit flatter, getting you closer to solvency. I think that's where we need to be more creative and think about how we could lower taxes for older workers so they stay in the labor force. Such reform could have bipartisan support.

Andrew Moylan: Let's talk the benefits side, which we've touched on. Rachel, we discussed your thoughts on a flat benefit structure. What do you think of a substantially more progressive benefit structure as a way to improve solvency and address other concerns?

Rachel Greszler: I'm all for a more progressive benefit structure, and a flat benefit would be significantly more progressive. It would increase the benefits for about a third of workers. I think that is important because Social Security is not keeping everybody out of poverty. We also need other programs, like Supplemental Security Income and SNAP [Supplemental Nutrition Assistance Program], to achieve that goal. However, the intent of the program was to prevent and alleviate poverty. So increasing benefits at the bottom while reducing them at the top makes sense. For example, millionaires are getting a $60,000 benefit, which doesn't make sense. We shouldn't take money from workers' paychecks to provide wealthy retirees with excessive benefits.

Andrew Moylan: Jason, what are your thoughts on moving toward a more progressive structure?

Jason Fichtner: I think it's very important because part of this is the intent of the program. High-income individuals don't need $60,000 from Social Security when they have substantial other income. I think we can find a way to cap the benefits at two or three times the poverty level. Additionally, Social Security has a minimum benefit that has not kept up with inflation. Let's make sure that there is a minimum benefit for poverty purposes.

Another part of the reform could be cutting payroll taxes to make labor more attractive. You want to tax things you don't like and subsidize the things you do. We are also making some savings more beneficial than others. For example, we overincentivize housing consumption. I do not need a mortgage interest deduction, but I will take it because it was offered to me. But the margin doesn't change my buying behavior. So we need to think about how we structure our tax system because some [reforms] level the playing field for taxation, while others don't.

Andrew Moylan: I want to shift gears for a moment. Jason, I'm going to pick on you to talk about demographics. Fundamentally, the challenge we are facing with Social Security is primarily one of demographics, essentially the baby boom. As baby boomers retire, fewer workers support them, and that's where the problem lies. When I joked about picking on you, I was pointing out that Rachel has six children, and I have four. We are doing our part.

Jason Fichtner: So among the three of us, we have about three children each.

Andrew Moylan: Rachel, let me start with you and ask on the demographic side. Do you think there is a role for the government in addressing some of those demographic factors, whether it is encouraging people to have more children or focusing on immigration? What are your thoughts on that as it plays into the Social Security debate?

Rachel Greszler: I think smart immigration policy is very important, especially as we try to address some of the workforce shortages we have. In terms of family policy, it's about enabling family formation rather than the government dictating the number of children people should have. We should make it easier for families to decide what is best for them. Currently, many barriers make it harder for families to get by. Some people avoid having more children because they cannot afford them. If we are talking about hiking Social Security taxes on families, that makes it harder for them to get by.

Before we start talking about a new government program or spending more money, let's discuss how we can break down the existing barriers.

Social Security was not supposed to be this way. It was primarily supposed to be self-funded in advance. However, the reality is that it is 100 percent financed by younger workers.

Jason Fichtner: You reminded me of an important point we haven't addressed directly. We've talked about Peak 65 and the millions of baby boomers retiring, but there's also a peak with millennials. In 2024, about 31 million of them are in their early 30s. Whatever Social Security reform we discuss today or 10 years from now is going to affect them as they approach retirement. That brings this concept of generational equity. If we raise taxes, millennials will be paying for future beneficiaries.

I am 52, and by the time the trust funds are depleted in 2033, I'll be 62. I'll be the guy here saying, "Don't touch my Social Security benefits." We need to think about the generational equity issue because if we start raising payroll taxes, millennials and the kids that come behind them will have a much harder time affording the things that we took for granted and could afford, such as housing, education, children, and family structures.

Andrew Moylan: So what do you think the political implications are of that generational challenge you just laid out? The political economy problem is that older Americans are much more likely to vote and are a much more active and wealthier demographic. How do you see helping break that cycle and raising some younger voices in this process in a way we wished happened some years ago? Rachel?

Rachel Greszler: That's a tough question. The government's massive debt forces younger generations to pay for it eventually. We haven't had to pay for it yet, which makes it seem sustainable. Older generations need to understand that Social Security reform is necessary for their children and grandchildren. If you told someone who's retired today, "Here's your benefit but tomorrow, that benefit has to come only from your children's and your grandchildren's paychecks," would they continue to take it? Probably, most of them would not. That's the problem with government spending and government programs. People don't know where the money's coming from.

So I think there needs to be a shift in how we talk about the reform, both for the older generation and younger workers. We have to confront the reality of imminent 21 percent cuts for everybody. In addition, recognizing the fact that no money was set aside in individual savings accounts is important. However, that's very difficult because politicians will demagogue anybody who wants to address the issue.

Andrew Moylan: It's a third rail for a reason. How do we deal with these generational concerns?

Jason Fichtner: This is a difficult question. Politicians don't want to touch it because it's the third rail, as you mentioned. So I'll go back to my first statement: We need to create a safe space for politicians to talk about the role of Social Security and other major programs. We need to talk about Social Security as an insurance program, explaining its purpose and how it works.

Insurance means you pay for something that has a high cost but a low probability. Now, we have a high-cost and high-probability retirement system. We need to have a say in how we tweak the system and get back to what an insurance program is.

Andrew Moylan: Let's prompt our audience for questions. While we get the mics to you, I'll share a personal note on Social Security. As a millennial, I've often heard that Social Security won't be around for me. I didn't give it a lot of thought other than my own policy concerns earlier in my life. Now, with baldness and unexplained knee pain, I suddenly have a newfound interest in the program. So I'm thinking about it more individually.

Q and A

Question 1: I started a project called the Center on Capital and Social Equity. I wanted to thank Rachel for mentioning low-wage workers and the longevity issue, which you uniquely did at this conference. I've been writing about individual accounts and want to reframe the discussion politically. Right now, you're left with a residual from the Bush years of chipping away Social Security to fund individual accounts, which Democrats will not accept. However, focusing on the 401(k) side, where half the people lack significant savings, could be more effective. You could provide a few hundred dollars when people get their Social Security card, encouraging savings. You've got $300 billion going into subsidizing 401(k)s, mostly for upper-income people. Move $30 or $40 billion down to the bottom, and you will end up with a supplement to Social Security after 30 to 40 years, financed by Wall Street. You're going to run up against the lobby, but I just wanted to throw that idea out there. Thank you.

Andrew Moylan: Rachel, you want to take a stab at that?

Rachel Greszler: Yeah. I think it's a great idea, education-wise, financial-well-being-wise, to start early, to have some form of account. Nowadays, with everyone having phones, it's easy to access and track these accounts, watching them grow over time. The education part of that would be worth it alone, but it's actual money that you have. From a behavioral economics perspective, if it's some account that is not locked up, it can be particularly important for lower-income Americans. They'll only withdraw when they need it, allowing the money to grow over time. I think that's something to look for: ways that could fund it. Currently, retirement savings are not so much tax-preferred. We just tax them once. But we could come up with other ways, such as creating a jump-start account.

Question 2 (Andrew Moylan): We have a question from a viewer, Dan, who suggests a fun idea. Jason, should we offer some sort of a buyout for current beneficiaries? He suggests 50 to 75 percent of the present value of the future stream of Social Security payments. Should we be thinking about buying people out?

Jason Fichtner: This idea has been mentioned by other scholars, such as offering a bonus payout or reduced benefit over time in exchange for a lump sum today. Again, there's no such thing as a free lunch. There are opportunity costs and tradeoffs. The thing is, who would be more likely to take it? You could have wealthy individuals saying: "Wow, I get to take my money today, lump sum. I'll invest it." If it helps the trust fund, maybe it's worthwhile. But you could also have lower-income workers who take it but don't have enough money in retirement. Then they're destitute, and we've done a bad service to them. We need to consider the consequences and who would likely take the offer. While it's not one of my preferred policy options, I'm open to discussing it.

Rachel Greszler: This is something that I've proposed. So say you are 40 years old, and you've been paying into the system. You've earned a benefit that is payable today. But going forward, if you want to have some of your taxes go into a personal account, you would have that option. In the beginning, it would be roughly half of what's currently coming out of your paycheck. It would go into your personal account, with the employer's pay going to the system. It's improving the system because there's no liability accruing going forward. In most cases, it's going to be a win-win situation. The reality is that even taking half of what Social Security is paying and investing it in something that grows over time will result in more money. Even lower-income workers could end up with more money, which they would own and could pass on to their children if they die early.

Jason Fichtner: That's a more creative idea. I appreciate thinking holistically about retirement security. Younger workers could see a combination of Social Security and personal savings accounts, offering both protection and growth potential.

Question 3: Tyler Bond, National Institute on Retirement Security. Rachel, so you conceded when talking about transitioning to a flat benefit that it would take two to three decades. I'm assuming you would eventually want to reduce the payroll taxes. So you're funding a smaller benefit with smaller revenue coming into the system. However, the system needs revenue now. How would you manage that tension between bringing money into the system now and transitioning to a smaller, flat benefit with less of a payroll tax feeding into the system?

Rachel Greszler: If you did it today, it's a lot easier, and there will be much lower transition costs. In the end, you come out ahead with solvency. To manage the interim period before upper-income benefits are reduced and lower benefits are increased, we could consider options like borrowing money or general revenue transfers.

Andrew Moylan: So in the few moments that we have left here, I want to prompt both of you to think positively. I try to be more optimistic about things. In programs like the Earned Income Tax Credit [EITC], improper payment rates are approaching 40 percent in some cases. Yet in the Social Security world, we have $1.4 trillion worth of payments to 70 million people, and improper payment rates are in the single digits, being as low as 1 percent in some components of the program. That's one element that is working better than at least some other areas of government. However, we don't want to get too excited about it.

Let me ask you both about something you are optimistic about or you think is working well in Social Security. Jason, I'll start with you.

Jason Fichtner: You mentioned improper payments, and that does not necessarily mean fraud, right? But the EITC is a very complicated thing to fill out. You're asking low-income Americans to fill it out, and they make a math mistake. Some of these improper payments are fraud, and we should definitely go after fraud.

I worked for both agencies, the IRS and Social Security. I worked for the most hated and most loved agencies in the government. There's an obvious difference. One takes your money, and one gives you money, and you can tell which one is liked and which one is hated. The improper payments happen if someone dies and you don't get the information back to the person to see if the payment keeps going. Complexity breeds complexity, which breeds improper payments. So keep things simple.

In some ways, Social Security is doing an amazing job of administering the program. They have some problems. The DI [Disability Insurance] is still a complicated issue, but I think we should take faith in knowing that the agency is trying to do its best, and we should find ways to help them while holding them accountable for those efforts.

Andrew Moylan: Rachel, what are you optimistic about?

Rachel Greszler: I am optimistic that the reality is that Social Security is solvable. There are common-sense reforms that can improve the system for those who need it most while benefiting the economy and personal incomes. The difficulty is politics, and I hope that we can get past that before we have a fiscal crisis.

Andrew Moylan: Well, thank you for that. I'd add my own note of optimism there that I am also optimistic this is a solvable problem, especially with the great wealth engine of the American economy.

PART TWO
Canada and New Zealand

7

THE CANADIAN RETIREMENT SYSTEM

The Canadian retirement system reduces old-age poverty through its basic flat-benefit pension while providing additional income for retirees through an earnings-related scheme. Neither of these programs offers excessive benefits, and both operate at relatively low costs. The earnings-related Canada Pension Plan (CPP) stands out for its long-term sustainability, largely a result of reforms adopted in the 1990s. The CPP also includes an automatic stabilizer that adjusts benefits and tax rates to ensure the system remains solvent and able to meet its obligations.

A notable aspect of the Canadian approach is the high degree of individual autonomy offered in retirement planning. Many workers save through various private retirement accounts, with a significant portion owning Tax-Free Savings Accounts (TFSAs). These accounts are especially popular among lower-income households and younger workers because they allow participants to access funds for nonretirement reasons. The Canadian model—which combines a strong anti-poverty benefit, a financially sustainable earnings-related scheme, and a broad array of private savings options such as TFSAs (which have no equivalent in the United States)—provides important insights for US legislators.

This chapter provides an overview of the Canadian retirement system and its financing structure, benefit provision, and impact on individual financial outcomes, against the benchmark of a libertarian system and by comparison with the Organisation for Economic Co-operation and Development (OECD) average and the US system.

The Canadian retirement system stands out for enabling private savings and wealth accumulation among a broad swath of the Canadian population, including by limiting government benefit provision. Programs like Old Age Security (OAS) and the Guaranteed Income Supplement (GIS) provide essential income security for seniors without paying excessively high benefits. Their benefits are not linked to preretirement earnings but are designed to safeguard retirees with limited earnings histories against old-age poverty. In contrast, Social Security, the US retirement system's primary public component, is earnings-related and provides overly generous benefits to high earners while often providing inadequate income support for retirees with low pre-retirement earnings.

Based on the OECD's measure of old-age poverty, Canada's senior poverty rate is below the OECD average, while the US rate is significantly higher than the average.[1] However, this OECD measure, which compares retirees' incomes with those of the general population, provides more insights about income inequality than about actual poverty levels. That is why it can sometimes produce counterintuitive results where wealthier nations appear to have higher senior poverty rates compared with much poorer countries. A more accurate method, used by both Canada and the United States to measure poverty, compares seniors' incomes with country-specific poverty thresholds.[2] Using this approach, the US rate of 10.2 percent was still higher than Canada's 6 percent in 2022.[3] However, the US poverty figure provided by the Census Bureau underestimates seniors' incomes, thus resulting in inflated poverty rates.[4] When using more accurate figures—available only for 2018—the United States had a slightly lower senior poverty rate than Canada that year.[5]

Canada's basic anti-poverty benefit structure is complemented by the CPP, a mandatory, earnings-related system that is structurally akin to Social Security but distinct in its financial sustainability. Specifically, according to the Chief Actuary's latest report, CPP revenues will be sufficient to cover the program's expenses over the next 75 years.[6] In contrast, borrowing based on the Social Security trust fund is projected to meet expenses only until 2033, after which the program faces automatic benefit cuts that could be indiscriminately applied.[7] In the late 1990s, Canada adopted benefit reforms that secured the CPP's long-term viability, prompted by an alarming actuarial report that highlighted funding shortfalls. Moreover, the CPP features an automatic balancing mechanism that safeguards the system against political inaction when actuarial reports identify that the system is financially unsustainable.

This is unlike the situation confronting the US Social Security system, where recurring actuarial reports have been sounding the alarm about the program's impending insolvency—yet politicians refuse to take corrective action. Social Security finances have been deemed unsustainable for decades, yet there is no effective mechanism in place to incentivize early political intervention. Instead, Congress is most likely going to wait until automatic benefit cuts loom at the trust fund's projected exhaustion in 2033.

Given the reluctance of Congress and presidents to address Social Security's financial problems, it would be helpful to adopt a CPP-like automatic stabilizer that kicks in well before the trust fund's exhaustion. Such a mechanism could make more gradual programmatic reforms to more closely align Social Security spending with revenues, including reducing benefit indexation formulas and adjusting eligibility ages for increases in expectancy, to name two easy-to-implement automatic adjustments.

While US policymakers should take note of CPP reforms, they should not raise payroll taxes, a component of the Canadian reforms in the 1990s. Congress has several available options that would address the program's financial problems without burdening workers with additional taxes. It should also resist calls to expand Social Security, similar to the recent CPP expansion that led to significant CPP tax increases.[8]

According to the OECD, Canada's public pension expenditure as a percentage of gross domestic product (GDP) is lower than that of the United States and the OECD average.[9] However, the OECD's methodology for calculating spending on pensions is broad, including not only main pension programs like the CPP and Social Security but also provisions such as veterans' benefits. When isolating the comparison to just the main pension components—OAS, GIS, and CPP—with US Social Security, Canada spent slightly more as a share of GDP on its general pension programs in 2023 than the United States did (without accounting for veterans' pension benefits).[10] It is worth noting that Canada's higher old-age dependency ratio—the number of seniors among 100 working-age individuals—partially explains its slightly higher pension expenditures.

Governmental provision is also complemented by various voluntary savings options, such as Registered Pension Plans (RPPs) and Registered Retirement Savings Plans (RRSPs), which offer tax incentives for voluntary private savings. Additionally, TFSAs provide flexible, tax-advantaged savings opportunities, appealing particularly to younger individuals and workers with low incomes. TFSAs are popular primarily because they allow withdrawals at any time for any purpose, not just at retirement. In contrast, US tax-advantaged savings tools such as 401(k) retirement accounts come with restrictions that discourage accessing savings before age 59½. Congress should consider adopting TFSA-like accounts in the United States, also known as universal savings accounts or USAs.[11]

Canada has one of the highest levels of voluntary retirement assets relative to GDP among OECD countries (not including TFSAs).[12] Additionally, Canada is one of eight OECD countries with widespread coverage of voluntary retirement plans, alongside Belgium, Estonia, Germany, Ireland, Lithuania, New Zealand, and the United States. For an average earner, these plans typically provide a replacement rate of 20 percent of preretirement earnings, more than a third of the total replacement rate of the Canadian retirement system.[13] Furthermore, sources other than public benefits (voluntary savings from retirement plans; work; and other savings) accounted for 62.4 percent of total senior income in Canada, which is slightly higher than their share in the United States, 60.7 percent.[14]

The Canadian model, with its blend of public provisions and voluntary savings mechanisms, offers valuable lessons for US policymakers.

It shows how to enhance retirement security and fiscal sustainability by focusing government provision on creating a base layer of financial security while enabling all individuals to save and invest to meet their own needs, leading up to and in retirement.

Overview of the Canadian retirement system

The Canadian retirement system relies on all the World Bank pillars except the second; similar to the United States, Canada has no mandatory private pension schemes. This is a good thing, as governments should not be in the business of forcing people to save a certain amount via a government-favored method for their own retirement—or to meet any other income need, for that matter.

The zero pillar consists of two programs: a basic flat-benefit program called Old Age Security and a targeted Guaranteed Income Supplement program for seniors with incomes below a certain threshold. The OECD reports that in 2022, the maximum OAS benefit was 9.8 percent of gross average wages, while the GIS maximum benefit amounted to 14.6 percent.[15] OAS benefits are subject to a recovery tax, with individuals earning over US$121,000 (C$142,600) receiving no OAS benefits.[16] However, GIS benefits are not taxed.

The CPP first pillar is an earnings-related scheme like Social Security. However, it does not have a progressive benefit structure like Social Security does; instead, it offers a flat replacement rate for all seniors regardless of their preretirement earnings.[17] Additionally, it includes an automatic balancing mechanism that stabilizes the system's funding shortfalls in the absence of policy intervention.

The CPP underwent significant changes in the late 1990s to address the program's funding problems.[18] These changes are relevant to Social Security's current challenges for two reasons.

First, before the reform, the CPP, like Social Security, was on its way to insolvency, with a 1993 actuarial report projecting that without intervention, the CPP fund would be exhausted by 2015.[19] This gave Canada 22 years to act, significantly more time than the 8 years that Social Security has as of 2025.

Second, during the reform process, Canada also faced large deficits and unsustainable debt, though these were less severe compared with the current fiscal situation of the United States.[20] The CPP funding shortfalls, coupled with Canada's shaky fiscal outlook in the '90s, led to bipartisan support for fiscal responsibility. As Canada's prime minister at the time stated, debts and deficits should be seen not as ideological issues but as arithmetic facts.[21]

The Canadian retirement system's third pillar, which includes voluntary employer-based schemes and individual retirement plans, is one of the strongest among OECD countries, with the total value of plan assets exceeding 100 percent of GDP.[22] These plans function similarly to American 401(k)s and individual retirement accounts (IRAs).

In addition, Canadians have access to TFSAs. As noted, TFSAs allow individuals to withdraw money at any time for any purpose, a feature particularly attractive to young and low-income individuals. Nearly 60 percent of Canadians owned these accounts in 2022.[23] Congress should consider establishing similar accounts to enable more Americans to save for immediate and future needs in accounts they own and control that benefit from similar tax treatment as retirement vehicles.[24]

Finally, the fourth pillar, comprising financial and nonfinancial assets outside of public pensions and retirement plans, is robust. More than 70 percent of Canadian seniors are homeowners,[25] and nearly half of retirees' income comes from sources beyond government pensions and retirement plans.[26] See Table 7.1 for a summary of the Canadian and the US retirement systems, along with select metrics to evaluate and compare their effectiveness.

The data featured in Table 7.1 are derived from the OECD's *Pensions at a Glance 2023* report and various national sources. For Canada, these include Statistics Canada and the Office of the Chief Actuary, while for the United States, the sources include the Congressional Budget Office and the Social Security Administration. The source for each metric is indicated in the table.

TABLE 7.1
Key highlights: Canada versus US retirement system

Category/metric	Canada	United States
Zero pillar	Old Age Security (OAS), Guaranteed Income Supplement (GIS)	Supplemental Security Income
First pillar	Canada Pension Plan/ Quebec Pension Plan	Social Security
Second pillar	None	None
Third pillar	RPPs, RRSPs, TFSAs (not exclusively retirement tool)	401(k)s, IRAs, Roth 401(k)s, Roth IRAs
Eligibility[a]	OAS/GIS: 65 years old, 10–40 years residency; CPP/QPP: 65 years old, early at 60, late at 70	Social Security: 66–67 years old, early at 62, late at 70
Old-age dependency ratio[a]	31.7	29.4
Zero-pillar benefit amount (percent of gross average wage)[a]	OAS: 9.8%, GIS: 14.6%	15.60%
Maximum taxable earnings for the first pillar (percent of annual average wage)[a]	79%	227%
Demographic impact ratio[a,b,c,d]	1.66	1.47
Total spending on public pensions per person (US$)[b,c,d]	$3,240	$4,020
Total spending on public pensions (percent of GDP)[b,d]	5.20%	5%
Total spending on public pensions, OECD (percent of GDP)[a,e]	5.30% (data from 2020)	7.50% (data from 2020)
Replacement rate (public pensions)[a]	36.80%	39.10%
Private retirement assets (percent of GDP)[a]	153%	138%
Replacement rate (public and private)[a]	57%	73%
Private replacement share[a,c]	0.35	0.47

(continued)

TABLE 7.1 *(continued)*

Category/metric	Canada	United States
Homeownership rate (percent of seniors)[b]	70% (aged 65+) (data from 2019)	78.4% (aged 65–74) and 82.4% (75+) (data from 2019)
Median net worth of seniors (US$)[b]	$444,245 (data from 2019)	$266,000 (aged 65–74) and $255,000 (75+) (data from 2019)
Poverty rate (national measure, percent of seniors)[b]	6% (data from 2022)	10.2% (data from 2022)*

Note: CPP = Canada Pension Plan; GDP = gross domestic product; IRAs = individual retirement accounts; OECD = Organisation for Economic Co-operation and Development; QPP = Quebec Pension Plan; RPPs = Registered Pension Plans; RRSPs = Registered Retirement Savings Plans; TFSAs = Tax-Free Savings Accounts.

a. Data from OECD's *Pensions at a Glance 2023* report.

b. Data from a Canadian/US government source.

c. Authors' calculations.

d. For Canada, includes Old Age Security, Guaranteed Income Supplement, Canada Pension Plan, and Quebec Pension Plan; for the United States, includes Social Security.

e. Broader definition of public pensions; for example, includes Supplemental Security Income for the United States.

* The US senior poverty rate is likely much lower because the official poverty measure does not account for most of the income seniors derive from private retirement accounts.

Zero pillar

The zero pillar of the Canadian retirement system includes the Old Age Security (OAS) and the Guaranteed Income Supplement (GIS) programs. The OAS program provides a flat benefit to individuals aged 65 years and older. To receive a full benefit, an individual must have lived in Canada for at least 40 years.[27] For those with fewer than 40 years of residence, the benefit is reduced proportionally (the minimum residence requirement is 10 years). In 2025, the maximum monthly benefit for seniors aged 65 to 74 is C$728 or US$617 (adjusted for purchasing power parity [PPP]).[28] According to the OECD, the maximum OAS benefit amounted to 9.8 percent of gross average earnings in 2022.[29] Furthermore, since 2022, the OAS benefit has increased by 10 percent for seniors over the age of 75, bringing their monthly benefit to roughly US$678 (C$800).[30]

The OAS is income-tested through taxation, with seniors earning more than US$73,600 (C$86,900) paying the OAS pension recovery tax. Individuals pay 15 percent of the difference between their income and this threshold.[31] The benefits are fully clawed back when an individual's income reaches US$121,000 (C$142,600). These thresholds are higher for seniors aged 75 and over. In 2022, about 95 percent of individuals over the age of 65 received OAS benefits.[32]

The second component of the Canadian retirement system's zero pillar is the GIS program, which supplements the OAS for individuals with an annual income below US$19,000 (C$22,000).[33] The maximum monthly GIS benefit of US$921 (C$1,087) is not subject to recovery tax but decreases if an individual has a partner who receives the OAS pension.[34] According to the OECD, the maximum GIS benefit amounted to 14.6 percent of gross average earnings in 2022, with about 31 percent of Canadian seniors receiving GIS benefits.[35]

Both the OAS and GIS benefits are indexed to prices and financed from general revenues.[36] In 2023, Canada spent US$64 billion (C$75 billion), or 2.59 percent of GDP, on these programs combined.[37]

It is interesting to see how the OAS and GIS programs fulfill their primary goal of reducing senior poverty. According to the relative poverty measure offered by the OECD, 12.1 percent of Canadian seniors lived in poverty in 2020, a figure lower than the OECD average of 14.2 percent and substantially below the US rate of 22.8 percent.[38] However, this relative poverty measure—which compares seniors' incomes with 50 percent of median household income within each country—is an indicator of income inequality rather than of actual poverty.

A more accurate indicator of poverty is Canada's Market Basket Measure (MBM), which is calculated based on the cost of a basket of goods and services required for a "modest, basic standard of living" (e.g., food, clothing, transportation).[39] Using the MBM, only 6 percent of Canadian seniors lived in poverty in 2022, less than half of the OECD figure. In addition, according to the same measure, the poverty rate among Canadian seniors was lower than the poverty rate of the overall population, which was 9.9 percent in 2022.[40]

According to the US Census Bureau's official poverty measure (OPM), which is based on the cost of basic necessities like food and other basic expenses, the US senior poverty rate in 2022 was 10.2 percent.[41] However, this figure overstates senior poverty in the United States, as it does not include most of the income American seniors receive from private retirement accounts.[42] To address this issue, the Census Bureau introduced the National Experimental Well-Being Statistics (NEWS), which is based on more comprehensive income data. The NEWS figures suggest that the Census Bureau significantly overestimated the senior poverty rate in 2018 (the only year examined by the study), with the initial estimate of 9.75 percent being substantially higher than the 5.73 percent calculated by NEWS.[43] While the Census Bureau has not yet provided revised senior poverty figures for 2022, we can assume they are lower than the suggested 10.2 percent. When comparing the 2018 senior poverty rates of the United States (based on NEWS) and Canada (based on MBM), Canada's rate of 6 percent is slightly higher than the 5.73 percent in the United States.[44] However, this comparison should be taken with caution, because although both the MBM and US thresholds aim to reflect the cost of a basic basket of goods, these thresholds differ significantly in how they are constructed and the specific items included.

First pillar

The first pillar of Canada's retirement system is the Canada Pension Plan, with a separate plan for Quebec workers called the Quebec Pension Plan (QPP). For simplicity, unless otherwise specified, both plans are referred to as CPP in this chapter and the provided figures include both plans.

The CPP is a mandatory, earnings-related scheme with a tax rate of 11.9 percent of earnings (12.8 percent for QPP), shared equally between employees and employers. In 2025, the maximum pensionable earnings, or the ceiling up to which the CPP tax applies, is US$60,000 (C$71,300).[45]

In addition, beginning in 2024, as part of the CPP expansion (discussed in more detail in the next section), an additional earnings limit was introduced. Starting in 2025, this new ceiling will be 14 percent higher than the original limit (in 2024, it was 7 percent higher). Earnings between the original and new thresholds will be subject to an additional 8 percent tax.[46] For reference, the OECD estimated the original maximum pensionable earnings to be 79 percent of average full-time gross wages in 2022 (since this threshold is indexed to wage growth, the ratio to average wages should not change over time).[47] In contrast, the maximum taxable earnings for Social Security amounted to US$147,000 or 227 percent of the annual average wage in the same year.[48]

The CPP offers a flat replacement rate of 33 percent of an individual's average lifetime earnings, irrespective of their earnings.[49] This differs from the progressive structure of Social Security, which provides higher replacement rates for lower-income earners and lower rates for those with higher incomes.[50] Furthermore, the CPP does not offer overly generous benefits to high-income seniors like Social Security does. As of 2025, someone retiring at normal retirement age would receive a maximum of US$1,214 (C$1,433) from the CPP in monthly benefits, which is more than three times lower than the maximum monthly Social Security benefit of US$4,018.[51]

Initial CPP benefits are indexed to average wage growth and are later adjusted according to price changes.[52] The full eligibility age is 65, with early and delayed retirement possible at 60 and 70, subject to benefit reductions or increases. Canada's old-age dependency ratio, which measures the number of individuals aged 65 and over per 100 working-age individuals (aged 20 to 64), was 31.7 in 2022. This figure was above the US dependency ratio of 29.4 and the OECD average of 31.3.[53]

The CPP includes an automatic balancing mechanism, which safeguards the system from political complacency. Every three years, the Chief Actuary publishes a report evaluating the actuarial status of the program. The Actuary calculates the minimum CPP tax rate needed to fund the system for 75 years. If this rate exceeds the current rate, the system is deemed unsustainable, prompting federal and provincial finance ministers to devise a plan to restore sustainability. If they cannot reach an agreement, the automatic balancing mechanism is activated, freezing benefit growth and increasing the tax by 50 percent of the difference between the existing and the calculated minimum tax rates.[54] In contrast, Social Security has a blunter, delayed balancing mechanism. When the trust fund's balances are insufficient to cover benefits, benefits are supposed to be automatically reduced to match revenues. This means that the mechanism is only activated in the final year when the trust fund is depleted. As a result, unlike the CPP, this system does not incentivize political action until it is too late.

Social Security's finances have been deemed unsustainable for decades, with the Social Security Board of Trustees projecting 75-year actuarial deficits in 1984, just one year after the 1983 reforms.[55]

Given Congress's complacency in addressing the program's financing problems, implementing an automatic stabilizer could help prompt more timely reforms. However, unlike the CPP's balancing mechanism, the US Social Security version should not include payroll tax increases, as higher taxes reduce disposable income for workers, increase labor costs, and displace private savings.[56] Instead, such a stabilizer should prioritize reducing spending to align benefits with revenues. This could involve automatically adjusting benefit indexation formulas and raising eligibility ages to reflect increasing life expectancy, thus ensuring that program costs align with revenues without placing additional financial burdens on American workers.

In 2023, the Canadian government spent more than US$65 billion (C$76 billion), or 2.66 percent of GDP, on the CPP and QPP combined.[57] Overall, Canada spent 5.24 percent of its GDP on CPP, QPP, OAS, and GIS in 2023, amounting to US$3,243 (C$3,794) per person.[58] In comparison, US spending on Social Security was US$1.35 trillion in the same year, equivalent to 5 percent of GDP or US$4,021 per person.[59] However, according to the latest OECD data, which uses a broader definition of public spending on retirement that includes programs such as veterans' benefits (for both countries) and the US Supplemental Security Income (SSI), Canada spent 5.3 percent of its GDP on public pensions, while the US spent 7.5 percent. In addition, Canada's public pension expenditure was 35 percent less than the OECD average.[60]

The demographic impact ratio (DIR) for Canada is 1.66. The DIR, which is calculated by multiplying a country's pension spending as a share of GDP by its old-age dependency ratio, allows us to better compare countries by accounting for the demographic pressures each country faces. If two countries have the same pension spending relative to GDP, a higher DIR indicates that one country is under more demographic pressure because it has a higher proportion of elderly individuals. The DIR for the United States is 1.47, 11.5 percent lower than that of Canada.[61] However, US pension spending as a share of GDP is only 4.6 percent lower than that in Canada. This discrepancy indicates that aging plays a more substantial role in the overall pension burden for Canada than for the United States.

According to the OECD, the CPP, QPP, and OAS replacement rate is 36.8 percent, lower than the Social Security rate of 39.1 and the OECD average of 50.7 percent for mandatory retirement programs.[62] While Canadian public pensions provide a lower replacement rate than the OECD average, the total replacement rate of Canada's retirement system, which also includes voluntary retirement plans, exceeds the OECD average. This suggests that Canada effectively maintains seniors' standard of living while offering them greater freedom in their retirement planning decisions. More details on this are discussed in the remainder of this chapter.

CPP reforms

In 1998, the Canadian federal government and provinces agreed to implement significant changes to the CPP system. The agreement was triggered by the CPP "Fifteenth Actuarial Report," which revealed that the program was massively underfunded, with its 1993 balance falling short of the previous report's projection by US$665 million (C$805 million). Additionally, in 1993, the CPP faced nearly US$413 billion (C$500 billion), or 66 percent of GDP, in long-term unfunded obligations, with the CPP fund projected to be depleted by 2015. The report estimated that the CPP tax rates would need to jump from 5.6 percent in 1996 to more than 14 percent by 2030 without reforms.[63]

To address the program's financial instability and prevent a steep hike in taxes, lawmakers agreed to freeze the basic exemption amount at US$2,870 (C$3,500, which is the income floor for paying CPP taxes), reduce the growth rate in benefits, sharply increase the CPP tax to 9.9 percent by 2003 (maintaining this rate indefinitely), and allow the newly created Canada Pension Plan Investment Board to invest accumulated surpluses in stocks and other assets (previously limited to investing in federal and provincial securities).[64]

According to the latest actuarial report (31st) on the CPP, investment income from the CPP fund represents about 30 percent of total program income.[65] Importantly, the same report states that the program is financially sustainable over the long term.

It is noteworthy that the 1990s CPP reforms coincided with a fiscal crisis in Canada. In 1993, Canada's federal budget deficit was 5.1 percent of GDP, the federal debt was 71 percent of GDP, and interest costs were 5.4 percent of GDP.[66] Recognizing the severity of Canada's fiscal outlook, the governing Liberal Party collaborated with members of the conservative Reform Party to address the crisis. As Paul Martin, then-Minister of Finance, stated:

> The debt and deficit are not inventions of ideology. They are facts of arithmetic. The quicksand of compound interest is real. The last thing Canadians need is another lecture on the dangers of the deficit. The only thing Canadians want is clear action.[67]

Among other reforms, from 1995 to 1997, Canada reduced government spending by 8.8 percent and reduced the number of federal employees by 14 percent. In 1998, this bipartisan cooperation led to the first balanced budget in 30 years. Therefore, the CPP reform was a logical step in the context of an overall fiscally responsible environment in Canada. As Finance Minister Paul Martin put it: "[O]ur National Pension Plan had an unfunded liability greater than the national debt and it could not be ignored."[68]

To put things into perspective, Table 7.2 compares the fiscal and pension system health of Canada in 1993 and the United States in 2024. Across almost every metric, except for interest costs, the US system is in a significantly worse situation than the Canadian system was in the

TABLE 7.2
Fiscal health and pension metrics: Canada's federal government (1993) versus the US federal government (2024)

	Canada (1993)	US (2024)
Deficit as a percentage of GDP	5.1	6.7
Debt as a percentage of GDP	71	99
Interest as a percentage of GDP	5.4	3.1
CPP/Social Security unfunded obligation as a percentage of GDP	66	89
Years before fund depletion	22	9

Source: For Canadian figures, see Office of the Chief Actuary, Actuarial Report (31st) on the Canada Pension Plan and Speer, Getting out of a Fiscal Hole. For the US figures, see Update to the Budget and Economic Outlook, Congressional Budget Office and "2024 Annual Report of the Board of Trustees," Social Security Administration.
Note: CPP = Canada Pension Plan; GDP = gross domestic product.

1990s. Canada adopted the aforementioned reforms with lower deficits, debt, and unfunded obligations and with a larger window to fix its pension system compared with the United States today. The longer US policymakers delay implementing fiscally responsible measures, including Social Security reform, the worse the fiscal outlook and Social Security's finances will become. Congress should consider how Canada set aside partisan differences in the 1990s to avoid a worse fiscal crisis and protect retirees from a pension system crisis.

Although Canada passed laudable fiscally responsible reforms in the 1990s, affecting both the CPP and the broader federal government, raising the payroll tax rate is the least desirable option for pension reforms. This change increased labor costs in Canada and displaced private savings among Canadians.[69] While Congress is encouraged to adopt Canada's proactive approach from the 1990s, Social Security reform must not include harmful payroll tax increases, especially given the wide array of other available options that would improve the program's financial outlook.

About 20 years after the 1990s reforms, Canada began expanding the CPP, gradually increasing its tax rate from 9.9 percent to 11.9 percent between 2019 and 2023.[70] In 2024, an additional threshold for taxable earnings was introduced, initially 7 percent higher than the original threshold, with the difference rising to 14 percent in 2025.[71] Earnings falling within this new range will be taxed at 8 percent.

These major tax hikes were justified by accompanying increases in CPP benefits, which now replace 33 percent of preretirement earnings, compared with 25 percent before the change.[72] However, Philip Cross, a senior fellow at the Fraser Institute and participant in the inaugural Cato Social Security Symposium, argued in 2016 that the push to expand the CPP was based on the myth that Canada had a retirement income crisis, stating that "the vast majority of Canadians are well-served by both the pension system and their own actions in providing for their retirement."[73] Furthermore, other experts at the Fraser Institute have criticized the CPP expansion as poorly targeted, focusing on middle-income Canadians who faced low risks to their retirement security, while doing little to help the most vulnerable seniors with low lifetime earnings.[74]

Congress should resist similar proposals to expand Social Security, such as the Social Security Expansion Act introduced by Sens. Bernie Sanders (I-VT) and Elizabeth Warren (D-MA). This legislation would increase Social Security benefits in exchange for saddling workers, investors, and business owners with a US$33.8 trillion tax hike.[75] Instead of relying on additional forced savings to increase the retirement income of seniors, Congress should pursue reforms that encourage more voluntary savings. As discussed in the following section, Canada offers valuable insights on this aspect.

Third pillar

The third pillar of the Canadian retirement system, voluntary retirement plans, is more robust than that of most other OECD countries. Combined, employer-based registered pension plans, individual registered retirement savings plans, and public pensions provide a 57 percent replacement rate, just above the OECD average.[76] In 2022, Canada's voluntary replacement share (VRS)—the share of voluntary private plans in the total replacement rate—was 35 percent. The total replacement rate for the US retirement system was even higher at 73.2 percent, with a VRS of 47 percent.

Voluntary private retirement plans in Canada benefit from tax concessions, whereby contributions and investment growth are not taxed but withdrawals are taxed as income. This is known as the EET regime (for Exempt-Exempt-Taxed). In 2022, Canada was one of seven OECD nations with private retirement plan assets exceeding 100 percent of GDP, reaching 153 percent.[77] Among these seven countries—Australia, Canada, Denmark, Iceland, the Netherlands, Switzerland, and the United States—only Canadian and US private plans are voluntary.

In 2021, 27.3 percent of Canada's working-age population participated in occupational plans like RPPs, while 25.6 percent participated in personal plans such as RRSPs, according to the OECD.[78] In comparison, the United States had a 56 percent participation rate in employer-sponsored plans such as 401(k)s in 2023 and a 25.3 percent participation rate in individual retirement accounts in 2019, according to the Congressional Research Service.[79]

The OECD statistics for Canada do not account for TFSAs, which allow anyone to contribute after-tax money, with both investment growth and withdrawals exempt from taxation. TFSAs offer considerable flexibility because funds can be withdrawn at any time for any purpose. Introduced in 2009, TFSAs quickly gained widespread popularity among Canadians. Statistics Canada reported a 39.4 percent participation rate for TFSAs in 2020, compared with 28.7 percent for RRSPs.[80]

Notably, in 2015, 15 percent of the low-income population owned a TFSA, while only 3 percent of this group contributed to a retirement plan. By 2022, 51 percent of those aged 18 to 34 had a TFSA, compared with 38 percent who owned a retirement plan. These figures underscore the advantage of TFSAs over traditional retirement schemes: low-income and younger individuals are more likely to save through these accounts because the funds are not locked away until retirement, allowing them to use their savings for immediate needs.[81]

As the 2024 Cato Tax Plan suggests, Congress should create universal savings accounts, which function similarly to TFSAs, to enable more Americans to save for immediate needs, including emergencies, in addition to their retirement.[82]

Finally, according to the OECD, in 2020, 62.4 percent of Canadian seniors' total income came from sources other than public benefits, including TFSAs. In comparison, 60.7 percent of American seniors' income was composed of nonpublic benefit sources.[83]

Fourth pillar

To have a comprehensive understanding of the retirement security of Canadian seniors, it is important to consider the strength of the fourth pillar, which encompasses retirement income sources beyond traditional pensions and private plans. According to Statistics Canada, in 2019, 70.1 percent of individuals aged 65 and older owned their homes, 16.8 percent owned additional real estate, 8.8 percent held stocks, and 51.6 percent had TFSAs.[84] The median net worth for the same age group in 2019 was US$445,245 (C$543,200).[85] Furthermore, about 48 percent of Canadian seniors' total income came from sources beyond government pensions and retirement plans.[86]

By comparison, 78.4 percent of US seniors aged 65 to 74 and 82.4 percent of seniors aged 75 and over owned their primary residences in 2019.[87] These age groups also owned other residential properties at rates of 18.1 percent and 16 percent, respectively. Furthermore, 15.3 percent of those aged 65 to 74 and 19.2 percent of seniors aged 75 or more held stocks.[88] The median net worth for both age groups was approximately US$260,000.[89]

Summary

While the Canadian retirement system is far from the libertarian model—where individuals are fully responsible for their retirement savings—it has attractive features that enable Canadians to provide for much of their own retirement security. It includes OAS, a basic flat-benefit pension focused on alleviating old-age poverty rather than replacing preretirement income. The CPP, the earnings-related component of the system, does not provide excessive benefits for wealthy retirees and thus costs less than Social Security and is more financially sustainable. Importantly, the substantial role of voluntary private plans and TFSAs in Canada's retirement system grants considerable autonomy to individuals for planning their retirement security rather than relying primarily on government-provided benefits.

Canada's zero-pillar OAS and GIS programs, designed to provide basic old-age income security, have reduced the senior poverty rate to 6 percent, which is significantly lower than that of the general population.

The system's first pillar, the CPP, is structurally similar to Social Security but does not face funding shortfalls and is financially sustainable in the long run. Financial stability was achieved through the late 1990s reforms that were triggered by an alarming actuarial report projecting the CPP fund's exhaustion in 22 years. In contrast, although the Social Security Board of Trustees has been publishing alarming reports about the program's finances for years, as of this writing, due to congressional inaction, only 8 years remain to address trust fund insolvency and avert automatic benefit cuts. US policymakers, like their Canadian counterparts in the 1990s, must find common ground and pass fiscally responsible measures. These measures should include reforming Social Security by reducing the growth in benefits so that they match the revenue collected from workers more closely. Importantly, Congress should avoid expanding Social Security, a mistake that Canada made with the CPP expansion from 2019 at the cost of higher CPP taxes. Instead, Congress should prioritize enabling more Americans to save for their retirement voluntarily, without additional forced savings.

Furthermore, Congress should consider a Canadian-style automatic balancing mechanism to safeguard the Social Security system from political complacency (which threatens both worsening shortfalls and reduced policy options) for extended periods.

The Canadian public pension system achieves poverty reduction and financial sustainability with relatively low overall pension spending. According to the OECD, Canada's expenditure on all old-age benefits, which includes the OAS, GIS, CPP, QPP, and veterans' benefits programs, is below the OECD average and that of the United States (which includes Social Security, SSI, and veterans' benefits).

Through a wide array of voluntary mechanisms, the Canadian system allows individuals to make many of their own retirement and saving decisions, with more than 60 percent of total retirement income coming from nonpublic sources. Employer-based RPPs and individual RRSPs offer tax concessions, empowering individuals to provide for their retirement through private savings and investments. These plans are popular, as evidenced by a high VRS, substantial assets accumulated in voluntary private schemes, and Canada's status as one of the eight OECD member countries with extensive voluntary retirement scheme coverage.

Notably, Canada also offers TFSAs, which are tax-advantaged accounts not limited to retirement savings. TFSAs are popular, with higher adoption rates than the RPPs or RRSPs because there are fewer restrictions attached to TFSAs. TFSAs are particularly attractive to low-income and younger Canadians, who are often reluctant to lock away funds until retirement, as required by RPPs and RRSPs. The United States should create USAs, similar to TFSAs, to enable more Americans to save for immediate needs and to expand opportunities among younger and lower-income workers to plan for their retirement.

8

THE NEW ZEALAND RETIREMENT SYSTEM

New Zealand's retirement system limits government old-age provisions to a basic flat-benefit pension, which successfully achieves its primary objective of reducing poverty among seniors. The benefit is set at a level that achieves a high replacement rate for low-income seniors while encouraging higher earners to rely more on voluntary savings for income replacement and consumption smoothing. By combining limited government provision with a strong voluntary savings component, the system remains low-cost while offering individuals significant freedom in planning for retirement. New Zealand offers a valuable lesson to US policymakers on the potential merits of transforming Social Security into a flat-benefit program, leaving the responsibility of additional savings to individuals. Depending on the benefit level, this structure could be less expensive, could better address senior poverty, and could promote greater self-reliance and autonomy in retirement planning.

This chapter evaluates the New Zealand retirement system, examining its key components, funding structure, effectiveness in reducing old-age poverty, and level of individual autonomy in retirement planning. Additionally, it compares the New Zealand system with that of the

United States and the average Organisation for Economic Development and Co-operation (OECD) member country, as reflected in the OECD metrics.

New Zealand is unique among OECD nations because it does not have a mandatory pension scheme in which workers pay dedicated taxes to qualify for future benefits. Instead, the New Zealand Superannuation (NZS) is a universal flat-benefit scheme, financed with general revenues. NZS's benefit is set at a level that is sufficient to safeguard most retirees from old-age poverty. This benefit is particularly significant for low-income retirees, for whom the program provides the highest preretirement income replacement rate, which is well above the OECD average and that of US Social Security.[1] Unlike NZS, Social Security is an earnings-related benefit that provides the highest benefits to the highest-income earners.

The New Zealand Ministry of Social Development (MSD), which adapted the European Union's material and social deprivation index for New Zealand, reported a 4 percent material and social deprivation rate in 2018, one of the lowest when compared with EU countries.[2] By prioritizing poverty elimination rather than focusing on replacing preretirement earnings of middle and high earners, the New Zealand public pension system is cost-efficient when measured as a percentage of gross domestic product (GDP). According to the latest OECD data, New Zealand's public pension expenditures were substantially lower than those of the United States and the OECD average.[3] However, the OECD's calculations encompass all public benefits for retirees, including veterans' benefits and in-kind benefits. In the case of the United States, this also includes the Supplemental Security Income program. When comparing only NZS and Social Security, NZS spending is still lower, albeit by a small margin.[4]

The structure of NZS gives New Zealanders substantial freedom in their retirement planning, as it leaves most consumption smoothing decisions to workers' discretion. The government employs a nudge strategy by automatically enrolling workers in the primary voluntary savings scheme, KiwiSaver. However, workers are free to opt out of the plan or access their savings early for specific needs, such as purchasing their first home or for financial hardship reasons. Furthermore, they are largely unconstrained in their contribution decisions, having the option to contribute from 0 to 10 percent of their wages to any of the 30 private providers of KiwiSaver in the country. They also have the option to pause their contributions for up to one year. Employers are obligated to match employees' contributions up to 3 percent of their pay, which creates incentives for employees to participate to access this match.

KiwiSaver has a high adoption rate among New Zealand workers, with assets amounting to about 24 percent of GDP held in these accounts.[5] Furthermore, New Zealand is one of eight OECD countries with broad coverage of voluntary retirement plans, along with Belgium, Canada, Estonia, Germany, Ireland, Lithuania, and the United States.[6] These plans replace about 15 percent of career earnings for an average earner, comprising about one-third of the total replacement rate achieved by New Zealand's public and voluntary schemes.[7]

The current structure of the New Zealand retirement system was shaped by reforms in the 1980s and 1990s that included reducing NZS's costs and reaching an agreement to preserve the existing system, in which individuals are responsible for securing any income beyond the basic government benefit.

This system, which combines a universal flat benefit with voluntary private provision, offers simplicity and flexibility to retirees. NZS benefits are not based on taxes paid into the system or on earnings. Rather, they are set at a flat rate, ensuring all recipients know exactly what they will receive. This simplifies retirement planning and eliminates the need for complex benefit calculations. Furthermore, KiwiSaver, where workers are auto-enrolled, is not restrictive, providing substantial freedom in individuals' consumption and saving decisions.

While the New Zealand retirement system involves relatively limited government intervention, it could trim the costs of NZS by targeting benefits only to those in need. However, by not means-testing benefits, NZS mitigates the disincentives to save and invest or game the system that typically accompany poverty-targeted government redistribution systems.

Congress should consider transforming Social Security into a flat-benefit regime similar to NZS. Such a model could be more cost-effective, depending on the benefit level, and more targeted toward reducing old-age poverty. If Congress is unwilling to support such a fundamental restructuring of Social Security, legislators should at least consider reducing benefits for wealthier retirees.

Overview of the New Zealand retirement system

Based on the World Bank's pension framework, old-age provisions in New Zealand are provided through the retirement system's zero, third, and fourth pillars. The only government-provided pension, the zero-pillar NZS, is a residency-based universal flat benefit. Among the schemes that are financed by general revenues instead of dedicated taxes, its benefit amount exceeds those of all other OECD nations when measured as a share of gross average wages.[8]

NZS's replacement rate of preretirement earnings for an average earner is 40 percent, which is roughly equivalent to that of Social Security and lower than the OECD average. However, for low earners, the NZS replacement rate is significantly higher than that of Social Security and nearly matches the OECD average.[9] Because it is particularly important for low-income retirees, NZS effectively reduces old-age poverty in the country. According to a 2021 study by the New Zealand MSD, the material and social deprivation rate among seniors was just 4 percent in 2018, significantly lower than the general population's rate. This placed New Zealand among the countries with the lowest deprivation rates when compared with European Union (EU) member states, even outperforming some wealthier nations.[10]

NZS accounted for 4.9 percent of New Zealand's GDP in 2023, slightly less than Social Security's expenditure of 5 percent of US GDP.[11] According to the latest OECD data, which includes a broader range of pension expenditures, New Zealand's public pensions cost substantially less than both the OECD average and what the United States spends on old-age programs.[12]

Another significant component of the New Zealand retirement system is its third pillar, primarily represented by KiwiSaver. This voluntary saving scheme, introduced in 2007, provides retirement benefits on top of NZS for many New Zealanders. All workers are automatically enrolled in the scheme but can opt out freely. In 2023, about 60 percent of the population were members of KiwiSaver.[13]

The fourth pillar of the New Zealand retirement system, which includes non–retirement plan income sources and assets, seems strong. About 75 percent of seniors own their homes, and roughly 35 percent hold financial assets such as bonds, stocks, and shares in mutual funds.[14]

The New Zealand model, combining a zero-pillar pension aimed at poverty prevention with a voluntary plan for additional income, achieves the primary objectives of a government retirement system while allowing significant individual autonomy in retirement planning.

Table 8.1 provides an overview of the New Zealand and US retirement systems and selected metrics to assess their effectiveness. The metrics data are sourced from the OECD's *Pensions at a Glance 2023* report and various national sources, including the New Zealand MSD, the New Zealand Treasury, the Congressional Budget Office, and the Social Security Administration. Each metric's source is noted in the table.

TABLE 8.1
Key highlights: New Zealand versus US retirement system

Category/metric	New Zealand	United States
Zero pillar	New Zealand Superannuation (NZS)	Supplemental Security Income
First pillar	None	Social Security
Second pillar	None	None
Third pillar	KiwiSaver	401(k)s, IRAs, Roth 401(k)s, Roth IRAs
Eligibility[a]	NZS: 65 years old, 10–20 years residency	Social Security: 66–67 years old, early at 62, late at 70
Old-age dependency ratio[a]	27.7	29.4
Zero-pillar benefit amount (percent of gross average wage)[a]	39.70%	15.60%

(continued)

TABLE 8.1 *(continued)*

Category/metric	New Zealand	United States
Maximum taxable earnings for the first pillar (percent of annual average wage)[b,c]	N/A	227%
Demographic impact ratio[a,b,c,d]	1.36	1.47
Total spending on public pensions per person (US$)[b,c,d]	$2,540	$4,020
Total spending on public pensions (percent of GDP)[b,d]	4.90%	5%
Total spending on public pensions, OECD (percent of GDP)[a,e]	5.10% (data from 2021)	7.50% (data from 2020)
Replacement rate (public pensions)[a]	39.70%	39.10%
Private retirement assets (percent of GDP)[a]	32%	138%
Replacement rate (public and private)[a]	57%	73%
Private replacement share[a,c]	0.28	0.47
Homeownership rate (percent of seniors)[b]	74.5% (aged 65+) (data from 2018)	76.1% (aged 65–74) and 81% (75+) (data from 2022)
Median net worth of seniors (US$)[b]	$290,000 (data from 2021)	$410,000 (aged 65–74) and $335,000 (75+) (data from 2022)
Poverty rate (national measure, percent of seniors)[b]	4% (data from 2018)	5.73% (data from 2018)*

Note: GDP = gross domestic product; IRAs = individual retirement accounts; N/A = not applicable; OECD = Organisation for Economic Co-operation and Development.

a. Data from OECD's *Pensions at a Glance 2023* report.
b. Data from a New Zealand/US government source.
c. Authors calculations.
d. For New Zealand, includes NSZ; for the United States, includes Social Security.
e. Broader definition of public pensions; for example, includes Supplemental Security Income for the United States.
* The US senior poverty figure is based on National Experimental Well-Being Statistics, which uses more comprehensive income data, addressing the limitations of the Census Bureau's official measure and resulting in a lower poverty estimate.

Zero pillar

New Zealand does not have first- and second-pillar pensions. New Zealand Superannuation serves as the zero pillar and is the sole public component of the country's retirement system. Notably, New Zealand is the only OECD nation without a mandatory pension scheme funded by dedicated taxes.[15] NZS is financed from general revenues and provides a flat-rate benefit. The NZS benefit is not means-tested, meaning it is available to all New Zealand residents, regardless of their income and assets. By avoiding means-testing, NZS reduces common disincentives to save and invest that arise under programs where individuals must limit their wealth to qualify for benefits. However, the universal nature of NZS also makes it more costly for taxpayers compared with a targeted, needs-based system that supports only those in financial need.

Individuals are eligible for NZS benefits if they are at least 65 years old and have a minimum of 10 years of residency after age 20, which is set to gradually increase to 20 years for those born in 1977 or later.[16] The benefit for couples is set at 66 percent of the net average wage (a single person receives 65 percent of the gross rate paid to couples), known as the "wage floor."[17] The maximum pre-tax biweekly benefit for a single senior is roughly NZ$1,214 or US$826 (adjusted for purchasing power parity [PPP]), totaling US$21,475 (NZ$31,560) annually.[18] In comparison, the maximum Social Security annual benefit for someone retiring at normal retirement age is US$48,216.[19] NZS is a taxable benefit, which reduces the maximum yearly NZS benefit to US$13,100 (NZ$19,257) for seniors in the top income tax bracket. Similarly, up to 85 percent of Social Security benefits are subject to income taxes above certain income thresholds. In 2022, every eligible senior aged 65 years and over received some amount of the NZS benefit.[20] The OECD reports that the NZS benefit value for single seniors was 39.7 percent of gross average earnings in 2022.[21]

Cost-of-living adjustments for benefits are made annually through a process that accounts for both wage growth and inflation. Generally, benefits are adjusted based on wage growth to align with increases in the wage floor. However, if the annual change in the Consumer Price

Index (CPI) exceeds wage growth, the benefits are adjusted based on the CPI. This process, performed every year on April 1, protects the NZS benefit from the negative effects of inflation.[22] However, the net NZS benefit for a couple is capped at 72.5 percent of the net average wage. Among OECD countries, NZS provides the highest pension benefit relative to gross average wages among schemes funded from general revenues.[23]

In New Zealand, individuals must wait until age 65 to start receiving benefits. However, there is no official retirement age, meaning beneficiaries can continue working beyond 65 while still receiving NZS benefits with no deductions.[24] This encourages workforce participation among older New Zealanders. Furthermore, population aging is less pronounced in New Zealand compared with some other developed nations. As of 2022, the old-age dependency ratio, indicating the number of seniors per 100 working-age individuals, stood at 27.7, lower than both the US ratio of 29.4 and the OECD average of 31.3.[25] The OECD projects that New Zealand's old-age dependency ratio will increase to 44.9 in 2052, which, while still below the OECD average, will exceed the US rate projected for that year.

In 2023, New Zealand spent US$13 billion (NZ$19.5 billion), or 4.9 percent of GDP, on NZS, which translates to roughly US$2,540 (NZ$1,728) per person.[26] In comparison, US expenditures on Social Security totaled US$1.35 trillion that year, representing 5 percent of GDP, or approximately US$4,021 per person.[27]

Based on the OECD's broad measure of public expenditure on old-age and survivor benefits, which includes benefits other than NZS, New Zealand spent about two-thirds of the OECD average on old-age pensions in 2019.[28]

The New Zealand demographic impact ratio (DIR), which highlights the influence of aging on public pension spending, stood at 1.36 in 2023. The DIR is determined by multiplying a country's pension spending as a percentage of GDP by its old-age dependency ratio, providing a clearer picture of how demographic pressures influence pension system costs. The US DIR was 1.47 in the same year. The larger gap between the two countries' DIRs, compared with the difference between their pension spending as a share of GDP, highlights the more substantial impact of aging on pension expenditures in the United States. In other words, the United States spends more on pensions than New Zealand does in part because its population is older.

NZS, representing the sole public part of New Zealand's retirement system, achieves a 39.7 percent individual replacement rate of lifetime earnings for average earners, which is below the OECD average of 50.7 percent.[29] However, the NZS replacement rate is significantly higher for lower earners (those earning half of average earnings), at 63 percent of preretirement earnings, closely aligning with the OECD average for this income group. By comparison, Social Security's replacement rate for lower earners is 49 percent. However, Social Security replaces 28 percent of preretirement earnings for higher earners (those in the category with 200 percent of average earnings), compared with 20 percent for NZS. Put simply, while Social Security provides more substantial benefits for higher earners, NZS focuses on supporting those with lower incomes, reflecting its emphasis on poverty alleviation rather than income replacement for retirees. Notably, the total replacement rate (public and voluntary) of the New Zealand retirement system is about the OECD average, indicating a strong role for voluntary savings and significant individual autonomy in retirement planning.

In terms of how well New Zealand achieves its primary objective of alleviating poverty, it is worth noting that the country does not have an official poverty measure.[30] Based on the OECD's relative poverty indicator, which measures the percentage of seniors with less than half the national median income, New Zealand's senior poverty rate is 16.8 percent, 2.6 percentage points higher than the OECD average and 6 percentage points lower than the OECD-based US poverty rate.[31]

However, this index also suggests that New Zealand's senior poverty rate is higher than those of some significantly poorer countries. For instance, New Zealand's rate is nearly triple that of Hungary and three points above Turkey's. According to the OECD, New Zealand has a substantially higher GDP per capita than both countries do (adjusted for purchasing power parity).[32] While a wealthier country can have a higher senior poverty than poorer countries, considering the robustness of the New Zealand retirement system and its focus on poverty elimination, this seems highly unlikely in this instance. These unexpected results should be attributed to the OECD's method for measuring poverty, which captures income inequality rather than actual poverty levels.

A 2021 material well-being study by the New Zealand MSD provides better insights.[33] That study employs non-income measures (NIMs) for measuring material hardship, directly assessing individuals' ability to purchase or access certain goods and services instead of inferring their material well-being from their income. The MSD replicated the material and social deprivation index from the EU statistics on income and living conditions (EU-SILC) survey for New Zealand.[34] This index includes 13 items, such as "capacity to afford a meal with meat, chicken, fish, or vegetarian equivalent every second day" or "having two pairs of properly fitting shoes" (see the appendix for the survey's full list). If an individual lacks 5 of these 13 items, they are considered to live in material hardship.

The study revealed that only 4 percent of New Zealand seniors aged 65 and over lived in material hardship in 2018.[35] Among 29 European countries (27 EU member states, Iceland, and Norway) and New Zealand, only seven countries—Denmark, Finland, Iceland, Luxembourg, Norway, Sweden, and the United Kingdom—had lower senior material hardship rates, with New Zealand ranking higher than wealthier European nations such as France, Germany, and the Netherlands (where a higher ranking indicates lower poverty).[36] In addition, the material hardship rate among New Zealand seniors was significantly lower than the 10 percent rate for the general population. Notably, despite Hungary having lower senior poverty according to the OECD, its material and social deprivation rate was four times higher than New Zealand's.

Similarly, using the DEP-17, an index developed by the MSD, the senior material hardship rate in New Zealand was 3 percent in 2018, one-third of the general population's poverty rate.[37] While the DEP-17 is conceptually similar to the EU-SILC index (EU-13), the two indexes have only seven items in common, with DEP-17 comprising 17 items in total.[38] For example, the DEP-17, like EU-13, includes a question about the ability to afford two pairs of shoes, but it also asks whether one has postponed a doctor's visit due to lack of funds—a question not included in EU-13.

Overall, considering the measurement methods and the outcomes, the EU-13 and DEP-17 senior poverty measures seem more reliable than the OECD's. Based on these indexes, NZS successfully achieves its primary objective of eliminating senior poverty. Importantly, by focusing on poverty elimination and not providing earnings-related benefits to high earners, the New Zealand system is less expensive than many other public schemes of OECD countries.[39]

The US Census Bureau measures senior poverty differently, assessing seniors' incomes against a fixed threshold rather than using NIMs. Based on this measure, the US senior poverty rate was 9.7 percent in 2018, below the general population rate of 11.8 percent.[40] However, this measure excludes much of the income seniors receive from their private retirement accounts, resulting in higher poverty numbers than in reality.[41] To address this issue, the Census Bureau provided updated poverty figures for 2018 through its National Experimental Well-Being Statistics (NEWS), which rely on more comprehensive income data. According to NEWS, the actual poverty rate in 2018 was much lower, at 5.7 percent.[42]

Making direct comparisons between the New Zealand and US poverty rates is difficult because of the different measurement methodologies used in the available data. However, it's clear that NZS has proven to be highly effective in reducing old-age poverty, with one of the lowest rates compared with EU nations. Furthermore, it operates at a relatively low cost.

When Congress begins to debate Social Security reform, it should consider replacing the program with a flat-benefit scheme like NZS that prioritizes old-age poverty reduction. Depending on the benefit level, such a scheme could be more cost-effective than the earnings-related structure of Social Security while being more effective at alleviating poverty. For example, according to the Congressional Budget Office, switching Social Security's benefit structure to a flat benefit set at 150 percent of the federal poverty level would save more than $280 billion by 2034 and fully eliminate the program's long-term funding shortfall.[43] At the very least, if Congress does not support transitioning to a flat-benefit structure, legislators should consider reducing overly generous benefits for wealthier seniors.

Third pillar

As mentioned, NZS is the only general public pension in New Zealand, meaning the country's retirement system does not include first and second pillars. Instead, additional retirement income is generated through voluntary private savings schemes. The most significant of these schemes is KiwiSaver, introduced by the government in 2007. KiwiSaver is an employer-based plan in which employees are automatically enrolled but have the option to opt out within the first eight weeks. To incentivize participation, the government contributes up to US$355 (NZ$521.43) to individual accounts each year. Participants can choose to contribute 3, 4, 6, 8, or 10 percent of their salary to the scheme, while employers are required to match only the 3 percent contribution (the default combined contribution rate is 6 percent). In addition, participants can always take a "savings break," stopping contributions to the system for up to a year without needing to provide a reason. There is no central fund managing contributors' investments. Instead, individuals can choose to invest in any of the 30 KiwiSaver providers.[44] According to the OECD, on average, KiwiSaver account holders contributed 4 percent of the national average annual wage to their accounts in 2022.[45]

KiwiSaver contributions follow the Taxed-Taxed-Exempt (TTE) regime, meaning contributions are made from after-tax income, investment earnings are taxed, and withdrawals are tax-free.[46] Thus, they are treated similarly to regular savings in bank accounts. In addition, since 2012, employer contributions to KiwiSaver accounts have been taxed as "income in kind." However, most KiwiSaver investment earnings are taxed at advantageous tax rates, known as the prescribed investor rates, which are 10.5, 17.5, and 28 percent,[47] compared with the default income tax rates of 10.5, 17.5, 30, 33, and 39 percent.[48] While withdrawals are not taxed, the funds are locked in the accounts until an individual reaches age 65, with some exceptions, such as buying a first home, suffering a significant material hardship, moving overseas, or facing serious health issues.

KiwiSaver has a high adoption rate among New Zealanders, with 3.3 million people, or more than 60 percent of the population, having accounts as of June 2023.[49] Furthermore, according to the OECD, KiwiSaver has achieved an 80 percent participation rate among the workforce.[50] A study covering 93 percent of KiwiSaver accounts found that by the end of 2021, assets worth US$58 billion (NZ$85 billion), or about 24 percent of GDP, were held in these accounts.[51] Besides KiwiSaver, New Zealanders also have the option to join other employer-sponsored plans, though their popularity has waned following the removal of tax concessions for private retirement savings in the late 1980s (see "Retirement system reforms in the 1980s and 1990s" in this chapter). According to the OECD data, total assets in voluntary retirement plans in New Zealand reached 32 percent of GDP in 2022.[52]

The OECD estimates that voluntary plans, the New Zealand retirement system's third pillar, replace an additional 15.2 percent of pre-retirement income for average earners. When combined with NZS, KiwiSaver and other voluntary plans achieve a 54.9 percent replacement rate for an average earner, slightly below the OECD average of 55.3 percent and significantly less than the US rate of 73.2 percent.[53] In New Zealand, the voluntary replacement share—the proportion of the total replacement rate attributed to voluntary retirement plans—is 0.28. In the United States, this share is 0.47, indicating that voluntary retirement savings play a more substantial role in the US retirement system, which may be at least in part attributable to the tax incentives built into Simplified Employee Pensions (SEPs), 401(k)s, individual retirement accounts (IRAs), and similar retirement savings vehicles in the United States.

Fourth pillar

In evaluating nonretirement plan assets and income sources that support New Zealand retirees (the fourth pillar in the World Bank framework), local sources report several relevant indicators. According to the Ministry of Housing and Urban Development, about 74.5 percent of individuals over 65 owned their homes in 2018.[54] Additionally, Stats NZ data from 2021 show that more than 13 percent of seniors owned real estate other than their primary residence, and about 35 percent held assets such as bonds, stocks, and shares in mutual funds.[55] The median net worth of New Zealand seniors was US$290,000 (NZ$423,000) in 2021.[56]

Homeownership rates among US seniors vary by age group. In 2022, 76.1 percent of seniors aged 65 to 74 owned their homes, and this figure rose to 81 percent for those aged 75 and older. Furthermore, 19 percent of the 65 to 74 age group owned other real estate beside their primary residence, compared with 15.5 percent of seniors aged 75 and over.[57] About 20 percent of the individuals in these age groups also held stocks. As of 2022, the median net worth stood at US$410,000 for those aged 65 to 74 and US$335,000 for those 75 and older.[58]

Retirement system reforms in the 1980s and 1990s

The New Zealand retirement system went through a major overhaul in the 1980s when tax concessions for retirement savings were eliminated as part of a broader tax reform.[59] Before these reforms, led by then-Minister of Finance Roger Douglas, retirement savings were taxed under the Exempt-Exempt-Taxed regime, which meant that only withdrawals from private retirement accounts were taxed. After the reforms, New Zealand adopted the TTE regime, where only withdrawals were not taxed, making it the only OECD country with no tax concessions for retirement savings. As of 2021, Australia, New Zealand, and Turkey were the only OECD countries taxing retirement savings under the TTE regime (Australia taxes contributions and investment returns at concessional rates).[60]

During the reform process, a consultative committee comprising five independent experts from various relevant fields was established, with the Government Actuary serving as the technical adviser.[61] The committee's goals were to suggest amendments to the Minister of Finance to ensure the smooth implementation of the reforms in alignment with the government's policy objectives. The committee also collected public comments. Most public submissions were critical of the reforms. The committee, while supportive of the government's objective of eliminating preferential tax treatment for retirement savings, recommended adopting the Exempt-Taxed-Taxed regime. According to the committee, such an arrangement would be less costly. However, the government proceeded with the TTE scheme.

The New Zealand government also cut Superannuation benefits and voted for an increase in the retirement age to reduce the cost of public pensions from 8 percent of GDP in the early 1980s to 5 percent by the late 1990s.[62] These cuts created public tensions, leading to the establishment of the Taskforce on Private Provision for Retirement in 1991.

The Taskforce, composed of experts from the public and private sectors, was responsible for finding ways to improve private retirement savings while considering the interactions between private and public retirement provisions.[63] It recommended maintaining the existing retirement system of flat-rate public pensions and voluntary private savings, explicitly rejecting a transition to an earnings-related scheme like Social Security. It also supported retaining the NZS income test. On the basis of these recommendations, major political parties signed the Accord on Retirement Income Policies (the Accord) in 1993, committing to not campaign on retirement policies, effectively removing them from electoral discussions.[64] However, this consensus was short-lived.

In 1997, the New Zealand First party, which was not part of the Accord but had joined the government in coalition with the National Party, led the efforts to introduce a compulsory savings scheme. A national referendum on the issue resulted in 92 percent of voters rejecting the proposal. Although this initiative failed, the New Zealand First/National Party coalition government abolished the NZS income test in 1998, transforming NZS into a universal pension.

Furthermore, in 2001, the New Zealand Superannuation Fund (NZSF) was established to ensure sustainable financing of NZS despite projected demographic shifts and associated financial challenges.[65] The NZSF invests government-provided funds in a diversified portfolio of assets, including global stocks and bonds.[66] According to the OECD, the NZSF and Sweden's AP6 fund averaged the highest real rate of return among public pension funds over a 20-year period.[67]

The funds will continue to accumulate in the NZSF until 2033, after which withdrawals will begin to help stabilize the program's cash flows over the long term. By 2085, the NZSF is expected to cover 11.9 percent of the projected cost of NZS.[68] As of 2023, the fund held about US$44 billion (NZ$65 billion), or more than 16 percent of GDP, in assets.[69]

US Sen. Bill Cassidy (R-LA) has suggested that Congress establish a similar government investment fund to finance future Social Security benefits, borrowing about US$1.5 trillion to invest in stocks, private equity, hedge funds, and other financial instruments. Andrew Biggs of the American Enterprise Institute critiques Cassidy's plan by arguing that it is a financing gimmick that acts like a hidden capital gains tax increase, while offering a superficial solution rather than addressing the core financial issues of Social Security. According to Biggs:

> Cassidy's plan uses a roundabout method of extracting a larger share of future GDP to help pay for Social Security benefits. The federal government borrows today, using the money to purchase stocks that currently are held by Americans. Future taxpayers must repay those loans. And instead of flowing to Americans, the returns from those stocks now flow to the federal government, which by the end of 75 years would own roughly one-third of the U.S. stock market. As Wharton School economist Kent Smetters has shown, Cassidy's approach is not meaningfully different from simply increasing the capital gains tax: When the stock market goes up, the federal government takes a slice of the gains. Everything else is simply window dressing.[70]

Summary

Among the retirement systems discussed in this book, New Zealand's approach most closely resembles what Congress should aim for in transforming the US retirement system. Ideally, governments should focus on alleviating poverty, while reducing overall levels of redistribution and keeping taxpayer costs low. The structure of the New Zealand retirement system, which includes a basic state pension supplemented by voluntary private plans, is straightforward and effective at reducing old-age poverty while providing retirees with considerable flexibility to enhance their savings based on individual retirement needs. Furthermore, the New Zealand Superannuation, by providing universal benefits, avoids disincentives to save and invest, which are more widespread in means-tested programs.

The public part of the New Zealand system, which relies solely on the zero-pillar NZS, achieves its primary goal of eliminating old-age poverty. In a comparison of non-income measures of senior poverty, New Zealand's material and social deprivation rate is lower than that of wealthier European nations and is less than half the rate observed in the general population.

NZS offers the highest benefit as a share of average wages among the OECD's schemes that are not financed with dedicated taxes, replacing a significantly higher share of low-income retirees' preretirement income compared with those of higher earners. The New Zealand public pension system, by relying on a basic benefit scheme instead of an earnings-related model, tackles senior poverty at a significantly lower cost as a share of GDP than the OECD average.

The New Zealand retirement system leaves most consumption-smoothing decisions to individuals' discretion, allowing them freedom in their retirement savings choices. The government incentivizes participation in KiwiSaver, a voluntary retirement plan, through automatic enrollment and a modest subsidy. However, individuals are free to opt out of the scheme. KiwiSaver participants have considerable flexibility in deciding their contribution rates and choosing private funds to manage their investments. In 2023, more than 60 percent of the population was enrolled in the plan.

New Zealand's retirement system underwent significant changes in the 1980s and 1990s. The government eliminated tax concessions for private retirement savings while reducing pension costs. Notably, a committee of independent experts played an important role in the process. The US Congress should consider a fundamental restructuring of the Social Security system and can learn a lot from how New Zealand provides a basic, predictable benefit for seniors while leaving most retirement income replacement decisions to individuals.

9

PANEL DISCUSSION: LESSONS FROM THE CANADIAN AND NEW ZEALAND PENSION SYSTEMS

PANELISTS

- **Philip Cross,** Senior Fellow, Fraser Institute
- **Michael Littlewood,** Honorary Academic and Former Co-Director, Retirement Policy and Research Centre, University of Auckland
- **Moderator: Chris Edwards,** Kilts Family Chair in Fiscal Studies, Cato Institute

KEY HIGHLIGHTS

- **Philip Cross:** "We had a significant debate about the CPP [Canada Pension Plan] and pension reform in the mid-1990s, which coincided with a massive fiscal crisis. Addressing both issues simultaneously concentrated everyone's attention and made it easier to implement reforms. . . . Given the overwhelming sense of crisis about both our government deficits and our pension system, the deal came together quite easily.

When people are staring into the abyss, partisan differences tend to fall by the wayside."

- **Michael Littlewood** explains the reasons behind low savings in KiwiSaver accounts: "**The reason that they're not saving much is that they save up to the tax concession limit and then put other savings elsewhere since KiwiSaver savings are locked up until age 65.** So people wouldn't voluntarily put more into those accounts than necessary."
- **Philip Cross:** "It's not surprising that **TFSAs [Tax-Free Savings Accounts] are incredibly popular.** There's a limit on how much you can contribute each year, usually around $7,000. Occasionally, the government allows higher contributions, like $10,000, but it's also cumulative. You can go two or three years without contributing, and that contribution room carries forward. You could theoretically not contribute for a decade and then contribute $100,000 all at once if you received a windfall, like an inheritance. You can pull money out anytime for any reason, whether you want to buy a house or help your child buy a house, and then you can put it back whenever your liquidity improves. . . . **They're incredibly flexible and easy for most Canadians to understand.**"
- **Michael Littlewood:** "We do have something called the New Zealand Superannuation Fund, which is a little bit like the senator's proposal [government investing in stock markets to fund pensions], which I think is an extremely bad idea. **Governments should not be in the business of investing in markets.** Governments should do only the things that only governments can do. Investing in financial markets isn't one of those."
- **Michael Littlewood:** "**New Zealand Superannuation looks after the basic retirement income needs of everyone.** It's generous enough that, as long as you've paid off your house, a married couple can survive on New Zealand Superannuation. Any savings on top of that are supplementary."

Transcripts have been edited for style and clarity.

Chris Edwards: My name is Chris Edwards. I'm the chair of fiscal studies here at the Cato Institute. Our panel today will be examining the retirement systems of New Zealand and Canada. We have experts from both countries here today, Phil Cross and Mike Littlewood

I'll start with Canada and a question for Phil Cross. As I understand it, Canada has four layers to its retirement system. At the basic level, there's the OAS [Old Age Security], a universal flat benefit funded by general government revenues. Then there's the CPP [Canada Pension Plan] system, similar to our Social Security, funded by payroll taxes to create earnings-related benefits. On top of that, there are employer-based RRSP [Registered Retirement Savings Plan] accounts, like our 401(k)s. Finally, there are Tax-Free Savings Accounts [TFSAs], which are similar to our Roth IRAs but much better. Phil, does the Canadian system work well, and what would you improve?

Philip Cross: The system works well in the sense that pensions aren't a matter of debate anymore. We had a significant debate about the CPP and pension reform in the mid-1990s, which coincided with a massive fiscal crisis. Addressing both issues simultaneously concentrated everyone's attention and made it easier to implement reforms.

And by the way, I should correct the senator who spoke earlier. We didn't solve Canada's pension crisis just by investing in the United States, although that is an excellent strategy. The real crisis happened in 1993 when the Chief Actuary said that the contribution rate would jump from 5.5 percent to 14.2 percent of earnings, which was clearly unacceptable. Such a tax hike in an already-weak economy would have been disastrous, so people recognized the need for reform.

So instead, we limited the contribution rate to 9.9 percent. The government tried really hard to keep it below 10 percent, understanding that exceeding this threshold would be unacceptable to the Canadian people. Another lesson is that dealing with our pension crisis, as part of a broader fiscal crisis, required a bipartisan consensus. Again, a speaker earlier talked about how the parliamentary system can be more effective for addressing such issues because it avoids the gridlock often seen in Congress and between the president and Congress.

What is important about the CPP is that it required federal and provincial governments to work together. The federal government could not act alone. Seven provinces, accounting for 50 percent of the population, had to approve it. If you think congressional squabbling is bad, you should see our federal–provincial squabbling. It's just as intractable as what goes on in Congress here. However, given the overwhelming sense of crisis about both our government deficits and our pension system, the deal came together quite easily. When people are staring into the abyss, partisan differences tend to fall by the wayside.

Another notable point about Canada is that while we fixed the pension system in the mid-'90s, the interesting aspect of pensions isn't just the CPP. The CPP is just one pillar. What's really interesting is that defined benefits from companies have basically died. They're no longer a factor, yet we don't see mass poverty. People have adapted through RRSPs and voluntary savings like TFSAs. People worked longer, made small adjustments, and it worked.

Sometimes the best solutions come from unexpected places. The C. D. Howe Institute, a think tank in Canada, floated the idea of TFSAs, and they're wildly popular. You can move money in and out whenever you need it. Over 50 percent of Canadians have TFSAs, compared to about a third with RRSPs. So sometimes the best solutions come from the most unexpected places.

Chris Edwards: Let's jump over to New Zealand and Michael. If I understand correctly, New Zealand has a three-layer retirement system. At the bottom layer, there's New Zealand Superannuation, which provides flat-rate government retirement benefits funded by general revenues. Above that, there are private superannuation plans provided by employers, though they aren't hugely popular. Finally, there are KiwiSaver accounts, introduced in 2007, which are private voluntary accounts.

What's the difference between the existing private superannuation accounts and the new KiwiSaver accounts? Maybe you can untangle some of that for us.

Michael Littlewood: They're essentially the same thing. They are all part of the same supplementary saving regime. Employer schemes, as with Canada, have largely disappeared as a result of KiwiSaver. The distinguishing feature of KiwiSaver is that it was a government-initiated program with auto-enrollment, allowing people to opt out if they don't want to continue or want to have a "savings suspension." Employers must match employee contributions up to 3 percent of pay. About three million Kiwis have one of those accounts. How much are they saving into them? Not very much at all.

Chris Edwards: What percentage of the workforce has KiwiSaver accounts?

Michael Littlewood: About 60 percent of the population. So it'd be a high proportion of the workforce. The reason that they're not saving much is that they save up to the tax concession limit and then put other savings elsewhere since KiwiSaver savings are locked up until age 65. So people wouldn't voluntarily put more into those accounts than necessary.

Chris Edwards: Let's discuss the tax treatment, which I find interesting. I was a bit confused about it. In the United States, our 401(k) plans are tied to employers. You get a tax deduction up front and then the benefits are taxed when paid out. However, it seems that the Australian or New Zealand superannuation accounts and KiwiSaver are taxed up front. But then, when the benefits are paid out, there's no further tax. Is that how it works?

Michael Littlewood: It goes further than that. You also pay tax on the investment income during the accumulation phase. So it's an income tax-neutral arrangement. Taxpayers have no stake in the outcome. It's like saving money through a bank account; it's exactly the same.

Chris Edwards: So are the benefits taxed as well?

Michael Littlewood: Benefits are tax-free. That's a withdrawal of capital.

Chris Edwards: So it is only taxed on one side then.

Michael Littlewood: It's TTE, which is tax-neutral on the income test.*

Chris Edwards: Do you favor that?

Michael Littlewood: I used to think that tax incentives were a good idea, but now I don't. Tax incentives are an extremely bad government intervention. They're very expensive. They're very complicated. Thickets of regulations have to be developed to control them. They're distortionary, they're very regressive, and they don't work.

Chris Edwards: Reading about the New Zealand tax treatment, it does seem very complicated. However, the tax treatment of the United States' Roth IRAs or the Canadian TFSAs is very simple. You just put after-tax money into the accounts, and then the benefits aren't taxed. It's very simple.

Michael Littlewood: So that deals with the beginning and the end. If your tax rate in retirement is the same as the tax rate at which you contributed, it's neutral, right? But what isn't neutral is the roll-up. The advantage you get through avoiding tax on the investment income is huge. It dwarfs the other two.

Chris Edwards: I will disagree with you on the tax treatment here. If you think the baseline tax system is an income tax, income tax systems double tax savings. They encourage people to consume now and not

---

*The Organisation for Economic Co-operation and Development TTE tax model refers to the taxation system of private retirement savings, where contributions are made from taxed income, earnings on the savings are also taxed, but withdrawals are exempt from taxes. The more common treatment internationally is EET, where contributions are deductible (or not regarded as indirect income in the case of an employer's contributions), earnings on the savings are tax-free, and the benefits at retirement are taxed. Chris Edwards's reference to Roth IRAs can be characterized as TEE. Contributions are from after-tax income; earnings on the savings are exempt, as are the benefits.

save. But on the other hand, economists like me believe that a more neutral system is a consumption-based system that does not favor current consumption over future consumption. It seems to me that you're saying you don't like the tax favoritism of these sorts of accounts, but aren't you actually favoring a sort of tax penalty? Wouldn't that encourage people to consume now rather than save for the future?

Michael Littlewood: My view is that all income should be taxed. And if you're getting a concession by contributing to a savings scheme, that bit of your income isn't being taxed.

Chris Edwards: Well, it is being taxed once, just not being taxed twice.

Michael Littlewood: Where is it being taxed?

Chris Edwards: Well, when you initially earn the income.

Michael Littlewood: But if you're contributing and getting a deduction for those contributions against your other income, that's a concession.

Chris Edwards: No, but you're taxed on the way out down the road.

Michael Littlewood: Yeah, that bit is neutral.

Chris Edwards: This is one of the differences between retirement systems in different countries. And Canada is more like the United States, where they employ a basic employer-based system. You get the deduction up front, and you're taxed on the future benefits. In contrast, the United States' Roth IRAs and the Canadian Tax-Free Savings Accounts are taxed up front, not in the future.

Let's go back to Canada for a minute. I wanted to follow up with the CPP system in Canada, which is like our Social Security system. You talked about the reforms in the 1990s, part of which were to prefund part of the future benefits in the system. In our Social Security system, there's no prefunding at all. It's basically fully pay-as-you-go: cash comes in, cash goes out. So the Canadian system is partly prefunded. Can you explain that a little bit? And has that system worked?

Philip Cross: Yes, Canada, starting in the late 1990s, transitioned from a pure pay-as-you-go system to what's called steady-state financing. As I said, actuaries had calculated that the contribution rate would need to jump from 5.5 percent to 14.2 percent over time. They preloaded all these increases into four years, raising the rate from 5.5 to 9.9 percent. All this extra money went into a fund that was then invested. But even today, the Canadian system is still almost 80 percent pay-as-you-go, with a little less than 20 percent paid by this fund. This fund was basically created to avoid that last increase from 9.9 to 14.2. They created this fund and prefunded it to avoid that level of increase. It's interesting that this reform had broad political and societal consensus.

A further change to the CPP was attempted by the Trudeau government in the mid-2010s, designed to increase benefits to the middle class. Unlike the reforms of the 1990s, there was a great deal of resistance to the 2015 reforms, resulting in a very watered-down version with a small increase, which is only being implemented now.

Before we hold up Canada as an example of what to do, remember that Canadians got lucky. They introduced this large increase in the contribution rate in the 1990s, when the economy was booming. We were benefiting from the same high-tech boom that drove the US. It was perfect timing, the ideal economic circumstances to introduce a tax increase with minimal damage.

Whereas today, we're hiking CPP rates during an extremely weak economy. I saw the GDP numbers for the US, which showed a 4.2 percent growth rate. The Canadian economy, conversely, is flat on its back. On a per capita basis, it is actually in severe recession. This is the worst possible time to introduce a tax increase. And that's what we're doing. Unfortunately, because of the nature of pensions, you have to look far ahead. Given our poor record of economic forecasting, it's almost impossible to perfectly time contribution rate increases with economic booms. Canada had that luck in the '90s; we don't have it today.

Chris Edwards: Let me jump back to Michael, and then I'll ask Phil the same question. The problem with our Social Security system is that it's a pay-as-you-go system, and we face a demographic problem: more older, gray-haired folks and fewer younger workers. It makes a pay-as-you-go system accounting very difficult. Does New Zealand face those troubles? And what should be done about it, in your view?

Michael Littlewood: The essence of a pay-as-you-go scheme is that you don't have to worry because you pay out what you receive or receive what you pay out. In New Zealand, we've got a formula that ties the tier one pension to the national average wage, calculated every first of April. So every first of April, there's a new national average wage applied to the pension, and that number goes into the budget. There's no particular mystery about that. We do have something called the New Zealand Superannuation Fund, which is a little bit like the senator's proposal [government investing in stock markets to fund pensions], which I think is an extremely bad idea. Governments should not be in the business of investing in markets. Governments should do only the things that only governments can do. Investing in financial markets isn't one of those.

Chris Edwards: The benefits as a share of GDP will be rising over time in New Zealand. You're sort of saying that's not a problem, but isn't it a problem that the government will be grabbing more resources and transferring more resources, which arguably isn't good for economic growth?

Michael Littlewood: Currently, the net cost of New Zealand Superannuation is about 4.3 percent of GDP, compared to the US Social Security's 4.8 percent, which is a bit more. You're going to add about 2 percent of GDP points to your current cost, as are we, and that's all built-in.

Chris Edwards: So you're saying there's no problem with the New Zealand system. You're saying you should have a general revenue funding of benefits.

Michael Littlewood: This raises a very important point: it should be for the taxpayers of the day to decide how much of the economy should be devoted to the old and the working populations. Today's voting population should not attempt to tie tomorrow's taxpayers to any particular basis. Each generation of taxpayers should assess and decide what's fair.

Chris Edwards: So you're saying the US Social Security system's complex accounting that tries to tie people over generations is nonsense? We should just tax people and pay people now, like a welfare system.

Michael Littlewood: I think the trust arrangements of Social Security in the US and the actuaries are actually an impediment to reform.

Chris Edwards: And Phil, what is your view on it? Is Canada facing a demographic crisis? In the United States, the demographic crisis will affect not only our Social Security system but our Medicare system too. Is that true for Canada as well?

Philip Cross: Not for our pension plan, but definitely with the aging society, we have a real problem controlling our health costs. Often, our Medicare system is held up as an example to the US. However, there's an increasing consensus in Canada that we spend the most on health care after the US among major countries, yet our results are below average. Canada faces a looming fiscal problem, not just due to pensions but also due to health care costs. This is where the real crisis or threat from our demographic profile is coming from. However, Canada has a relatively young population with the highest rates of immigration in the world, which creates other problems like housing but prevents a declining labor force and shrinking population as seen in some European countries and Japan.

Chris Edwards: Philip, I wanted to follow up with you for a bit on the Tax-Free Savings Accounts in Canada. In 2009, Canada introduced new accounts called Tax-Free Savings Accounts [TFSAs]. They're like the US Roth IRAs, where you put in after-tax money. With Roth IRAs, you can only pull the money out many years or decades later when you retire.

The Canadian accounts are very interesting. They're like universal savings accounts. You put in after-tax money now and can take out the money any time, for any reason. The idea is that by allowing people to take money out anytime without further tax, you're increasing liquidity and encouraging people to save. These accounts are remarkably popular in Canada, with over half of the population having them.

Philip Cross: I should clarify, just following up on an earlier discussion, that in both RRSPs and our TFSAs, the money earned in investment is not taxable. The difference is that in RRSPs when you take the money out, it's taxed, whereas in TFSAs, it's never taxed. It's not surprising that TFSAs are incredibly popular. There's a limit on how much you can contribute each year, usually around $7,000. Occasionally, the government allows higher contributions, like $10,000, but it's also cumulative. You can go two or three years without contributing, and that contribution room carries forward. You could theoretically not contribute for a decade and then contribute $100,000 all at once if you received a windfall, like an inheritance.

You can pull money out anytime for any reason, whether you want to buy a house or help your child buy a house, and then you can put it back whenever your liquidity improves. It's not surprising that TFSAs are so popular. They're incredibly flexible and easy for most Canadians to understand.

Michael Littlewood: And costly to the taxpayers?

Philip Cross: That's why the upper limit is $7,000.

Chris Edwards: These accounts have been discussed in the United States for a decade or two. After the Republicans passed their Tax Cuts and Jobs Act in 2017, there was a follow-up bill in the House that included these sorts of accounts for the United States, which I'm a fan of.

I think that encouraging people to save for any and all types of reasons is a good idea. The beauty of these accounts is that people can use them to save for retirement, health care, or any purpose. So I think those are going to be on the agenda here.

I wanted to go back to New Zealand a bit. So we have three layers: the government superannuation benefits, employer-tied superannuation accounts, and the KiwiSaver voluntary accounts introduced in 2007. What did New Zealanders do before then, aside from the government benefit? Did they just save in regular taxable accounts?

Michael Littlewood: Well, tax breaks disappeared finally in 1990, the withdrawal having started in 1987. So between 1990 and 2007, there were no tax incentives at all.

Coincidentally, a longitudinal household study covering the period starting in 2000 found that by 2004, New Zealanders were actually slightly oversaving for retirement. That was before KiwiSaver started.

You might ask, why do we have KiwiSaver then? The finance minister at the time, who was left of center, didn't want to give income tax reductions and preferred to provide New Zealanders a tax reduction they couldn't spend, which is largely how KiwiSaver came about.

Money is now locked up until age 65. Yes, you get a tax concession on the way in. There's no tax incentive on the investment income, and there's no tax on the benefit at the end of the day, but it is locked up until age 65.

Chris Edwards: So before KiwiSaver, there were employer superannuation accounts. But I understand not very many employers had those. Why weren't they popular?

Michael Littlewood: Because New Zealand Superannuation looks after the basic retirement income needs of everyone. It's generous enough that, as long as you've paid off your house, a married couple can survive on New Zealand Superannuation. Any savings on top of that are supplementary. Employer schemes essentially disappeared when the tax breaks were withdrawn, which says something about the tax incentive regime.

Chris Edwards: So the basic New Zealand benefit is a flat-rate amount. What percentage of average wages does it cover?

Michael Littlewood: Well, the calculation for the married couple's pension is a 66 percent of the net average wage, with half paid to each.

Chris Edwards: As I understand it, at the top end, those benefits are taxed away.

Michael Littlewood: It's ordinary income. So it's added to all your other income and taxed at normal rates. No concessions.

Chris Edwards: We talked about this a little bit earlier, Michael. Next door, Australia has a well-known private account–based retirement system. About 30 years ago, they moved to a system with a now 11 percent mandatory payroll tax contribution to these private accounts. Do you like the Australian system?

Michael Littlewood: Well, not only do I not like tax incentives for retirement saving, but I also don't like compulsion. Australia can justify compulsion because they have an income- and means-tested state pension, the tier one pension. So you can justify having compulsion, but it's hugely complicated. And anyone who wants to think about means testing Social Security in the US should take a close look at what goes on in Australia because it has all sorts of unintended consequences. For example, the primary residence is exempt from the capital test; so naturally, Australians invest more in primary residences than New Zealanders. The supplementary savings are locked up until the preservation age, which currently is 60. People tend to retire as soon as they hit 60 to spend those savings and then go on to the state pension in full. There's also a lot less work in retirement because the income test actively discourages it. So I'm against income and asset tests; they're too complicated and have unintended effects.

Chris Edwards: You're saying you don't like compulsion. The Australian private accounts are compulsory because it's mandatory for people to contribute. But isn't the New Zealand system, mainly based on government flat-rate general-funded revenue, also a form of compulsion?

Michael Littlewood: Anything the government does is a form of compulsion.

Chris Edwards: So you're saying you prefer some forms of compulsion over others.

Michael Littlewood: Yeah. In the retirement income business, the government has four potential roles. The first is to either eliminate or alleviate poverty in retirement, which only the government can do by collecting taxes and redistributing them. The second is to level the tax playing field so that the government doesn't send a signal that one form of saving is preferred over another. The third is to develop impeccable data on what households are actually doing, which we don't do in New Zealand but should, so everyone understands what's happening. The fourth role, which only the government can fulfill, is to develop an information and education program. Outside of these four roles, the government should stay away.

Chris Edwards: The US Social Security system has a funding shortfall. In other words, payroll taxes aren't enough to pay benefits. What should the United States do?

Michael Littlewood: Get rid of the trust fund for a start. Get rid of the actuaries. Start running it on a proper pay-as-you-go basis so that people actually understand what's going on. Change the benefits as well; I like flat-rate benefits. Life would be so much simpler if you got rid of the actuaries.

Chris Edwards: So, Phil, what would you suggest to the United States? The Canadian system seems very successful to me.

Philip Cross: I'm not sure I'd call it a success. Yes, it's successful in the sense that pensions and retirement aren't issues. But on the other hand, our economy is a train wreck, and I don't think you can completely break the link between the two. We live next door to the most innovative, productive economy in the world. If you step across the Quebec–

New York border, per capita incomes double. That's a shocking gap and a severe threat to our long-term survival. As a young person, why would I stay in Canada when we have a free trade agreement with the US? Why not set up your business in the US, in a much more pro-business, entrepreneurial culture, and export back to Canada if you can find a market?

The point of the economic system is to generate jobs and growth, not to fund retirement. This is not the most important thing. Perhaps this is the wrong thing to say at a retirement conference, but when forming the system, don't lose track of the bigger picture. Don't do things that break your economic model. Joe Biden may lose his election because Americans perceive the economy isn't doing well, but ask anyone else in the world which economy they'd like to be in, and 100 percent would say the US. Don't do things that mess up this recipe for growth that you uniquely seem to have discovered.

Chris Edwards: Great, thank you. We can open up to questions from the audience.

Q and A

Question 1: I'm Bill Arnold with the National Academy of Social Insurance. Canada has an automatic balancing mechanism that says if its reserves go below a certain amount, Parliament is removed from the scene, and there's an automatic adjustment of both the contributions and the benefits. Is that a feasible target for a country like the United States?

Philip Cross: Fortunately, we're not even faced with that. There's no actuarial projection that our pension system is going into deficit. This was also true back in the mid-'90s. Automatically, our contribution rates were going to go from 5.5 percent over time up to 14.2 percent. Politicians intervened and said: "No, this is not acceptable. We're not going to allow contribution rates to go up like that." They cut back on benefits, especially for disability, increased the income subject to contribution-rate taxation, cut costs, and tinkered with the system.

I find it hard to imagine a system ever being allowed to go on automatic, particularly with something that involves taxes and is as important as pensions. Politicians are going to get involved; there's nothing automatic about these systems. I certainly wouldn't advocate for anything automatic, partly because I just don't believe it's possible. This is too important an issue not to be resolved in the political arena. I agree, death to actuaries.

Question 2: My name is Leila Saldana. I'll be collecting Social Security next year. My question is, we are talking about a program that gives cash, but we haven't discussed other safety nets like SNAP [Supplemental Nutrition Assistance Program] and Medicaid, which supplement low-income people. Is there an equivalent of SNAP, for example, in Canada or New Zealand, where low-income people get free food?

Philip Cross: In Canada, the floor is uniquely established by the Old Age Security program. There aren't other benefits, except for the myriad of things offered to older people. For example, I get a 20 percent discount at my local pharmacy if I buy on a Wednesday. It's also worth noting that there are many in-kind transfers, especially within families, that aren't measured. Just because we don't measure something doesn't mean it's not important.

Ten percent of Canadian seniors live with their family. Twenty-five percent of Canadians say they are providing care to elderly parents. These are enormous contributions, and we never talk about them in debates about retirement systems. All these unmeasured contributions exist, and we should be more aware of them.

Michael Littlewood: In New Zealand, we have something called the Accommodation Supplement, which provides additional benefits to people who don't own their homes. It also supplements the income of very low-income earners, even if they do own their homes, although that's a smaller part of the program. Apart from that, there are no formal government programs to support low-income individuals.

Question 3: The real question is, how you transform the dialogue in Washington, especially in an election year, to have a credible and honest conversation about this issue instead of perpetuating it as a political campaign issue?

Chris Edwards: Both presidential candidates now say they won't touch Social Security, which is unfortunate. We've heard a bit from Phil about how Canada faced crises in the '90s that led to reforms. New Zealand also had trouble and passed major reforms in many government programs. How was that possible? Did they wait for a crisis, and then an entrepreneurial politician took advantage of it?

Michael Littlewood: Yes, we had such an experience. It was resolved when we got a Labour government, left of center, which was captured by a free-market finance minister, Roger Douglas. Most of the major reforms started in 1984 and cleared out a lot of the old policies, including tax incentives for retirement savings, which was his initiative.

Then the conservative government attempted to put an income test on the state pension, and all hell broke loose politically. That was resolved by appointing a task force, a traditional government response. I was on that task force and got my political education during the 15 months I spent there. At the end of that process, almost magically, the major political parties agreed that retirement incomes should be taken off the political agenda. A formal accord was signed, although it didn't last long. Since then, it has essentially stayed out of political discourse.

Chris Edwards: In the 1990s, Canada had a left-of-center Liberal government that pursued all kinds of fiscal reforms, including spending cuts and privatization, along with pension reforms. Similarly, in New Zealand, it was a Labour government. This is an interesting contrast to the United States. Back in the 1990s, there was substantial interest in fiscal reforms within the Democratic Party, with President Bill Clinton showing considerable interest. Unfortunately, we don't see that much anymore here.

Michael Littlewood: We have a very easy system politically. We have a unicameral government. So whoever has the majority passes the law.

Question 4: Hi, I'm Linda Stone. I'm the senior retirement fellow with the American Academy of Actuaries. I don't know if I'm the only actuary in the room here, but I just feel compelled to have you qualify your statements. I'm sure you were commenting not on specific actuaries or the profession in general but more on the structure of the program that actuaries are involved in. Thank you.

Philip Cross: Well, I will elaborate on my comment. You know, I criticized statisticians as well, not just actuaries. It's because both tend to approach problems with the mindset that "if we just had enough data and applied enough brainpower, we could solve it."

In that sense, a fiscal crisis—whether it's a Liberal government in Canada or a Labour government—surprisingly makes it easy to find consensus. But sometimes you have to walk up to the abyss first. That goes back to Milton Friedman's famous comment about the role of think tanks: their place is to keep ideas like this alive until they're needed in an emergency.

Michael Littlewood: I quite like Romina's earlier suggestion [to establish an independent fiscal commission]. I think this institution could play a role in establishing a kind of exchange or free market for ideas in this area. It needs someone outside the political discourse to gather that information and address politicians who talk rubbish, telling them they don't know what they're talking about.

Philip Cross: Actually, one last thought. I spoke too quickly about actuaries. It was the Chief Actuary of Canada in 1993 who really made that debate bipartisan. He came out with the report three days before the famous Paul Martin austerity budget, saying, "The pension plan is in crisis, and this is break-the-glass time." That helped build a bipartisan, consensual view and took the whole issue out of politics. So you're quite right. I spoke too soon.

Question 5: Should disability be split from Social Security?

Chris Edwards: Social Security includes both the retirement system and the Social Security disability system, which is massively complex, problematic, and expensive on its own. In Canada and New Zealand, is disability tied in with Social Security?

Philip Cross: In Canada, disability was tied in. The reforms in the mid-'90s addressed this because disability payments were exploding and getting out of control. The provinces, which administer health care, basically told the medical system to tighten up on this. They weren't going to sign off on someone retiring 20 years early because of soft-tissue issues.

Chris Edwards: This is interesting. Ronald Reagan tried to cut back on the disability costs that were exploding at the time. But there was a big backlash, and his reforms were reversed. Disability has really exploded here. But in Canada, you cut back on benefits, and it sort of stuck.

Philip Cross: That's right. Disability was a part of the reform. There was an attack on disabilities made through the health care system, managed by the provinces. But the benefits were also cut back within the CPP. So both demand and supply were applied to this. It's really not an issue anymore. We have lots of problems in our health care system, but excessive demands for disability isn't one of them.

Michael Littlewood: New Zealand is a bit different in this regard. We have an Accident Compensation Corporation, which is a no-fault workplace or accident insurance system. Everyone pays premiums for that. It is fully prefunded, like an insurance company, and effectively government-owned. This means you can't sue anybody for personal losses as a result of an accident.

PART THREE
Germany and Sweden

10

THE GERMAN RETIREMENT SYSTEM

An expensive, government-run, earnings-related scheme dominates the German retirement system. The already-high taxes that workers pay are insufficient to cover the program's rising costs, with taxes projected to rise further over time. Although participation in occupational and personal retirement plans is relatively high, the majority of senior income still comes from government benefits, indicating that voluntary savings play a limited role. Nonetheless, the United States can still draw important lessons from the German experience.

First, in the German system, the earnings-related pension features an automatic balancing mechanism that regularly adjusts system parameters to prevent insolvency, which Social Security is projected to face in less than a decade.

Second, Germany's Bundestag has been more proactive than Congress in reforming its primary pension scheme in response to unfavorable demographic and economic projections. Congress has been reluctant to address Social Security's severe financial challenges.

This chapter explores the primary components of the German retirement system, examining its financial sustainability, benefit structure, and outcomes for German seniors. It compares the German system with that of the United States and an average member nation of the Organisation for Economic Co-operation and Development (OECD) across various metrics.

Statutory Pension Insurance (Gesetzliche Rentenversicherung, or GRV), a first-pillar pension, is the primary component of the German retirement system, offering earnings-related benefits to German seniors. GRV benefit calculation is points-based, where individuals earn points proportional to their income. Consequently, GRV does not have the progressive benefit structure found in Social Security.

Notably, since 2023, the program no longer imposes limits on additional earnings beyond GRV pensions for individuals choosing to retire early. This change was implemented to increase labor force participation among seniors.[1] A similar rule in the Social Security system, called the retirement earnings test (RET), reduces senior benefits between early and full retirement ages but compensates for this reduction later.[2] However, many seniors perceive the RET as a permanent penalty, which discourages them from continuing to work after retiring early. Congress should consider removing the RET from Social Security to eliminate any disincentives for Americans to stay in the workforce longer.

Removing the additional earnings limit was also relevant in the context of Germany's demographic challenges. The country currently faces one of the most serious aging problems within the OECD, with only six member nations—Finland, France, Greece, Italy, Japan, and Portugal—confronting worse demographic situations.[3] This demographic strain is also reflected in Germany's high pension expenditures, which significantly exceed those of the United States and the OECD average.[4]

The GRV system automatically adjusts both benefits and taxes. It includes an automatic stabilizing mechanism, called the sustainability factor, which slows benefit growth in response to unfavorable demographic trends. This mechanism, implemented in 2004, has proven to be an important factor in controlling long-term pension expenditures as Germany's population ages.[5] Additionally, GRV tax rates are reviewed annually and are raised if the system's reserves fall below a predefined threshold.[6] Benefit growth also slows if pension tax rates increase.

German legislators have also actively pursued reforms to tackle the system's financing problems. In the 1990s, they substantially reduced benefits for periods during which workers were not paying GRV taxes. Then in the early 2000s, they enacted legislation to gradually increase the retirement age from 65 to 67 by 2031 and introduced the aforementioned sustainability factor and a new voluntary retirement scheme.[7]

Despite these reforms, GRV continues to experience financing difficulties. It receives significant transfers from the federal government to cover the difference between program revenues and benefit costs. The GRV tax rate is already higher than the OECD average, and it is expected to rise alongside a decline in benefit levels over time, as the German population continues to age.[8] The fact that most of the senior population's income comes from public provisions makes these prospects even more dire.[9]

These factors place the German retirement system far from the libertarian ideal, which is not surprising considering that Germany is the birthplace of government-run old-age pensions. In 1889, under the leadership of Chancellor Otto von Bismarck, Germany introduced the social insurance model, which is now known as the "Bismarckian model." This system links pension benefits to workers' earnings. Since its implementation in Germany, the model has been adopted by various countries around the world, including the United States.[10]

A key lesson for US lawmakers from the German experience is to make policy corrections in the face of the looming Social Security crisis. Unlike German lawmakers, who have been proactively implementing pension reforms over the years, US politicians have not implemented major reforms since 1983, even though the program has faced long-term actuarial deficits since 1984.[11] If US policymakers remain hesitant to act, they should at least consider adopting automatic stabilizers like those in the German system, which operate to rebalance taxes and benefits without requiring political action.

Overview of the German retirement system

According to the World Bank classification of retirement system components, the German system includes government-run zero- and first-pillar pensions, occupational and personal third-pillar retirement plans, and a fourth pillar that comprises income sources beyond government pensions and retirement plans.

The zero-pillar program—Basic Income Support in Old Age and in Case of Reduced Earning Capacity (Grundsicherung im Alter und bei Erwerbsminderung)—offers means-tested flat benefits along with various supplemental benefits to seniors who cannot provide for their basic needs (such as food and housing).[12] The program plays a limited role in the German retirement system, covering only 4 percent of seniors, with total expenditures amounting to less than 1 percent of German gross domestic product (GDP).[13]

The first pillar, Statutory Pension Insurance, is an earnings-related scheme, which provides old-age, survivor, and disability benefits.[14] Overall, the German pension system is designed to be much less progressive than Social Security in the United States. Benefits are calculated based on an individual's lifetime points, and the system does not feature Social Security–like progressive elements in benefit assessments. Current legislation aims to maintain the program's benefit level, defined as the net replacement rate for an average earner, above 43 percent until 2030.[15] GRV, similar to Social Security, includes a cap on taxable earnings, but the threshold is set much lower. In 2022, the GRV taxable ceiling was US$116,380 (€84,763 adjusted for purchasing power parity [PPP]), or 154 percent of average earnings in the country. In comparison, Social Security's maximum taxable earnings stood at US$147,000, or 227 percent of average earnings.[16] Conversely, the GRV tax rate, currently at 18.6 percent, is significantly higher than Social Security's 12.4 percent.

However, as in the United States, GRV's payroll tax revenues are insufficient to cover the program's expenditures, which exceeded 9 percent of GDP in 2023. Approximately 30 percent of the program's spending is financed through transfers from the federal government.[17] Some of these transfers cover shortfalls created by paying out benefits for periods during which individuals are not paying GRV taxes (e.g., during child-rearing), but the system also requires external transfers to mitigate its inherent imbalances, such as those arising from the population aging.

Concerns about the system's long-term financial sustainability because of its aging population led Germany to implement an automatic stabilizer in 2004.[18] This mechanism, which inversely links benefit growth to the increasing pensioner-to-worker ratio, has proven important in mitigating the aforementioned unfavorable financial projections.

During the same period, with the aim of encouraging retirement savings, the government introduced voluntary Riester pensions, named after former Federal Minister of Labour and Social Affairs Walter Riester. These retirement plans are incentivized through deferred taxation and state subsidies for low-income earners.

Riester pensions and occupational schemes make up the third pillar of the German retirement system. The government does not provide fixed subsidies for occupational schemes (as it does for Riester pensions), but payments into these plans are treated under the Exempt-Exempt-Taxed regime and are exempted from payroll taxes (up to a certain threshold).[19]

Participation rates are significantly higher in occupational plans, at 54 percent, compared with 30 percent in Riester pensions.[20] This discrepancy could be partially explained by the presence of strong labor unions, which negotiate occupational plans with employer representatives on behalf of workers.[21] Furthermore, the relatively slow adoption of Riester pensions may be attributed to overly stringent investment rules that require plan providers to guarantee at minimum 100 percent of the principal invested. This rule effectively decreases returns on these plans, as providers mostly choose to invest in safe assets such as bonds.[22] Even so, the overall participation rate in voluntary schemes—both Riester pensions and occupational plans—is one of the highest among OECD nations.[23]

The fourth pillar of the German retirement system is relatively weak, with notably lower homeownership rates compared with those in the United States.[24] German seniors also hold other properties, as well as financial assets such as stocks, at much lower rates than their American counterparts. One likely explanation for low homeownership is strong protections for renters, including limits on rent increases, that make renting a more attractive choice than owning a property.[25]

Table 10.1 compares the German and US retirement systems, based on selected metrics. The data for these metrics are drawn from the OECD's *Pensions at a Glance 2023* report, as well as various national sources such as the Federal Ministry of Labour and Social Affairs, Deutsche Bundesbank, the Congressional Budget Office, and the Social Security Administration. The source for each metric is specified in the table.

TABLE 10.1

Key highlights: German versus US retirement system

Category/metric	Germany	United States
Zero pillar	Basic Income Support in Old Age and in Case of Reduced Earning Capacity	Supplemental Security Income
First pillar	Statutory Pension Insurance (GRV)	Social Security
Second pillar	None	None
Third pillar	Occupational plans, personal (Riester) pensions	401(k)s, IRAs, Roth 401(k)s, Roth IRAs
Eligibility[a,b]	GRV: 66–67 years old, early at 63	Social Security: 66–67 years old, early at 62, late at 70
Old-age dependency ratio[a]	38	29.4
Zero-pillar benefit amount (percent of gross average wage)[a]	19.50%	15.60%
Maximum taxable earnings for the first pillar (percent of annual average wage)[a]	154%	227%

168 Reimagining Social Security

TABLE 10.1 (continued)

Category/metric	Germany	United States
Demographic impact ratio[a,b,c,d]	3.50	1.47
Total spending on public pensions per person (US$)[b,c,d]	$6,545	$4,020
Total spending on public pensions (percent of GDP)[b,d]	9.20%	5%
Total spending on public pensions, OECD (percent of GDP)[a,e]	10.40% (data from 2019)	7.10% (data from 2019)
Replacement rate (public pensions)[a]	43.90%	39.10%
Private retirement assets (percent of GDP)[a]	7%	138%
Replacement rate (public and private)[a]	55%	73%
Private replacement share[a,c]	0.20	0.47
Homeownership rate (percent of seniors)[b]	60% (aged 65–74) and 49% (75+) (data from 2021)	76.10% (aged 65–74) and 81% (75+) (data from 2022)
Median net worth of seniors (US$)[b]	$330,000 (aged 65–74) and $185,000 (75+) (data from 2021)	$410,000 (aged 65–74) and $335,000 (75+) (data from 2022)
Poverty rate (EU/national measure, percent of seniors)[b]	8.8% (data from 2023)	9.7% (data from 2023)*

Note: EU = European Union; GDP = gross domestic product; IRAs = individual retirement accounts; OECD = Organisation for Economic Co-operation and Development.

a. Data from OECD's *Pensions at a Glance 2023* report.
b. Data from a German/EU/US government source.
c. Author's calculations.
d. For Germany, includes GRV; for the United States, includes Social Security.
e. Broader definition of public pensions; for example, includes Supplemental Security Income for the United States.

* The US senior poverty rate is likely much lower as the official poverty measure does not account for most of the income seniors derive from private retirement accounts.

Zero pillar

The German retirement system's zero-pillar pension is relatively small in scope and does not exclusively cover retirees. Basic Income Support in Old Age and in Case of Reduced Earning Capacity provides means-tested benefits for seniors who have reached the statutory retirement age of 66, as well as for individuals aged 18 and older with permanent disabilities that fully reduce their ability to work. The program offers financial assistance to those whose incomes—which include other government benefits such as the earnings-related pension—and assets (the income and assets of a spouse are also considered) are insufficient to cover their basic needs such as food, housing, and clothing.[26]

Seniors seeking this benefit must apply to the relevant agency, which evaluates their need-based eligibility. A rule of thumb is to apply for this benefit if one's monthly income is below US$1,455 (€1,062), which corresponds to 24 percent of the average monthly income in Germany in 2023.[27] Once eligibility is confirmed, a single senior receives a standard flat benefit of US$771 (€563), about 13 percent of the average monthly income.[28] This amount is annually adjusted based on a mixed index that factors in both price and wage developments.[29] Beneficiaries may receive benefits in addition to the standard rate, depending on their individual need. For example, seniors may receive supplemental transfers to cover their rental costs or heating expenses.[30]

According to the OECD, the average benefit value of the Basic Income Support in Old Age and in Case of Reduced Earning Capacity program amounted to 19.5 percent of gross average wages in 2022.[31] The program covers only 4 percent of the German population aged 65 and over, indicating its limited role in the broader German retirement system.[32] In 2023, the German government spent US$14.4 billion (€10.1 billion), or 0.24 percent of its GDP, on this basic income support program for seniors.[33]

First pillar

Much like the central role of Social Security in the American retirement system, the German system primarily relies on its first pillar, known as Statutory Pension Insurance. This scheme, following the Bismarckian social insurance model, shares the core principles of Social Security.[34] It operates on a pay-as-you-go, earnings-related basis, and it provides old-age, survivor, and disability benefits. Participation is mandatory for everyone except civil servants, some self-employed persons (depending on the profession), workers earning below a certain threshold, and those in short-term employment (three months or less).[35]

As of 2024, the full retirement age is 66, gradually increasing to 67 by 2031. Early retirement, while possible at 63, reduces benefits permanently by 3.6 percent for each year before the statutory age. Conversely, late retirement increases benefits by 6 percent for each year beyond the legal retirement age. Early retirement is only possible for individuals with at least 35 years of paying GRV taxes. In addition, those with 45 years or more of paying GRV taxes are eligible for the "Exceptionally Long Service Pension," which allows them to retire at 64 with full benefits, with this threshold increasing to 65 in 2029.

Notably, on January 1, 2023, the additional earnings limits for early retirement, which reduced pensions for seniors earning above a certain threshold, were lifted.[36] The aim of this reform was to remove the disincentives created by the earnings limit and encourage seniors to stay in the workforce longer.[37] Currently, Social Security has a similar limit, known as the RET, which applies to seniors receiving benefits between the early and full retirement ages.[38] Once these seniors reach the full retirement age, their benefits are increased to compensate for the earlier reductions. Put simply, their benefits are not lost. However, few seniors opting for early retirement recognize this adjustment and work less so as to avoid exceeding the income limit. To encourage American seniors to remain in the workforce, Congress should consider repealing the RET.

The GRV tax of 18.6 percent is split equally between employees and employers. According to the OECD, the 2022 contribution assessment ceiling (i.e., maximum taxable earnings) was US$116,380 (€84,763) or 154 percent of gross average earnings for full-time employees.[39] In comparison, the total US Social Security tax is 12.4 percent, with significantly higher maximum taxable earnings of US147,000 or 227 percent of average earnings in 2022.

The calculation of benefits in the German Statutory Pension system is based on a points system. Each year, workers earn points based on how their income compares with the average income of all insured persons that year. For example, if a worker's income matches the average, that worker will earn one point for that year. Upon retirement, the accumulated points are multiplied by a set pension point value to determine the monthly pension amount. Importantly, the points are awarded proportionally to a worker's income (up to the contribution assessment ceiling), meaning that GRV does not operate on a progressive basis like Social Security does.

As of 2024, the law specifies that the pension level, or replacement rate—which represents the ratio of a standard pension (earned by an average earner after paying GRV taxes for 45 years) to the current average worker's earnings—will not drop below 48 percent until 2025, with legislators discussing an extension of this provision through 2039.[40] Additionally, when comparing individuals' benefits to their lifetime earnings—rather than to the current average earnings—GRV offers the same replacement rate for everyone with a work record of equal length (the rate decreases with shorter work lives), regardless of their earnings. According to the OECD, which projects replacement rates for current workers when they retire at 67, GRV offers a 43.9 percent replacement rate for the average earner. This rate is slightly higher than Social Security's 39.1 percent and lower than the OECD average of 50.7 percent.[41]

As noted, Germany is currently facing one of the most severe demographic challenges among OECD nations. In 2022, Germany's old-age dependency ratio—the number of seniors aged 65 and over among 100 working-age individuals—was 38. This is considerably higher than the US ratio of 29.4 and the OECD average of 31.3.[42] Only six OECD countries confront worse demographic situations: Finland (41.5), France (39.3), Greece (39.3), Italy (41.0), Japan (55.4), and Portugal (39.0). Looking ahead to 2052, the aging issue in Germany, like that in every OECD nation, is expected to worsen. The old-age dependency ratio in Germany is projected to reach 59.1, which will be higher than the US projection of 43.4 and the OECD average of 53.8.

The expenditures of the German Statutory Pension Insurance scheme totaled US$544 billion (€381 billion adjusted for PPP) in 2023, or 9.2 percent of GDP.[43] This amounted to roughly US$6,545 per person (€4,582).[44] In comparison, Social Security expenditures for the same year were US$1.35 trillion, corresponding to 5 percent of GDP, or US$4,021 per person.[45] According to the OECD, which relies on a broader definition of pension expenditures (including veterans' benefits and civil servant benefits), Germany's pension spending amounted to 10.4 percent of GDP in 2019. This figure is significantly higher than the OECD average of 7.7 percent and US pension expenditures of 7.1 percent.[46]

The German demographic impact ratio (DIR) is 3.5, compared with the US DIR of 1.47. This metric, which multiplies total pension spending as a share of GDP by a country's old-age dependency ratio, emphasizes the influence of aging on the total pension burden. For example, comparing only the two countries' pension spending shows that Germany spends about 46 percent more on pensions than the United States does. However, when adjusting for the impact of aging, Germany's DIR is 138 percent higher than that of the United States. This discrepancy highlights the more pronounced demographic challenges in Germany compared with those in the United States.

Importantly, taxes in neither the German Statutory Pension Insurance nor Social Security in the United States are sufficient to fully cover their respective expenses.

For example, in 2023, workers' taxes covered only 71 percent of total GRV expenditures. The remaining 29 percent was financed through transfers from the federal government.[47] A portion of these transfers is allocated to compensate for periods when individuals are not paying into the system, such as during vocational training and child-rearing, yet these periods are still counted toward pension benefits.[48] Additionally, these substantial government transfers bridge shortfalls in the system arising from factors such as pronounced population aging, and they prevent further increases in tax rates or reductions in benefit levels (more details on these dynamics are discussed later in this chapter).[49]

Payroll taxes and taxation of benefits covered 92 percent of Social Security expenses in 2023.[50] However, unlike GRV, Social Security does not provide benefits for periods when individuals are not paying payroll taxes (except for survivor and dependent benefits, which are based on the primary workers' history). Social Security follows a progressive benefit structure and indexes initial benefits on the basis of economy-wide wage growth, thus reducing benefits' link to payroll taxes.

According to the World Bank, the first pillar's primary objective is to replace a portion of preretirement earnings.[51] However, given that first-pillar programs also contribute to old-age poverty protection and that GRV is the only major public pension in Germany, it is interesting to examine how effective it is in tackling senior poverty. Based on the latest OECD data, which defines poverty as having an income lower than 50 percent of median household income, Germany's senior poverty rate was 11 percent, lower than the OECD average of 14.2 percent. In comparison, the OECD reports the US senior poverty rate as 22.8 percent.[52]

However, this definition of poverty may capture income inequality more than actual poverty in which an individual is deprived of basic needs such as food and housing. It may overstate a country's poverty rate because having an income below half of the median does not necessarily imply living in actual poverty, especially in wealthier countries with high median incomes. Arguably, a better income measure of poverty would tailor the poverty line to each country's specific context. Alternatively, a non-income-based measure of poverty, which does not depend on country-specific circumstances, could be used to make comparisons across different countries.

The European Union statistics on income and living conditions (EU-SILC) survey offers such a non-income measure. The survey defines material and social deprivation as "the inability to afford a set of specific goods, services, or social activities that are considered by most people essential for an adequate quality of life." Rather than comparing individuals' incomes, the survey asks respondents whether they can afford at least 5 of 13 predefined essentials for an adequate quality of life. These essentials include items such as having an internet connection, access to a car, the ability to afford a meal with meat or a vegetarian equivalent every other day, and the ability to replace worn-out clothes (see the appendix for the survey's full list).[53] According to this measure, the senior material and social deprivation rate in Germany in 2023 was 8.8 percent, lower than that of the general German population rate of 12.7 percent and the EU average for seniors, which stood at 11.2 percent.[54]

In contrast, the US Census Bureau uses an income-based measure that compares individuals' incomes to a fixed poverty threshold. These thresholds are calculated based on the cost of minimum food and other necessary family expenses.[55] According to the Census Bureau, the 2023 senior poverty rate in the United States was 9.7 percent, lower than that of the general American population.[56] However, this figure overstates actual poverty because it excludes most of the income seniors receive from private retirement accounts.[57] The Census Bureau conducted a study in 2025 to address this issue, using more comprehensive income data to determine poverty. The National Experimental Well-Being Statistics report found that the Census Bureau's 2018 poverty figure of 9.75 percent was significantly higher than the adjusted estimate of 5.73 percent.[58] While there is no study adjusting the 2023 poverty figure, it is safe to assume that the actual senior poverty number for that year was lower than the 9.7 percent reported by the Census Bureau.

The German statutory insurance system includes an automatic stabilizer that slows benefit growth in the face of adverse demographic developments. The annual benefit increases, which are tied to gross wage changes, are reduced based on the sustainability factor, defined as the ratio of pensioners to contributors.[59] Put simply, if the ratio increases, indicating an aging population, annual benefit increases are trimmed. What is more, on January 1 of each year, the GRV tax rate is adjusted to rebalance expenditures with revenues, increasing or decreasing based on the available reserves for pension expenditures.[60] Pension benefit increases are also linked to these changes in tax rates; when taxes rise, benefit growth slows. Thus, the benefit levels are inversely related to the old-age dependency ratio and pension taxes. These features of the German statutory pension ensure that the burdens of paying pensions to an aging population are distributed across generations.

As of 2024, the same rule that guarantees that benefit levels will not drop below 48 percent until 2025 also caps GRV tax rates at 20 percent during the same period.[61] In addition, the federal government must adopt measures if the tax rate projections exceed 22 percent by 2030 (an increase of 3.4 percentage points). The government must also act if the projections show a decline in benefit levels from the current 48 percent to 43 percent by 2030 (a decrease of about 10 percent).

In contrast, the latest Social Security Trustees Report suggests that payroll taxes would need to be increased immediately by 3.33 percentage points to 15.73 percent to maintain the 75-year solvency of the combined Old-Age and Survivors Insurance and Disability Insurance programs.[62] Alternatively, benefits could be indiscriminately decreased by 21 percent for all retirees. Unlike German law, which requires proactive government measures in response to projected increases in pension taxes or significant benefit reductions, US law does not impose such obligations on the government.

Furthermore, Social Security does not have an automatic balancing mechanism to adjust benefits in line with demographic changes, nor do payroll taxes increase to balance the system's costs with revenues. The only balancing mechanism is automatic benefit cuts projected for 2033 when the program's trust fund balance is projected to be exhausted. This delayed mechanism allows politicians to avoid taking responsibility until the very last minute. If the United States adopted a system similar to Germany's, in which imbalances are regularly adjusted to secure system solvency, politicians would have more incentives to take timely actions. That is because voters—both workers and retirees—would feel the negative effects of the system's financial imbalances well before the insolvency date. Doing so would also allow for more gradual tweaks over time, rather than blunt policy changes as automatic benefit cuts loom. Congress should consider adopting a stabilizing mechanism for Social Security that forces preventive actions well in advance of system insolvency.

Unlike Social Security, the GRV program does not have a projected insolvency date because benefit and tax levels are adjusted regularly to keep the system in balance and general revenue transfers often make up for shortfalls. However, this does not mean the program is free from financial challenges. Tax rates are expected to increase from 18.6 percent to 20.2 percent by 2030 and to 21.1 percent by 2037. Simultaneously, benefit levels, which are inversely related to tax rates and the old-age dependency ratio, are projected to decrease from 48 percent of average worker wages in 2025 to 45 percent in 2037.[63] Longer-term projections indicate that by 2060, the GRV tax could reach 25 percent, with the benefit level dropping below 40 percent of average earnings.[64]

In 2021, Germany introduced the Grundrente (basic pension) aimed at low-earning seniors with a long history of paying GRV taxes. The Grundrente provides a supplement on top of the statutory pension for seniors whose average income during their working years did not exceed 80 percent of the national average earnings.[65] To qualify for the Grundrente, individuals must have paid statutory insurance system taxes for at least 33 years, with full benefits available after 35 years (including child-rearing periods). While research on the effects of the Grundrente is scarce, initial studies show that significantly fewer people benefit from this pension than anticipated.[66] Only 4.3 percent of all pensioners receive this benefit, with an average monthly supplement of US$124 (€90) per person in 2022.[67] The limited coverage of the Grundrente is partially explained by the fact that many seniors are disqualified by the income test, which considers almost all sources of income, including that of a partner. Additionally, the requirement for a long employment history—something many low earners often lack due to inconsistent working patterns—excludes many individuals from qualifying for this pension supplement.[68]

Third pillar

The third pillar of the German retirement system, voluntary retirement plans, stands out from other OECD nations. Germany is one of the nine OECD member countries—alongside Belgium, Czechia, Iceland, Ireland, Japan, Poland, Slovakia, and Slovenia—where voluntary plans have broad coverage, as defined by the OECD.[69] There are two types of retirement schemes in Germany.

The first type is occupational retirement plans. These plans are provided by employers, who choose a provider to manage employee contributions. Since 2002, employees have been able to request to contribute a portion of their earnings to an employer-sponsored plan, although employers are not required to match these contributions.[70] The government incentivizes participation in occupational plans by applying the Exempt-Exempt-Taxed regime to contributions. Additionally, payments into these plans are exempted from GRV taxes. As of 2024, the maximum tax-free contribution stood at US$10,067 (€7,248), with a maximum exemption from GRV taxes of US$5,033 (€3,624) annually.[71] According to the 2024 EU aging report, participation in these plans grew from about 15 million in 2001 to 21 million in 2021.[72] According to the OECD, 54 percent of German workers participated in these plans in 2019, compared with a participation rate of 56 percent in voluntary US occupational plans (e.g., 401(k)s) in 2021.[73] A relatively high participation in occupational plans can be explained by strong labor unions in Germany that negotiate these pensions on behalf of workers.[74]

The second type of voluntary retirement scheme is personal retirement accounts, commonly referred to as Riester pensions. The government encourages workers to participate in this scheme through deferred taxation. Specifically, annual contributions up to US$2,877 (€2,100) can be deducted from taxable income. Withdrawals are taxed and can begin from age 60 for those who signed their Riester contracts before 2011; for contracts signed after 2011, the earliest withdrawal age is 62.[75] Additionally, for low earners, the government provides a fixed matching subsidy of US$240 (€175) per year, with an additional US$411 (€300) for each child born after 2008.[76]

The OECD reports that Riester pensions had a 30 percent coverage rate in 2019, which is significantly lower than that of occupational plans.[77] While coverage grew after the introduction of these plans in 2002, adoption rates have slowed considerably since 2010. One reason for this slowdown is the low returns. Providers are required to guarantee that participants will get at least 100 percent of their paid-in contributions in nominal terms, leading them to primarily invest in bonds and avoid higher-risk investments such as stocks.[78] The OECD reports that the voluntary "assets earmarked for retirement" in Germany amounted to 6.5 percent of GDP in 2022, compared with 137.5 percent in the United States.[79]

Voluntary retirement plans in Germany contribute an additional 10.9 percent to the income replacement rate, bringing the total replacement for an average earner to 54.7 percent, which is close to the OECD average of 55.3 percent.[80] In Germany, the voluntary replacement share, which measures the proportion of income replaced by voluntary plans, is 20 percent. In comparison, the US voluntary replacement share is 47 percent, with retirement plans replacing 34.1 percent of pre-retirement income, resulting in a total replacement rate of 73.2 percent. Furthermore, in 2019, public benefits made up 68 percent of total senior income in Germany, whereas in the United States, this figure was only 39.3 percent in 2021.[81]

Fourth pillar

The last component of the German retirement system is its fourth pillar, which includes assets and income sources outside of public pensions and voluntary retirement plans. In 2021, 60 percent of seniors aged 65 to 74 owned their homes, but only 49 percent of those aged 75 and over owned theirs. One factor contributing to Germany's relatively low senior homeownership rates could be the country's strong protections for renters, including regulations that limit rent increases, which make long-term renting a more attractive option than homeownership for some.[82] In addition, 22 percent of the 65 to 74 age group owned additional properties, compared with 16 percent of those over 75. Ownership of stocks was equal across both age groups, with about 15 percent holding shares. The median net worth for the 65 to 75 age group was US$330,000 (€231,000), decreasing to US$185,000 (€129,500) for those aged 75 and over.[83]

In comparison, in the United States in 2022, homeownership among seniors was more prevalent, with 76.1 percent of those aged 65 to 74 and 81 percent of those aged 75 and over owning their primary residences. Additional nonresidential property ownership was reported at 19 percent of the younger group and 15.5 percent among the older group. Stock ownership among seniors was higher, with 20.4 percent of the 65 to 74 group and 19 percent of those 75 and older holding shares. Finally, the median net worth of seniors in the 65 to 74 group was $410,000, compared with $336,000 for those aged 75 and over.[84]

German retirement system reforms

The German government has been significantly more proactive in addressing the challenges facing the Statutory Pension Insurance scheme compared with the US government's reluctance to address Social Security. Social Security last underwent major reforms in 1983 and has been running 75-year actuarial deficits since 1984.[85]

In Germany, bleak demographic projections, coupled with steady increases in structural unemployment, prompted GRV reforms in the 1990s and early 2000s.

The 1990s reforms were primarily focused on strengthening the actuarial fairness of the program, including the removal of privileged treatment for education periods and reductions in disability and survivor benefits.[86] Additionally, with the expected rise in pension tax rates, the formula for annual benefit adjustments was modified. Previously, benefits were indexed to workers' gross wages. This meant that workers' gross wages increased faster than their net wages. To address this discrepancy, annual benefit adjustments shifted from being indexed to gross wages to being indexed to net wages (gross wages minus pension taxes), reducing the growth of benefits over time.[87]

The next wave of reforms, implemented between 2001 and 2007, aimed to further strengthen the system's financial sustainability. In 2004, recognizing that maintaining benefits at constant levels was impossible, the sustainability factor was introduced in the benefit adjustment process. This automatic stabilizer (discussed in more detail earlier in this chapter) inversely links benefit levels to the rising pensioner-to-worker ratio. Furthermore, in 2007, Germany enacted legislation to gradually raise the statutory retirement age from 65 to 67, a reform whose implementation began in 2012 and will be fully phased in by 2031. These reforms have helped mitigate the pressures of population aging on long-term pension expenditures.[88]

In 2002, to compensate for the projected reduction in benefit levels, the government introduced Riester pensions. Initially intended to be mandatory with a 4 percent contribution rate, the plan was made voluntary after public opposition because of the high combined tax and contribution rates for the GRV and Riester plans. Although Riester pensions did not achieve the success initially envisioned because of a combination of low returns and limited public education about their benefits, they demonstrate the German government's proactive approach to retirement system reforms.[89]

More recently, the German government has introduced the supplemental Grundrente pension in 2021, as discussed earlier in this chapter.

Summary

The German retirement system strays far from a libertarian model of minimal government involvement. The system, with its high tax rates and significant expenditures as a share of GDP, is costly for German taxpayers, reducing incentives to work and constraining German discretionary income significantly. Additionally, government-provided benefits represent nearly 70 percent of total senior income, which is in contrast with the libertarian principles of self-reliance and autonomy in retirement planning. However, the automatic stabilizers within the system and the proactive efforts of the German government to reform the scheme in response to adverse demographic and economic challenges offer valuable insights for US policymakers.

Similar to the American retirement system, the German system's primary government provision is the first-pillar pension, known as Statutory Pension Insurance or GRV. While this scheme also follows the Bismarckian model, where benefits are strongly related to earnings, it has several notable features that differentiate it from Social Security.

First, to encourage seniors to remain in the workforce longer, the German government eliminated additional earnings limits for those retiring early. In contrast, the US Social Security system still imposes a retirement earnings test or RET, which reduces current benefits if a beneficiary earns above a certain threshold before reaching full retirement age. Although benefits are later adjusted upward to account for these reductions, many seniors are unaware of this and choose to work less—or discontinue working—to avoid a temporary cut in benefits. RET should be eliminated from the Social Security system.

Notably, GRV features an automatic stabilizing mechanism that is inversely linked to population aging. This mechanism, known as the sustainability factor, reduces benefit growth as the pensioner-to-worker ratio rises. Additionally, benefits decrease as tax rates, which are adjusted annually, increase. These features ensure that the program avoids sharp benefit cuts or tax hikes, as the system is regularly adjusted. More importantly, they incentivize politicians to act as their voters experience the negative effects of unsustainable program finances. In contrast, US lawmakers are only incentivized to act at the very last minute, when Social Security's insolvency date approaches. Congress should consider incorporating similar mechanisms into the Social Security system that can balance the system's finances earlier and encourage timely political action.

What is more, German lawmakers have been more active in reforming the system when faced with bleak financial projections. The system underwent significant changes in the 1990s and early 2000s, including the trimming of benefits, raising of the retirement age, and introduction of the aforementioned automatic stabilizer. Additionally, relatively minor but still important changes have been made to the system after 2020. In contrast, despite the Social Security Board of Trustees projecting 75-year actuarial deficits since 1984, the last major change to the system occurred in 1983. American legislators should similarly take a more proactive approach to adjusting Social Security's imbalances more regularly, to allow for more gradual policy adjustments based on the principle of equity across the generations.

11

THE SWEDISH RETIREMENT SYSTEM

The Swedish retirement system stands out because of the significant reforms in the 1990s that set it on a long-term sustainable path. The transition from a defined-benefit (DB) to a notional defined-contribution (NDC) scheme, along with the introduction of an automatic balancing mechanism, ensured that the primary program of the Swedish pension system is always balanced, avoiding unexpected benefit cuts or tax rate increases. Furthermore, during this period, a partial privatization of the system occurred, with a portion of the total pension taxes directed to individual accounts. To further strengthen the finances of the system in the face of demographic challenges, Sweden recently legislated gradual increases in pension eligibility ages and linked them to average life expectancy. The Swedish system also effectively reduces old-age poverty through means-tested benefits such as the Guarantee Pension, which covers about half of seniors and costs less than 1 percent of gross domestic product (GDP). These aspects offer valuable lessons for US policymakers aiming for a more sustainable and equitable retirement system. However, it is worth noting that the Swedish model provides limited individual autonomy in retirement planning, relying heavily on government-run and collectively bargained plans, with private savings primarily limited to self-employed individuals.

In this chapter, we analyze the Swedish retirement system with respect to its effectiveness in protecting Swedish retirees from poverty in old age, the size and scope of benefits provided, the fiscal sustainability of the model, and the degree of individual freedom afforded to Swedish workers in retirement planning. We evaluate the Swedish system using various metrics and compare it with the US retirement system and the average across Organisation for Economic Co-operation and Development (OECD) member countries.

Sweden provides basic anti-poverty protection through the Guarantee Pension, a means-tested benefit that covers roughly half of the elderly population. The Guarantee Pension, alongside other targeted benefits, is effective at reducing senior poverty. The European Union statistics on income and living conditions (EU-SILC) survey indicates that Sweden has the lowest material and social deprivation rate among seniors across the EU, which is also substantially lower than the poverty rate among the general Swedish population.[1] Notably, Sweden achieves these outcomes while spending only 0.77 percent of its GDP on these anti-poverty provisions, illustrating how targeted basic benefits can significantly reduce poverty at a low cost.[2] In contrast, Social Security operates based on a costly earnings-related structure that provides expensive benefits to wealthy retirees. The success of the Guarantee Pension in reducing poverty highlights the potential advantages of transitioning Social Security to a more simplified and cost-effective flat-benefit scheme, which could be more effective in addressing poverty while also reducing the burden on taxpayers.

The Swedish retirement system also features earnings-related components—the Income Pension (Inkomstpension) and the Premium Pension (Premiepension). The Income Pension, introduced in the 1990s, replaced the previous defined-benefit model with a more sustainable notional defined-contribution scheme.[3] However, like Social Security, it operates on a pay-as-you-go basis, where current workers pay the benefits of current retirees. This structure makes the system susceptible to demographic pressures and to economic downturns that negatively affect employment levels. To address these risks, the Income Pension includes an automatic balancing mechanism that slows benefit growth when the system's liabilities exceed its assets. This mechanism, without requiring political intervention, automatically balances the Income Pension to avoid drastic benefit cuts or increases in tax rates. It was triggered after the Great Recession in 2008 and was deactivated in 2017 when the system regained stability.[4]

In contrast, Social Security faces looming insolvency within the next eight years, at which point the law calls for automatic benefit reductions.[5] And unlike in Sweden, there is no mechanism to automatically fix system imbalances in a more measured and forward-looking way, without political action.

US policymakers have few incentives to take corrective actions before the Social Security trust fund's projected insolvency date, due to the unpopularity among voters of measures that would reduce benefits or raise taxes. This puts the United States in a bad position, where reforms will most likely take place at the 11th hour against the threat of automatic benefit cuts that could affect the lowest-earning beneficiaries. Congress should consider adopting an automatic stabilizer mechanism that balances the Social Security system to correct for demographic and economic changes as shortfalls occur, well in advance of trust fund exhaustion.

The Premium Pension, also introduced as part of the 1990s reforms, is a relatively minor earnings-related component of the Swedish retirement system into which all workers must contribute. However, unlike most other government-run pensions, Premium Pension contributions are saved in individual private accounts, where asset growth depends on the individual's investment choices and market performance. Since its inception, returns in Premium Pension accounts—which are defined-contribution personal savings accounts—have consistently outpaced those of the Income Pension, which is essentially a notional defined-contribution pay-as-you-go scheme.[6]

In addition, about 90 percent of workers participate in occupational retirement plans, which were established through collective bargaining agreements.[7] As a result, most workers are required to participate in three earnings-related schemes (Income Pension, Premium Pension, and occupational schemes). Very few workers (primarily the self-employed) contribute to voluntary savings plans. In fact, 95 percent of total retirement income comes from mandatory public and occupational schemes.[8] Swedish citizens have little freedom in retirement planning; low levels of old-age income self-reliance; and almost no individual autonomy in retirement consumption-smoothing decisions. All these factors place the Swedish retirement system far from the libertarian North Star.

Nonetheless, Sweden's proactive approach to reforming its unsustainable pension system in the 1990s, the implementation of the balancing mechanism in the Income Pension in 2001, the gradual increase in eligibility ages since the 2020s, and the transition to partial privatization by allowing Swedes to invest a portion of their contributions in individual accounts provide valuable lessons for Congress. Despite political challenges, Sweden has repeatedly managed to adopt prudent retirement reforms over time. Like the Swedish Parliament, Congress should overcome partisan differences and work together to enact Social Security reforms that ensure the program's long-term sustainability. Among other measures, these reforms should include increasing the Social Security retirement age and linking the eligibility threshold to life expectancy, as Sweden has done, which would improve Social Security's long-term financial outlook.

Overview of the Swedish retirement system

Sweden is the only country discussed in this book with a retirement system that incorporates all five pillars of the World Bank pension framework.

The main element of the zero pillar is the Guarantee Pension, which is a residence-based pension financed from general revenues. This pension is means-tested against pension income but is not affected by work income. This means that the basic benefit is intentionally designed to not deter work among older Swedish citizens, a particularly compelling feature as Swedes are living longer productive lives. The maximum benefit, about 24 percent of the gross average wage in Sweden, gradually reduces with increases in the first-pillar pension.[9] Roughly

50 percent of Swedish seniors received some amount from the Guarantee Pension in 2023.[10]

The Swedish zero pillar includes other means-tested benefits with significant coverage, such as the housing supplement and the Income Pension supplement. Notably, Sweden has the lowest senior material deprivation rate in the EU, with poverty affecting just 1.9 percent of the elderly population under this definition.[11] In 2023, Sweden spent about US$5.7 billion (SEK 48 billion), or 0.77 percent of its GDP, on zero-pillar benefits.[12] The eligibility age for these benefits is set to increase from 66 to 67 in 2026, with the age threshold linked to life expectancy afterward.[13]

The first pillar of the Swedish retirement system is the Income Pension, an earnings-related NDC scheme. Unlike a DB scheme, which calculates retirement benefits based on a predefined formula, benefits in an NDC scheme depend on a predefined notional rate. For example, Social Security is a DB scheme in which retirees receive benefits based on a formula that depends on their average lifetime earnings. In contrast, workers' payments in the Income Pension grow at the rate of average wages in the country, and upon retirement, the accumulated funds (which only exist on paper) are transformed into an annuity. The Income Pension includes an automatic stabilizer that adjusts the system's growth rate (i.e., indexation to average wages) to maintain a balance between revenues and expenditures. Furthermore, five buffer funds, managed by independent boards of directors, invest in various asset classes and cover the gaps between the taxes paid by workers and benefit costs.[14]

The second pillar includes two components: the Premium Pension and occupational pensions. The Premium Pension is a mandatory private scheme in which workers' contributions are deposited into individual accounts that grow based on individual investment choices. Swedes are free to choose between 500 available funds or the default government-provided option. The Premium Pension is basically a compulsory savings scheme with accounts owned and investment choices controlled by participating individuals. The growth in assets in the Premium Pension accounts, which has averaged around 10 percent annually, exceeds the approximately 2 percent growth of Income Pension notional accounts. That means that this semiprivatized component of the Swedish system will grow to encompass a larger share of Swedes' retirement income in the future.[15]

Government-benefit provisions, which include the Guarantee Pension, the Income Pension, and the Premium Pension, achieve a 49 percent income replacement rate for an average earner, higher than Social Security's 39.1 percent and higher than the OECD average.[16] Combined, expenditures on these government programs amounted to 6.9 percent of GDP, compared with 5 percent of GDP for Social Security.[17] In 2023, Sweden raised the earliest eligibility ages for the Income Pension and Premium Pension from 62 to 63, with plans to further increase these thresholds to 64 in 2026 and then link them to life expectancy.[18]

The second component of the second pillar—occupational plans—while not government-mandated, are compulsory for 90 percent of workers because of collective bargaining labor agreements. Contribution rates for these plans sharply increase for wages above the taxable maximum for the Income and Premium pensions (108 percent of the average wage), rising from 4.5 percent of earnings to 30 percent. As a result, higher earners contribute a larger share of their income to these plans.[19]

The three mandatory earnings-related plans leave little room for the third pillar, voluntary retirement savings. The most active participants in voluntary plans are the self-employed, who do not qualify for occupational plans. Consequently, voluntary savings play a minimal role in the system, with only 5 percent of total government pension and retirement plan income coming from this source.[20]

A lack of data makes the estimation of the Swedish fourth pillar difficult. Based on homeownership statistics—the only available relevant data—more than 70 percent of Swedish seniors own their homes.[21]

Table 11.1 compares the Swedish and US retirement systems along selected metrics to evaluate their effectiveness. The data for these metrics are sourced from the OECD's *Pensions at a Glance 2023* report, as well as various national sources such as the Swedish Pensions Agency (Pensionsmyndigheten), the Swedish National Financial Management Authority, the Congressional Budget Office, and the Social Security Administration. The source for each metric is specified in the table.

TABLE 11.1
Key highlights: Swedish versus US retirement system

Category/metric	Sweden	United States
Zero pillar	Guarantee Pension	Supplemental Security Income
First pillar	Income Pension	Social Security
Second pillar	Premium Pension, occupational pensions	None
Third pillar	Voluntary pension plans that offer tax incentives for the self-employed	401(k)s, IRAs, Roth 401(k)s, Roth IRAs
Eligibility[a,b]	Guarantee Pension: 66–67 years old, Income/Premium Pension: earliest at 63–64	Social Security: 66–67 years old, early at 62, late at 70
Old-age dependency ratio[a]	35.9	29.4
Zero-pillar benefit amount (percent of gross average wage)[a]	23.70%	15.60%
Maximum taxable earnings for the first and second pillars (percent of annual average wage)[a]	108%	227%
Demographic impact ratio[a,b,c,d]	2.48	1.47
Total spending on public pensions per person (US$)[b,c,d]	$4,625	$4,020
Total spending on public pensions (percent of GDP)[b,c,d]	6.90%	5%
Total spending on public pensions, OECD (percent of GDP)[a,e]	7% (data from 2019)	7.10% (data from 2019)
Replacement rate (public pensions)[a]	49%	39.10%
Private retirement assets (percent of GDP)[a]	N/A*	138%
Replacement rate (public and private)[a]	62.30%†	73%
Private replacement share[a,c]	N/A*	0.47

(continued)

TABLE 11.1 *(continued)*

Category/metric	Sweden	United States
Homeownership rate (percent of seniors)[b]	73.60% (aged 60–69), 74.30% (70–79), 64.70% (80+) (data from 2023)	76.10% (aged 65–74) and 81% (75+) (data from 2022)
Median net worth of seniors (US$)[b]	No data	$410,000 (aged 65–74) and $335,000 (75+) (data from 2022)
Poverty rate (EU/national measure, percent of seniors)[b]	1.90% (data from 2023)	9.70% (data from 2023)[‡]

Note: EU = European Union; GDP = gross domestic product; IRAs = individual retirement accounts; OECD = Organisation for Economic Co-operation and Development

a. Data from OECD's *Pensions at a Glance 2023* report.
b. Data from a Swedish/EU/US government source.
c. Author's calculations.
d. For Sweden, includes the Guarantee Pension and other means-tested benefits, the Income Pension, and the Premium Pension; for the United States, includes Social Security.
e. Broader definition of public pensions; for example, includes Supplemental Security Income for the United States.
* OECD data on private retirement assets in Sweden include mandatory occupational schemes, but for this field, we focus exclusively on voluntary schemes.
† Includes occupational plans, which are mandatory in Sweden, unlike the private plans in the United States.
‡ The US senior poverty rate is likely much lower as the official poverty measure does not account for most of the income seniors derive from private retirement accounts.

Zero pillar

The Guarantee Pension is the primary component of the Swedish retirement system's zero pillar. It is a basic anti-poverty benefit funded from general revenues. The benefit is means-tested against pension income from the earnings-related part of the retirement system (the Income Pension, discussed in the "First pillar" section) but not against work income. The maximum monthly benefit is US$1,409 (SEK 11,907 adjusted for purchasing power parity), which fully phases out for individuals receiving more than US$2,144 (SEK 18,118) per month from the Income Pension. Additionally, the Guarantee Pension benefit is related to one's years of residency. The full benefit is proportionally reduced for each year below 40 years of residency.[22] According to the OECD, the maximum benefit value, which is indexed to prices and is fully taxed, amounted to 23.7 percent of the gross average wage in the country.[23] In 2023, about 50 percent of seniors received the Guarantee Pension.[24]

In addition to the Guarantee Pension, seniors may be eligible for a means-tested housing supplement (Bostadstillägg), the amount of which depends on one's housing costs and income.[25] In 2024, about 15 percent of Swedish seniors received this supplement. Also, a minor portion of seniors (around 1 percent), mainly immigrants with few years of residency, receive additional means-tested support (äldreförsörjningsstöd). Furthermore, in 2020, the Swedish government introduced the Income Pension supplement (inkomstpensionstillägg) for seniors with long earnings histories but relatively low pension incomes.[26] In 2023, about 57 percent of seniors received this supplement, although the maximum amount was only US$71 (SEK 600) per month.

It is interesting to examine how these anti-poverty benefits—the Guarantee Pension and other zero-pillar components—tackle old-age poverty in Sweden. According to the OECD, which defines poverty as having an income below half of the median national income, Sweden's senior poverty rate in 2021 was 11.8 percent.[27] It was lower than the OECD average of 14.2 percent and less than half the US senior poverty rate, according to this OECD measure, of 22.8 percent.

However, applying the OECD's methodology may overestimate poverty levels in wealthier nations such as Sweden and the United States, where earning less than 50 percent of the median income does not necessarily equate to living in poverty. The OECD figures provide more insights about income inequality than they do about poverty. A more accurate assessment might be found in country-specific income thresholds or universal criteria that define poverty based on tangible needs rather than relative income levels.

The EU offers the latter type of poverty measure. Specifically, the EU-SILC survey defines "material and social deprivation" as "the inability to afford a set of specific goods, services, or social activities that are considered by most people essential for an adequate quality of life." The survey applies a non-income threshold for all member nations, asking respondents whether they can afford at least 5 out of 13 items deemed essential for adequate quality of life, including basics such as the ability to keep one's home warm and having two pairs of properly fitting shoes (see appendix for the survey's full list).[28] Being unable to afford five of these essential items arguably indicates that an individual is living in poverty, regardless of whether one resides in a wealthy or poorer country.

The 2023 EU data show that the material and social deprivation rate among Swedes aged 65 and older was just 1.9 percent, the lowest in the EU.[29] For comparison, the average rate among the 27 EU countries was 11.2 percent, and it was 5.5 percent for the general Swedish population.

In contrast, the US Census Bureau measures poverty using a fixed income threshold, which is calculated based on the minimum cost of food and basic expenses.[30] However, this measure inflates senior poverty because it does not account for a significant portion of senior income, such as private retirement savings.[31] For example, the Census Bureau reported that 9.75 percent of American seniors were living in poverty in 2018. A 2025 study, using more comprehensive income data, adjusted the 2018 figure and found that the senior poverty rate was actually 5.73 percent.[32] Thus, the 2023 senior poverty figure, which is 9.7 percent, should be interpreted with caution, as the true rate is likely much lower.[33]

The Swedish retirement system's zero pillar successfully fulfills its primary objective of reducing poverty at a very low cost. In 2023, the Guarantee Pension, combined with other means-tested supplements, cost US$5.7 billion (SEK 48 billion), just 0.77 percent of Swedish GDP.[34]

The Guarantee Pension is a good example of how a basic pension can effectively reduce senior poverty at a low cost. Congress should consider shifting from the expensive earnings-related structure of Social Security to a well-designed basic pension. Depending on its features, such as the size of benefit levels, this system could be both more cost-efficient and more effective in tackling old-age poverty.

Sweden has also proactively addressed the financial implications of its aging population on its retirement programs. Sweden's old-age dependency ratio, defined as the number of seniors per 100 working-age individuals, was 35.9 in 2022, higher than the US ratio of 29.4 and the OECD average of 31.3.[35] To address rising old-age dependency, Sweden increased the eligibility age for its anti-poverty provisions from 65 to 66 in 2023 and will further increase it to 67 in 2026. From 2026 on, the eligibility ages for targeted benefits and income-related pensions will be linked to increases in life expectancy. Specifically, the threshold will increase by eight months for every one-year increase in average life expectancy at age 65.[36] The earliest eligibility age for the Guarantee Pension is expected to reach 70 by 2069.[37] It should be noted that one in four OECD countries link their pension eligibility ages to life expectancy.[38]

In contrast, despite a 16-year increase in life expectancy at birth since Social Security's inception, Congress has raised the program's full eligibility age by only two years in all that time.[39] Congress should raise the early and full retirement ages by three years, to 65 and 70, respectively. According to the Congressional Budget Office, raising the full retirement age to 70, with the early retirement age remaining at 62, would reduce the program's cash flow deficits by US$95 billion from 2026 to 2034.[40] Importantly, after increasing eligibility ages, these thresholds should be indexed to increases in life expectancy, similar to Sweden's approach.

First pillar

The primary component of the Swedish retirement system is the Income Pension, a first-pillar, pay-as-you-go earnings-related scheme. Sweden is among five OECD nations—alongside Italy, Latvia, Norway, and Poland—where the primary public pension operates on an NDC basis. In NDC schemes, participants have individual notional accounts where their contributions are accounted for and grow over time.

However, these are not "real accounts," meaning contributions are not saved and invested in financial markets. As described by the OECD, "The accounts are 'notional' in that the balances exist only on the books of the managing institution."[41] Similar to other pay-as-you-go schemes, current workers' contributions pay for current retirees' benefits. Therefore, it is more accurate to refer to the Income Pension as being funded by workers' taxes rather than by their contributions, since it is simply a government transfer program. The taxes that workers pay into these schemes are reflected in notional accounts that grow at a notional interest rate, which varies depending on the design of each country's system. For example, in the Italian pension scheme, the notional accounts grow in line with GDP growth.

In Sweden, notional accounts are indexed to the growth rate of average wages. Upon retirement, an initial annuity is calculated by dividing accumulated on-paper assets by a divisor that depends on the average remaining life expectancy and a 1.6 percent discount factor. The inclusion of the discount factor—which results in a higher initial benefit than a strictly actuarial calculation would provide—helps smooth the transition from work to retirement. This approach avoids a sharp decline in an individual's income and front-loads pension benefits.[42]

A person retiring at age 65 has an average remaining life expectancy of 20 years. If that person has accumulated US$350,000 in their Income Pension account, a strictly actuarial calculation would result in an initial annuity of US$17,500 (accumulated assets divided by the remaining life expectancy). However, the 1.6 percent discount factor reduces the annuity divisor to 17.07, resulting in a higher annuity of US$20,500.[43] Importantly, during retirement, the annual wage indexation of the initial annuity is adjusted downward by 1.6 percent to offset the initial increase provided by the discount factor.

The Swedish pension system tax is set at 18.5 percent of earnings, but its distribution follows a more complex formula than the typical 50/50 split between an employee and an employer. First, only 16 percent is dedicated to the Income Pension while the remaining 2.5 percent goes to the fully funded Premium Pension, which is explored in the next section. Of the total 18.5 percent, employees pay only 7 percent directly, up to the taxable ceiling, with their employers furnishing the rest. According to the OECD, this threshold stood at US$61,030 (SEK 534,000), or 108 percent of the average gross earnings in 2022. For comparison, Social Security had a higher taxable maximum of US$147,000, or 227 percent of the average wage.[44]

Importantly, the 7 percent employee portion is fully deducted from income taxes. The remaining portion—93 percent of gross earnings—is called the pensionable income. The employer share is paid on this pensionable income, which equals 10.21 percent of gross earnings $[(0.185 \times 0.93) - 0.07]$. In other words, the total tax is 17.21 percent of gross earnings. While the employee portion is capped at the taxable ceiling, the employer portion is not. Whatever the employer pays above this threshold goes to the central government budget and is not factored into the Income Pension benefit calculation.[45] This policy raises labor costs for Swedish firms and thus reduces take-home wages for workers and depresses overall employment levels. In contrast, the US payroll tax is fully deductible for US businesses.

The Swedish Income Pension includes an automatic balancing mechanism that guarantees the system can afford to pay its obligations without increasing the tax rate, regardless of adverse demographics or economic downturns.[46] The balancing mechanism is activated if the system's "balance ratio"—calculated as the ratio of assets to liabilities—falls below 1. The system's assets are composed of the present value of future taxes and the buffer fund balances (see in more detail later in this section), while its liabilities consist of pension balances of active workers and the present value of future pension payments.

When the balancing mechanism is activated, the way that notional account assets and pension benefits are adjusted changes. Specifically, the system transitions from using the income index, which adjusts assets and benefits based on average wage growth, to the balance index. The balance index is lower than the income index, increasing benefits and assets less than the rate of wage growth, whenever the system's assets fall short of its payout obligations. Indexation gradually returns to using wage growth as system assets catch up with liabilities. The balancing mechanism was activated in 2010 following the 2008 financial crisis—which precipitated the Great Recession—and was deactivated in 2017. As of 2025, the balance ratio is projected to be 1.1206, indicating that assets will outstrip liabilities by 12.06 percent.[47]

Congress should consider implementing a similar automatic stabilizer for Social Security. Social Security's old-age trust fund has been running cash flow deficits since 2010, with the Department of the Treasury borrowing from the public to cover these shortfalls.[48] An automatic mechanism to balance the system should align costs with revenues over time. Regular benefit adjustments could incentivize politicians to address the program's unsustainable finances, as voters would feel the impact sooner. Currently, with cuts delayed until insolvency in 2033, there is little incentive to act. Such a system would also reduce the harm of inaction by self-correcting over time.

In addition, politicians have taken proactive steps to address the Swedish pension system's demographic challenges, a major issue for any pay-as-you-go scheme. In 2020, the minimum eligibility age for receiving the Income Pension increased from 61 to 62. In 2023, this threshold was further increased to 63, and it will be maintained at this level until 2026. In 2026, the early eligibility age will increase to 64, and like the Guarantee Pension threshold, it will be indexed to life expectancy. Eurostat projects that the minimum eligibility age for the Income Pension will rise to 67 by 2069.[49] As previously mentioned, the Social Security eligibility age should also be raised further and linked to life expectancy.

Notably, Sweden does not have a mandatory retirement age. One can start collecting benefits while continuing to work. However, claiming benefits earlier reduces the size of annual benefits (see the annuity calculation as discussed earlier in this chapter). Still, the Income Pension includes a target retirement age, intended to act as a nudge for retirement. This age will be set at 67 in 2026 and will also be indexed to life expectancy.[50]

The Income Pension system is supported by five buffer funds (AP1, AP2, AP3, AP4, and AP6), each with different investment mandates. These funds, established in 1960 and initially financed by system surpluses, smooth the differences between the system's costs and revenues from workers' taxes, a common problem in pay-as-you-go systems.[51] From January 2026, the number of buffer funds will be reduced to three, through the merger of AP6 into AP2 and the liquidation of AP1, whose assets will be split equally between AP3 and AP4. The change aims to reduce fund management costs.[52] As of 2023, the buffer fund assets amounted to 16 percent of total system assets, supplementing revenues generated from workers' taxes.[53] The total value of fund assets was equivalent to 31 percent of Sweden's GDP. Notably, current tax revenue covers only 94 percent of benefit costs, while the remaining 6 percent is financed through investment income generated by these buffer funds.[54]

In comparison, revenues from payroll taxes and the taxation of benefits covered only 92 percent of Social Security's expenditures, while the remaining 8 percent was covered by borrowing based on the program's trust fund.[55] However, unlike the Swedish buffer funds, which are invested in real assets like stocks, the Social Security trust fund holds no real assets, only IOUs—promises to pay—from the federal government. When the program runs cash-flow deficits, the government must borrow to bridge the gap.

US Sen. Bill Cassidy (R-LA) has proposed creating a fund similar to Sweden's AP funds, which would invest in real assets. However, since Social Security runs deficits and has no surpluses, the government would need to borrow US$1.5 trillion to launch the fund, which would then invest in stocks, private equity, and other financial instruments. Andrew Biggs from the American Enterprise Institute critiques Senator Cassidy's plan, arguing:

> Cassidy's plan uses a roundabout method of extracting a larger share of future GDP to help pay for Social Security benefits. The federal government borrows today, using the money to purchase stocks that currently are held by Americans. Future taxpayers must repay those loans. And instead of flowing to Americans, the returns from those stocks now flow to the federal government, which by the end of 75 years would own roughly one-third of the U.S. stock market. As Wharton School economist Kent Smetters has shown, Cassidy's approach is not meaningfully different from simply increasing the capital gains tax: When the stock market goes up, the federal government takes a slice of the gains. Everything else is simply window dressing.[56]

In 2023, Sweden spent US$43 billion (SEK 360 billion), or 5.8 percent of its GDP, on the Income Pension. This figure includes spending on the Supplementary Pension (Tilläggspension), which is a benefit provided to those born before 1953 as part of the older, earnings-related pension system, gradually being phased out as younger generations retire.[57]

Second pillar

The Premium Pension

The first component of the Swedish retirement system's second pillar is the Premium Pension, a mandatory, fully funded defined-contribution scheme. As previously stated, 2.5 percent of workers' gross pensionable earnings, up to the taxable maximum, are allocated to the Premium Pension. The government supplements the Premium and Income Pension payments for individuals who are unemployed, disabled, or on parental leave.[58] Unlike the Income Pension, workers' contributions to the Premium Pension are paid into real private accounts and are invested in real assets (which is why payments into the Premium Pension are referred to as "contributions" rather than "taxes"). Thus, the accounts grow at market rates. Since its introduction, the Premium Pension has delivered a 10 percent annual return for an average participant, compared with the 2 percent average annual return of the Income Pension.[59]

Workers can choose to invest among approximately 500 funds, with the ability to distribute their portfolio among 5 funds.[60] While these are private funds, the Swedish Pensions Agency administers the system, including managing fund trading, handling pension accounts, acting as the insurer, providing information to savers, and verifying participants' savings before the determination of pensionable income.[61] Additionally, the contributions of workers who do not choose a fund are automatically invested in the state-provided default option, the AP7 Såfa fund.

As of 2025 individuals can begin withdrawing their Premium Pension benefits at 63, which will be increased to 64 in 2026 and linked to life expectancy afterward (i.e., similar to the eligibility criteria for the Income Pension). Upon retirement, individuals can choose a fixed or variable annuity. If they choose the fixed option, the accumulated assets in the funds are transferred to the Swedish Pensions Agency, which then pays a fixed monthly amount. The variable option keeps the assets in the funds, and the annuity amount depends on market performance.[62] Furthermore, individuals can choose to add a survivor's benefit to their premium pension, which allows the accumulated funds to be transferred to a partner in the event of the pensioner's death. However, because the benefits are expected to be paid out for a longer period under this option, the annuity amount is lowered.[63]

According to the OECD, the combined Guarantee Pension, Income Pension, and Premium Pension provide a 49 percent replacement rate for an average earner, higher than the OECD average of 42.3 percent (excluding mandatory occupational pensions, which are discussed later in this chapter). For comparison, Social Security achieved a 39.1 percent replacement rate for average earners.[64]

In 2023, the Swedish Pensions Agency reported that the total expenditures of the Premium Pension amounted to US$2.6 billion (SEK 22 billion), or 0.36 percent of Sweden's GDP. Expenditures on all public pensions, including the Income Pension, Premium Pension, and Guarantee Pension (including other means-tested supplements), totaled US$51.3 billion (SEK 430 billion), or 6.9 percent of GDP, corresponding to US$4,840 (SEK 40,564) per capita.[65] For comparison, the United States spent US$1.35 trillion on Social Security in the same year, equating to 5 percent of GDP, or US$4,021 per person.[66]

Based on a different methodology for calculating pension expenditures, which includes other pension components for both countries (e.g., Supplemental Security Income for the United States), Sweden's public pension expenditure was 7 percent of GDP in 2019, lower than that of the United States at 7.1 percent and the OECD average of 7.7 percent.[67]

Sweden's demographic impact ratio (DIR)—which is derived from multiplying total pension spending as a percent of GDP by a country's old-age dependency ratio—is 2.48, significantly higher than the US DIR of 1.47, by almost 70 percent. In contrast, when comparing pension spending alone, Sweden spends 38 percent more as a share of its GDP on pensions. The greater discrepancy between DIRs and spending figures suggests that the pressure of demographic aging on total pension spending is more pronounced in Sweden than in the United States.

Occupational plans

Sweden is one of five OECD nations—along with Denmark, Iceland, the Netherlands, and the United Kingdom—that have mandatory occupational retirement plans. These plans are established through collective bargaining agreements between trade unions and employer representatives and have broad coverage. In Sweden, about 90 percent of public and private employees are covered by these occupational plans.[68] Those not covered include the self-employed and employees who are not union members and who work for companies that have not signed collective bargaining agreements.[69] However, to compensate for this exclusion, the self-employed, unlike other workers, get tax concessions for voluntary savings (see more on this in the "Third pillar" section of this chapter).[70]

There are four major types of collective bargaining agreements, covering (a) central government employees, (b) municipal and county council employees, (c) private sector white-collar workers, and (d) private sector blue-collar workers.[71] The specific plan an employee belongs to is determined by the industry in which he or she is employed.

Contributions to these plans are paid by employers. For employees earning up to the Income Pension ceiling, or 108 percent of average earnings, the contribution rate stands at 4.5 percent. For wages that exceed this threshold, 30 percent of the portion above the 108 percent limit is deducted and goes toward occupational plans.[72] This sharp increase in the contribution rate is intended to offset the lack of Income and Premium Pension benefits for those earning above the ceiling. In other words, the government requires higher earners to contribute a larger share of their earnings to occupational plans because they do not receive benefits from the Income and Premium Pensions on their full income.[73]

Depending on the collective bargaining agreement, savings in occupational plans can be withdrawn from the age of 55, either as a lifetime annuity or for a shorter period (with options of 5, 10, 15, or 20 years).[74]

Occupational plans provide an additional 13.3 percent replacement rate of preretirement income for an average earner. Altogether, the Swedish system achieves a 62.3 percent replacement rate for an average earner, which is higher than the OECD average of 55.3 percent, a figure that includes voluntary retirement plans in some countries (including the United States).[75] In comparison, the total replacement rate for the US retirement system, which includes Social Security and voluntary plans, is 73.2 percent. In Sweden, the replacement rate for wealthier retirees—who earn twice the average income—is 76.4 percent, higher than that of an average earner. This pattern, which is rare among OECD nations where lower-income retirees typically get higher replacement rates, is largely due to the higher occupational contribution rates and higher occupational plan retirement incomes for higher-earning workers.

Total payments from occupational schemes reached roughly US$20 billion (SEK 167 billion), or 2.7 percent of GDP in 2023. The total mandatory pension expenditures, including public and occupational schemes, amounted to US$71.3 billion (SEK 597 billion), or 9.6 percent of Swedish GDP, or US$6,726 (SEK 56,500) per person.[76] This is significantly higher than Social Security expenditures that amount to 5 percent of US GDP or US$4,021 per person.[77] Our discussion excludes similar occupational pension benefits, such as those affecting certain US state and local public sector workers and those covered by single- and multi-employer plans.

Third pillar

The third pillar of the Swedish retirement system, voluntary retirement savings, is weak and plays a minimal role. The OECD does not consider Swedish voluntary plans to have broad coverage and does not report their share in the total replacement rate, which makes the calculation of the voluntary replacement share impossible.[78]

Until 2016, all Swedish workers received tax deductions for private retirement savings.[79] Since then, only the self-employed, who do not have occupational plans, are eligible for these deductions. They can deduct up to 35 percent of their business income, with a maximum deduction of US$68,000 (SEK 573,000) in 2024.[80] While contributions are exempted from taxation up to this threshold, investment gains and withdrawals are taxed (i.e., voluntary savings fall under the Exempt-Taxed-Taxed regime).

As noted, voluntary savings are not an important component of the Swedish pension system. In 2021, voluntary savings accounted for just 5 percent of total retirement income, while government-run plans contributed 67 percent and occupational plans made up the remaining 28 percent.[81] Mandatory public and occupational plans made up 71 percent of total senior income for Swedes in 2021, according to the OECD. The share of mandatory pensions in total senior income was much lower in the United States, at 39.3 percent.[82] Eurostat projects that voluntary retirement plans will gradually decline in Sweden, with only a small proportion of workers, mainly the self-employed, continuing to contribute to the system.[83]

Fourth pillar

The fourth pillar of Sweden's retirement system covers assets and income sources beyond government pensions and retirement plans. This pillar includes personal wealth accumulated outside traditional pensions and retirement assets, such as stocks, bonds, real estate, and other investments. However, in 2007, Sweden stopped collecting wealth statistics covering household assets and liabilities because the wealth tax and its related reporting requirements were abolished.[84] This complicates the evaluation of the Swedish fourth pillar.

However, data on a significant component of the fourth pillar—senior homeownership rates—are available. According to Statistics Sweden, 73.6 percent of Swedish seniors aged 60 to 69 owned their homes in 2023. Homeownership rates were slightly higher at 74.3 percent for those aged 70 to 79 and decreased to 64.7 percent for those 80 and older, which is attributed to the increasing number of seniors in this age group living in residential care facilities.[85] Senior homeownership rates were higher in the United States in 2022, with 76.1 percent of seniors aged 65 to 74 and 81 percent of seniors older than 75 owning their homes.[86]

The above OECD data—suggesting mandatory public and occupational plans made up 71 percent of total senior income in Sweden in 2021—provide additional insights. According to the OECD, the remainder of senior income comes from capital (12.4 percent)—defined as savings from personal retirement plans and returns on nonpension and nonretirement plan savings—and work (17 percent).[87]

Swedish retirement system reforms

Before the 1990s, when Sweden underwent substantial pension reforms, the retirement system consisted of two main components: the earnings-related, pay-as-you-go DB scheme known as *allmän tilläggspension*

(ATP) and a universal basic pension called folkpension. In a DB scheme, the pension benefits are predetermined based on a formula that typically factors in a worker's earnings and years of paying dedicated taxes. The ATP system provided benefits corresponding to 60 percent of the average earnings from a worker's 15 highest-earning years.[88] Similarly, Social Security is also a DB scheme, calculating benefits based on workers' 35 highest-earning years. A common issue with DB schemes is the weak link between taxes paid in and benefits paid out, as the benefits are predefined based on a portion of an individual's lifetime earnings rather than their tax payments, often leading to financial imbalances over time.

In the early 1990s, projections showed that the ATP scheme was on track to become insolvent in less than a decade—similar to the current position of Social Security.[89] This projection, coupled with an economic crisis, prompted a major overhaul of the Swedish retirement system.[90] In 1994, a Parliamentary Working Group on Pensions led the reforms that replaced the ATP scheme with the Income Pension, a pay-as-you-go NDC scheme, and the Premium Pension, a fully funded DC scheme.[91] Additionally, the 1990s reforms replaced the universal folkpension with the means-tested Guarantee Pension.

Unlike DB schemes, defined-contribution schemes do not promise a predefined level of benefits to contributors; instead, the pension amount depends on contributions and their investment performance. In the case of the Income Pension, which is an NDC scheme, investment performance refers to the growth of average wages. The idea was to link the system to the country's economic performance, with slower economic growth accompanied by weaker wage growth, which would decrease the rate of return in the notional accounts.[92] By having a stronger link to contributions, or more precisely paid taxes, the Income Pension is more financially robust than the ATP system. However, the Income Pension is still a pay-as-you-go scheme and is therefore vulnerable to challenges posed by an aging population.

That risk is why, in 2001, Sweden introduced the automatic balancing mechanism for the Income Pension. This mechanism protects the system from demographic risks as it regularly adjusts its parameters (see a more detailed discussion of this mechanism earlier in this chapter.).[93] Social Security is also a pay-as-you-go scheme, where young workers pay the benefits of senior retirees. Congress should also consider adopting a similar mechanism to mitigate the impacts of an aging population by adjusting benefits accordingly.

Furthermore, the introduction of the fully funded Premium Pension moved Sweden's public pensions toward partial privatization. Although it plays a relatively small role and is compulsory, transitioning part of public pensions to individual, private accounts is a positive step. Fully funded DC schemes such as the Swedish Premium Pension ensure that workers' contributions are set aside for their own retirement through investment in marketable assets. Notably, since its inception in 1995, the Premium Pension's average annual return has been 10 percent, significantly higher than the Income Pension's 2 percent average annual return.[94]

The Parliamentary Working Group on Pensions, which facilitated the 1990s reforms, is still the main body overseeing the Swedish pension system. It consists of members from all parties. The group adopted further reforms in 2020 that increased eligibility ages and linked these thresholds to life expectancy.[95]

The Swedish experience offers valuable lessons for US policymakers on setting aside partisan differences to address critical issues like population aging and their negative impacts on pension program sustainability. As Johan Norberg, a senior fellow at the Cato Institute, noted about the success of Sweden's 1990s pension reforms in putting the system on a fiscally sustainable path:

> No doubt, part of the explanation is that Swedish politicians prepared their citizens with an adult conversation about costs, benefits and what was possible, instead of merely rehearsing slogans and ignoring the inevitable crash.[96]

Summary

Sweden's retirement system does not align with libertarian ideals of self-reliance and freedom in retirement planning. In contrast to a system closer to the libertarian model, which would rely heavily on voluntary private savings, the role of voluntary retirement plans in Sweden is minimal, with only 5 percent of total senior pension and retirement plan income coming from voluntary savings. Individual autonomy over retirement planning decisions is virtually nonexistent, as most savings decisions are dictated by the government-run earnings-related pensions and compulsory occupational plans established through collective bargaining agreements.

Still, the Swedish pension system has several positive features that can offer valuable insights for US policymakers: an effective means-tested basic benefit, proactive reforms addressing demographic and economic challenges, an automatic balancing mechanism within its pay-as-you-go program, and a fully funded DC scheme with individual accounts.

The Guarantee Pension is the zero pillar of the Swedish retirement system. It is a means-tested basic benefit, with roughly 50 percent of seniors qualifying for it. Combined with other targeted benefits, the Guarantee Pension effectively achieves its primary objective of reducing old-age poverty, with Sweden's senior material and social deprivation rate being the lowest in the EU. Importantly, Sweden spends less than 1 percent of its GDP on these zero-pillar provisions, demonstrating how a well-designed targeted basic system can be both cost-efficient and effective in tackling poverty. Congress should consider transitioning from Social Security's costly earnings-related structure to a basic benefit system. Depending on its features, this system could be less expensive than Social Security and provide more robust anti-poverty protection.

Importantly, in the 1990s, Swedish lawmakers successfully reformed the primary earnings-related program, shifting from an unsustainable defined-benefit structure to a defined-contribution scheme known as the Income Pension. In 2021, to further strengthen the new scheme against the challenges posed by an aging population and unexpected economic downturns, Sweden introduced an automatic balancing mechanism that reduces pension benefits when system finances are deemed unsustainable.

In contrast, Social Security, which has been deemed financially unsustainable for decades, does not include a mechanism that regularly adjusts its elements to rebalance its finances. Instead, under current law, benefits will automatically be reduced by 21 percent when Social Security's trust fund is depleted in less than a decade. The lack of a rebalancing mechanism creates dangerous political incentives to delay implementing needed reforms until the last minute, when the program faces imminent benefit cuts. Incorporating a balancing mechanism similar to Sweden's would ensure Social Security avoids imbalances and encourage timely interventions by policymakers before massive automatic benefit cuts loom.

Moreover, as part of the 1990s reforms, Sweden introduced the Premium Pension, where workers' contributions are saved in individual private accounts. While participation in the Premium Pension is compulsory, this partial privatization of the retirement system was a positive step, given that workers are free to choose from hundreds of investment funds with high average returns.

In 2020, Sweden began gradually raising eligibility ages for public pensions. By 2026, the eligibility age for basic pensions will increase from 66 to 67 and the early eligibility age for the Income Pension will increase from 63 to 64, with both of these thresholds linked to life expectancy afterward. By establishing a pension working group with participation from members across all parties, Sweden created a political mechanism to adopt retirement reforms through a "we're all in this together" approach. Congress, like the Swedish Parliament, should work across party lines to raise Social Security eligibility ages and link them to life expectancy. Doing so would be a prudent step toward achieving a more financially sustainable system.

12

PANEL DISCUSSION: LESSONS FROM THE GERMAN AND SWEDISH PENSION SYSTEMS

PANELISTS

- **Kristoffer Lundberg,** Deputy Director, Policy Analysis Units, Swedish Ministry of Health and Social Affairs
- **Martin Werding,** Chair, Social Policy and Public Finance, Ruhr University Bochum
- Moderated by **Romina Boccia,** Director of Budget and Entitlement Policy, Cato Institute

KEY HIGHLIGHTS

- **Martin Werding** discusses major reforms in the German retirement system: "Most importantly, the formula for annual increases, which followed gross wages, was adjusted. Previously, this formula meant pensions grew faster than the net earnings of the working population, if contribution rates had to be increased. The reform switched to a mode guaranteeing a constant net benefit level for pensions. That was step one in the late 1980s.

[In the early 2000s,] we introduced an automatic stabilization mechanism in the benefit uprating formula. This adjustment slowed down annual pension increases as the demographic situation worsened. Consequently, the net benefit level decreases over time, necessitating attention to the second and third pillars—occupational and private pensions. So there was an attempt to strengthen private provisions. We also increased the legal retirement age from 65 to 67, with this change being gradually implemented until 2031."

- **Kristoffer Lundberg:** "During the '90s, Sweden had the highest dependency ratio among the three countries represented on this panel [the United States, Germany, and Sweden], coinciding with our latest reform period. . . . **During our reform, we focused on the real economy. In the situation of the increasing dependency ratio, you need to focus on employment. Prioritizing employment and economic growth is crucial, more so than discussing taxes or contributions.** . . . Additionally, there should be a focus on enabling people to work more and longer, as this is part of the solution."
- **Kristoffer Lundberg** discusses the automatic stabilizer in the Swedish system: "During our reforms in the '90s, it was clear that increasing the contribution rate further was not a preferred option. Therefore, adjustments needed to be made in other areas, such as benefits or pension age. . . . **The balancing mechanism makes it difficult to increase the contribution rate.** So the pressure is on the other two elements, which is challenging. It is a tough medicine."
- **Martin Werding:** "Once you've entered the business of **trying to keep up living standards at old age for workers, which is what the US does, even with the progressive elements, you need actuarial adjustments to demographic changes.** . . . The increase in contributions is not a good idea

for many reasons. It increases total wage costs, harms international competitiveness, and introduces or expands intergenerational redistribution, where young people pay for high benefits for older individuals who might not need them due to good occupational provisions."

- **Kristoffer Lundberg:** "We had an economic crisis in the early 1990s. As the saying goes, **don't waste a crisis** when you need to implement difficult reforms."

Transcripts have been edited for style and clarity.

Full Transcript

Romina Boccia: Our discussion is about lessons learned from the German and Swedish pension systems. For those who might detect a bit of an accent, I am originally from Germany but have spent my entire working career in the United States, so I'll be learning about the German system along with you.

I'd like to start with a quick question for both of you. Kristoffer, let's begin with you, and then we'll move on to Martin. Could you briefly describe the key structures of your country's pension system? What are the main components?

Kristoffer Lundberg: Thank you very much. First of all, a big thank-you for having me here. It's a great pleasure to meet our American friends and allies here in Washington. Pensions or Social Security, as it's called in the US, are complex topics. Don't worry. I won't delve into all the intricate details of our pension system and its interactions, as it involves many components, including the taxation system. Analyzing the full effects of this requires expertise in economics and actuarial science, along with a dedicated team.

To keep it simple, think of our retirement scheme like a smartphone—not everyone knows the technical workings, but everyone relies on it. Similarly, not everyone knows all the formulas involved in the pension system, but it's crucial for everyone at some point in their lives.

The Swedish setup is based on a publicly provided social security system, which forms the base. It includes several components. On top of this, we have occupational pensions, which are sector-wide and negotiated between unions and employer organizations, providing significant income replacement for workers. Finally, there are private savings, similar to most other countries. These three pillars—public social security, occupational pensions, and private savings—vary in proportion based on an individual's income level.

Romina Boccia: Are occupational pensions widely available? What percentage of the population has them?

Kristoffer Lundberg: Well, 90 percent. The only exception is the self-employed, as they are both employer and employee and thus need to provide for themselves.

Romina Boccia: And if you know the answer to this, for an average Swedish worker, what percentage of their retirement income might come from the social security component versus their occupational pension or retirement savings?

Kristoffer Lundberg: Well, that is very individual. I come from a small country. We are only 10 million people. Our economy thrives on producing and selling products globally at competitive prices. So we depend on free trade and strong international relationships with you in the US and elsewhere. We also value individual freedom highly, which influences our cultural context.

In Sweden, each unit of currency contributed has a direct connection to the benefits received. Our system emphasizes individual contributions through taxes or contributions, and benefits are returned in proportion to what has been paid in. To alleviate poverty, we have targeted systems that address specific situations. We are not in favor of having a flat-rate system where everyone gets the same regardless of how much they contribute. On the contrary; for us, it's very important that you get what you paid in.

Romina Boccia: We'll talk more about that notional defined-contribution system in a minute. But, Martin, could you also give us a quick overview of the basic German pension system structure and how much people rely on the government versus their own private savings?

Martin Werding: In Germany, the first pillar—government provision of public pensions—is very important compared to many other countries. The German public pension scheme is one of the oldest in the world, rooted in the Bismarckian tradition, as opposed to the Anglo-Saxon tradition of poverty relief as the main goal of public intervention in old-age provision.

The German system is rather similar to the US system but without progressive elements in assessing pension benefits. You pay in contributions and get additional benefits for each euro that you pay in. Also, contributions after age 63 are fully reflected in higher pensions, avoiding the disincentives mentioned in earlier discussions.

We also have occupational pensions covering 60 percent of the population, with efforts to strengthen the third pillar initiated 20 years ago, attracting 30 to 40 percent participation. Additionally, the fifth pillar encompasses any other income sources for old-age provision. Unfortunately, about 20 percent of the population relies solely on public pensions in old age, particularly poorer individuals, who have been working in small enterprises without occupational pensions. Germany also faces one of the largest demographic challenges in the developed world over the next two decades.

Romina Boccia: Yeah. I'd love to pull up a slide [see figure 12.1] that you prepared for us on this point to talk a little bit about the [demographic] differences. Could you walk us through what we're looking at on the slide and how it matters?

Martin Werding: It's the old-age dependency ratio, defined as the number of individuals aged 65 and older per 100 individuals ages 20 to 64. You could choose the age brackets in a different way. That would make a difference in levels but not in trends. The graph includes the United

FIGURE 12.1
Old-age dependency ratios, 1950–2060

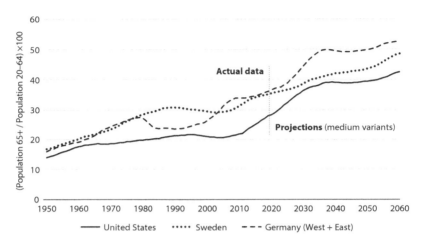

Source: Data compiled by the Organisation for Economic Co-operation and Development.

States, Sweden, and Germany, the three countries in a sense represented on this panel. The solid line represents the US, showing a relatively flat trend until around the 2010s, followed by a significant increase due to the aging baby-boom generation. Sweden had similar levels as the US in the 1950s and 60s, with an increase in dependency that eventually flattened out and then accelerated again.

That's the demographic situation in Sweden, which is unfortunate but not as unfortunate as in Germany. The dashed line represents Germany, where a decrease in the 1980s reflects the German baby boomers entering the labor market. Germany's baby boom was relatively late and small by international standards, but it mattered already then [i.e., in the 1980s], partly due to the impact of World Wars I and II on the size of earlier birth cohorts. The significant issue now is that these baby boomers are retiring from the 2020s to 2035, a problem we've anticipated for four decades but haven't fully resolved.

Romina Boccia: Let's discuss how Germany is addressing this demographic shift, particularly the lopsided dependency ratio, where a growing number of retirees depend on a shrinking workforce despite increased immigration. How is Germany tackling this issue?

Martin Werding: When focusing on pensions, migration is one potential solution, but it brings political challenges. Health care is another significant issue with an aging population. Regarding public pensions, Germany undertook reforms in the late 1980s when demographics looked favorable, but the labor market's performance was poor. Anticipating an increase in the dependency ratio post-2000, we tightened the system by eliminating many noncontributory benefits, such as those for training and education periods that primarily benefited academics. At the time, people with academic training were between 10 and 20 percent of the population. Also, until then, there were generous options for leaving the labor market early and drawing a pension without any actuarial reductions. That was abolished.

Most importantly, the formula for annual increases, which followed gross wages, was adjusted. Previously, this formula meant pensions grew faster than the net earnings of the working population, if contribution rates had to be increased. The reform switched to a mode guaranteeing a constant net benefit level for pensions. That was step one in the late 1980s.

Then, we had a second round of reforms in the early 2000s, where we somehow understood that guaranteeing a constant net benefit level is out of reach with our demographic situation. So we introduced an automatic stabilization mechanism in the benefit uprating formula. This adjustment slowed down annual pension increases as the demographic situation worsened. Consequently, the net benefit level decreases over time, necessitating attention to the second and third pillars—occupational and private pensions. So there was an attempt to strengthen private provisions. We also increased the legal retirement age from 65 to 67, with this change being gradually implemented until 2031.

Romina Boccia: Kristoffer, tell us how Sweden has been addressing population aging through the pension program.

Kristoffer Lundberg: First, I'd like to comment on the figure. During the '90s, Sweden had the highest dependency ratio among the three countries, coinciding with our latest reform period. Relative to many other countries, the US has a very positive structural outlook, as you can see from the graph.

So coming from a country in the far north, where it's cold and dark half of the year, where you really have to struggle, we like to trade with everyone who has a better outlook.

During our reform, we focused on the real economy. In the situation of the increasing dependency ratio, you need to focus on employment. Prioritizing employment and economic growth is crucial, more so than discussing taxes or contributions.

Combining US productivity with Sweden's high employment rate would be ideal for us and would solve many financing issues, providing more resources for political preferences across the spectrum.

So I think that's where the focus should be—not so much on the technicalities or the preferred toolkit used in your country. But it's very important that governments protect people in need from poverty. That has to be the role of government.

Additionally, there should be a focus on enabling people to work more and longer, as this is part of the solution. So incentivizing employment is very important and can be achieved within the pension system, tax system, or by providing necessary services to support labor-market participation.

Romina Boccia: Is there a particular reform that has had outsize benefits for Sweden? If there's one reform you would encourage countries to look at because it was the most impactful in the Swedish context, what would that be? Would it be within the pension system, the tax system, or perhaps, say, providing childcare support for single mothers?

Kristoffer Lundberg: Well, I think it's all of these things. You need to work across many dimensions because every bit counts. If you can find ways to increase growth, wherever that opportunity lies, you should utilize it. This is something we do, and I believe focusing on these aspects would be highly beneficial.

Romina Boccia: Let's talk a little more about how the notional defined-contribution system works and some of the automatic balancing mechanisms in the Swedish system. This is particularly interesting to the United States because we've spent the past 40 years without making any reforms to Social Security despite facing significant demographic challenges. What are some of these marginal balancing mechanisms or automatic triggers that the US should consider as it looks to reform its system before 2033 to avoid another long period without necessary adjustments?

Kristoffer Lundberg: Well, this is very important. Policy decisions should align with the will of the people. During our reforms in the '90s, it was clear that increasing the contribution rate further was not a preferred option.

Therefore, adjustments needed to be made in other areas, such as benefits or pension age. That does not apply to recipients of targeted pensions, ensuring they aren't adversely affected. For everyone else, there's a strong push to work more and longer, with adjustments linked to increases in longevity.

The balancing mechanism makes it difficult to increase the contribution rate. So the pressure is on the other two elements, which is challenging. It is tough medicine. But it was perceived that we had reached a contribution level slightly higher than in the US, and we didn't want to go further.

Romina Boccia: It seems this is the opposite of the situation in Germany. Is that right, Martin? Do contribution rates tend to be the primary balancing mechanism to ensure pensions are paid out?

Martin Werding: That's right. But there are similarities, and it's important for the US to consider Kristoffer's points. The Swedish pension system shows one thing very clearly. Once you've entered the business of trying to keep up living standards at old age for workers, which is what the US does, even with the progressive elements, you need actuarial adjustments to demographic changes. If you have a poverty relief system, then you cannot reduce benefits, if demographics are becoming adverse.

The increase in contributions is not a good idea for many reasons. It increases total wage costs, harms international competitiveness, and introduces or expands intergenerational redistribution, where young people pay for high benefits for older individuals who might not need them due to good occupational provisions.

By fixing the contribution rate and incorporating adjustment mechanisms, Sweden distributes what goes into the pay-as-you-go system to the elderly in line with actual living standards.

This is something Germany should have implemented 20 years ago, as it's now a bit late to make such adjustments. The Swedes also did one additional important thing: if you fix the contribution rate and accept that benefit levels of the pay-as-you-go system may go down, then you need an effective prefunded element. Given the traditions of European countries, you also need some degree of compulsion because you cannot wait for one generation to understand that they should have saved on top of their pension contributions.

This approach is quite different from what we've heard about New Zealand. The question is how one could transition from one system to another. The US, situated between these two worlds, might not learn much from European countries if it leans toward New Zealand's model. However, if the US wants to maintain living standards without increasing poverty risk, European countries, especially Sweden, offer valuable lessons.

In Germany, rules require the contribution rate to rise to maintain a balanced system budget. The system also receives federal government funds, allegedly to make up for still-existing noncontributory benefits. So if this is correct, all other benefits are to be financed from contributions. The need to increase contributions creates a problem for Germany over the next two decades. The challenge is how to avoid this.

Romina Boccia: How much of the German system is impacted by the fact that Germany was divided and then reunited? Does that contribute to some of these financing challenges requiring general revenue transfers? How was that negotiated?

Martin Werding: It has a minimal impact. One advantage of pay-as-you-go systems is their ability to integrate regions like East Germany, incorporating both contributors and pensioners. If demographics, employment, and labor-market performance had been similar to the West, it wouldn't have made a difference at all.

However, the situation was slightly different. Wages were lower, and employment declined after the reintegration. This was problematic for a while because the transition from the old East German pension system to the existing federal system was relatively generous. There is some percentage of additional benefits that are simply there because of these generous rules. But it makes up for less than 10 percent of our current annual expenditure in the pension system, and it will disappear over time. For a while, we also had slightly different values attached to one pension point, which is what you receive as a basis for your pension entitlement if you pay in contributions on an average income for one year. The way preretirement wages were converted into pension points was also different between East and West. But these differences have now disappeared. Some follow-up issues still linger in the system.

Romina Boccia: Kristoffer, I understand Sweden has a buffer fund to enhance the income pension program. How does that work? How big is the buffer fund, and where does the revenue come from?

Kristoffer Lundberg: Our social security system has experienced positive cash flows when contributions exceeded payouts. These funds have been invested over the years, contributing to the system and smoothing fluctuations due to varying birth cohort sizes. The investments have been successful, and the fund has grown significantly.

Romina Boccia: Was this money a surplus from the pension program?

Kristoffer Lundberg: Yes, during years of positive cash flows, the surplus was allocated to these buffer funds and invested. The idea is to use this reserve during times when contributions are lower than payouts.

Romina Boccia: And who oversees the fund management? Are there any political tensions about what that money could be invested in, driven more by political preferences rather than maximizing returns?

Kristoffer Lundberg: Historically, there were political divisions about this. However, after having these funds for such a long time and seeing how professionally they are managed and how they're detached from governmental control, there's now broad political support. Everyone recognizes that the fund managers are doing a very good job and maximizing returns effectively. So we are very happy with their work.

Romina Boccia: Tapping into economic growth seems to be a successful strategy. Martin, is that something Germany is also considering—creating a fund to bolster the German pension system? What are your views on that kind of system?

Martin Werding: The current German government's plan should be considered an amendment rather than a reform. They aim to fix the benefit level, which was supposed to decrease over time according to rules established 15 to 20 years ago. This is what they want to stop. To finance this, they propose a system similar to what Senator Cassidy presented this morning. The basic idea is that the system borrows money at relatively low interest rates, given the rating of German Treasury bills, and then invests it in the international stock markets, expecting that there can be a higher return, which is sensible.

The question is how significant and stable this difference in returns will be over the long term. The German credit rating could suffer, and this approach is intended to continue for 15 years. When the baby boomers fully enter the pension system, they plan to use the difference between the interest paid and the stock-market returns while not touching injections to comply with our debt break. This is a kind of trick that might work. But with the concentration on just the difference between stock-market returns and the interest that needs to be paid, it cannot make up for the extra contributions that are needed when the benefit level is fixed. We made a rough calculation in the German Council of

Economic Experts and found that it would only cover pension expenditures for a few days in 2035.

Romina Boccia: That seems like a very risky proposition for a very little return.

Martin Werding: Yeah. If it works, it can contribute a few billion euros. But it's nothing that will solve our problem.

Romina Boccia: It's not a silver bullet.

Martin Werding: No.

Romina Boccia: Kristoffer, could you talk to us about the roles of the Parliamentary Pension Commission and the Working Group in the reforms Sweden underwent in the mid-'90s?

Kristoffer Lundberg: Certainly! We had an economic crisis in the early 1990s. As the saying goes, don't waste a crisis when you need to implement difficult reforms. Given that social security and retirement systems are long-term, often taking 30 to 40 years to mature, it's crucial to have broad support. This means forming a coalition of the willing that is as broad as possible. Considering the various governments and coalitions over the past decades, it's clear that having each government implement its reforms periodically doesn't lead to effective outcomes.

We created a parliamentary group with members from all willing parties to discuss the issues, focusing on policy rather than politics. This process was reiterated over time to build trust among all involved. Senior politicians from various fields became friends and understood the issues, allowing them to negotiate compromises that satisfied everyone. This approach was highly successful, and the financial crisis certainly provided the impetus for necessary action.

Romina Boccia: Was there any role played by independent experts, or was it all worked out by elected officials?

Kristoffer Lundberg: Well, it depends on what kind of structure you have in your country. Once again, we're a small European country with a robust civil service. People such as me stay forever and work for the winners. Due to our limited pool of personnel, we utilize whoever we have and make the best of it. We reach out to academics, but the civil service provides the backbone, and we bring in experts from those willing to help.

Romina Boccia: I want to ask Martin a question, and then I'd like to take a few questions from the audience. In 2001, Germany introduced the Riester pension. Why do you think adoption rates are so low? Is there a way to increase its use as a vehicle for retirement savings? How do you shift from a system where the population relies primarily on the government to one where they rely more on their private savings?

Martin Werding: The Riester pension was designed as a new program for third-pillar provisions but wasn't widely embraced by the public due to several design flaws. Initially, it was supposed to be mandatory, but then chancellor [Gerhard] Schröder stopped this at the last minute due to public backlash against compulsory measures. If you do not have compulsion, then you need a good design.

The biggest issue is the requirement for providers to guarantee the return of 100 percent of the contributions paid in. This guarantee is costly because it hinders investment in the stock market and therefore yields poor returns. I mean, after 40 years of investment, only getting back 100 percent of what you paid in is a nightmare of a result for a private pension plan. Together with the low-interest period that followed from 2010 onward, it made it entirely unattractive to invest. Another thing is that the German financial services industry has extremely high costs that ate up what was left of the potential returns. Given these flaws, it's probably fortunate that only 30 to 40 percent of the target population took up these contracts. Some of them are relatively good, but most of them are not worth investing one euro. Many people have stopped investing and are waiting for it to be disbursed so they are not losing their subsidies.

Q and A

Question 1: Hi. Wendell Primus with the Brookings Institution. In the United States, our fertility rate now is below 1.7. Some of us believe we're facing a significant workforce shortage problem down the road, especially as the baby boomers require long-term care services. My question is, how did your two countries address immigration? While it's not a silver bullet, we think increasing legal immigration could solve about a sixth of our Social Security financing problems. How do immigration and workforce shortages work together in your countries?

Martin Werding: It took Germany some time to realize it's an immigration country. Initially, we thought of immigrants as guest workers who might eventually return home. But since the late 1990s, we've been actively trying to design immigration policies. We have lots of open doors for labor immigrants, but the challenge in Germany is that many people are using other doors, such as claiming asylum or refugee status. While the total number of immigrants is high, the composition isn't always what we need for the labor market.

As I emphasized earlier, immigration isn't something politicians can make work instantly. You need to build networks of immigrants with specific qualifications and origins. If a group successfully integrates into the labor market, it's beneficial to keep that door open, as others with similar backgrounds are likely to follow. We're also working hard to integrate refugees into our labor markets. And while their performance isn't bad, it's challenging due to language barriers and skill levels. So the situation could be better, but at least we've understood what the problem is, and we're working on it. We're trying to keep those on board who resist immigration. Yeah, that's politically difficult.

13

CONCLUSION

Amanda looked in the rearview mirror as she pulled out of the hospital parking lot, the setting sun casting a soft glow on the cars. It had been a long shift—another 10-hour day—but tonight she didn't feel the same heaviness in her chest. Instead, as she thought about the future, there was a quiet sense of relief.

A commission on Social Security had succeeded in getting reforms done. The program had been restructured into a more predictable, sustainable one. The constant discussions of insolvency, future cuts, and political stalemates had finally been addressed. A panel of independent experts, with Congress's blessing, had modernized the system, averting benefit cuts for her parents while also protecting working families like hers. Now Amanda knew what to expect.

As she headed home, she turned on the radio. Once again, NPR was discussing Social Security—but this time the tone was different. Experts talked about the success of the reforms. While several benefit adjustments had been made, the foundational changes ensured that Amanda's generation could rely on the system's basic benefits without fear of sudden cuts or escalating taxes. The introduction of universal savings accounts (USAs) had given her and millions of other workers new flexibility, allowing them to save for the future on their own terms. Amanda and Dave had opened their own USA accounts shortly after the reforms passed, and every month, they contributed to their savings, confident that this additional nest egg would complement the basic security that Social Security provided while also being there for them in an emergency.

"Mom, can Josh stay for dinner tonight?" her son asked as she walked through the door, pulling her out of her thoughts. She smiled, setting her bag down and heading to the kitchen, where Dave was shredding a slow-cooked chicken that smelled of paprika, lemon, and onion. Her mouth was watering, and she could feel her stomach growl a little. Life was still busy—filled with work, bills, and parenting—but the looming fear of a broken system had been replaced with a sense of control. She and Dave weren't just hoping things would work out anymore; they had a plan.

As she settled down on the couch later that night to rewatch *Lessons in Chemistry*, her favorite show, Amanda felt something new—confidence. She was no longer passively relying on the promises of an old system. The reformed Social Security program, with its simple, flat benefits and new USAs, had empowered her family to take charge of their future. There was clarity now, something she hadn't realized was missing before. She knew what she could count on from Social Security and how she could build on that foundation with her own savings.

The world had shifted, and Amanda was ready. The future, once a cloud of uncertainty, now looked manageable, even promising. The weight of the past few years had lifted. As Dave came to sit next to her, she smiled. They would be okay.

* * *

Amanda's story reminds us that this is not just an academic exercise or a policy debate—it's a question of real lives, real futures, and real stakes for millions of Americans. Like Amanda, countless workers are caught between the promises of a system designed for a different era and the economic realities of today.

Throughout this book, we have examined the lessons learned from other nations—Canada, Germany, New Zealand, and Sweden—all of which have undertaken significant reforms to their public pension and retirement security systems. These countries show that reform is possible without undermining the well-being of retirees, and that proactive measures can prevent the kind of crisis the United States now faces with Social Security.

Each of these nations has employed different strategies: raising the retirement age, creating flexible savings accounts, or transitioning to flat-benefit models focused on poverty alleviation, among other ideas. These approaches can guide US policymakers toward reforms that balance fiscal sustainability with security for future retirees, while protecting younger generations from burdensome taxes or unsustainable debt and higher inflation.

Social Security—the primary component of the US retirement system—has been running cash-flow deficits since 2010. Its only sources of revenue, payroll taxes and the taxation of benefits, have been insufficient to cover the program's expenditures for the past 15 years, with the Treasury raising new debt to cover these funding shortfalls. Between 2010 and 2023, the US government borrowed US$1.08 trillion so the program could continue paying full benefits to retirees. This unsustainable borrowing strategy will allow Social Security to meet its obligations until 2033, contributing about US$4.1 trillion to federal deficits during this period. By 2033, the program's trust fund will be depleted—or, more precisely, the Treasury will no longer have authority under current law to borrow to pay Social Security benefits. At that point, scheduled benefits for all beneficiaries, regardless of income, assets, or age, could be cut by 21 percent.

The looming insolvency of Social Security is not a new story or an unforeseen problem. In fact, since 1984, the Social Security Board of Trustees has been warning that the program is unsustainable over a 75-year horizon. Despite these warnings, Congress last enacted major reforms in 1983. Moreover, Social Security is a flawed program not only because it is financially unsustainable, but also because it discourages personal savings and misallocates resources. By reducing individuals' incentives to work and save for their own retirement,

Social Security creates dependency on government support and unfairly redistributes wealth across generations. It is time for a fundamental reimagining of retirement security for Americans, with Social Security playing a much smaller, less burdensome part.

Not all reforms to cover Social Security's funding shortfalls are worth adopting. For example, the Congressional Budget Office (CBO) estimates that raising the payroll tax from 12.4 percent to 16.7 percent could cover the program's 75-year actuarial deficit. Yet this significant tax hike would hurt younger American workers, increasing the payroll taxes paid by a median earner by US$2,600 per year and pushing their annual payroll tax over US$10,000. Apart from the economic damages of such a steep hike in payroll taxes, saddling younger workers with additional tax burdens to pay the retirement benefits for significantly wealthier retirees is simply unfair.

Some have suggested eliminating the payroll tax cap to shore up the program's finances. But like increasing payroll taxes across the board, abolishing the limit on taxable earnings would be an economically damaging reform. Such an increase in the marginal tax rate on higher earners would stifle innovation and slow economic growth. Importantly, uncapping the payroll tax is not a sufficient solution to Social Security's financial challenges. This reform would cover only half of the program's long-term funding shortfall, while producing payroll tax surpluses during early years of the reform that Congress would spend elsewhere and saddling younger workers with deficits just a few years later. Focusing on achieving 75-year solvency instead of matching the annual balance is a flawed reform approach that risks repeating past mistakes. The Social Security Expansion Act, proposed by Sens. Bernie Sanders (I-VT) and Elizabeth Warren (D-MA), aims to build up the trust fund through massive tax increases, only to spend it down again. This strategy fails to address the underlying issue—excessive benefit increases that are out of balance with available revenues. Their plan, which includes four benefit expansions and significant tax hikes, would impose a $33.8 trillion burden on workers, savers, investors, and the owners of small businesses. Even with these tax hikes, the system would revert to cash-flow deficits by 2038, demonstrating that long-term solvency isn't a sustainable goal for a system that operates on a pay-as-you-go basis with no real savings or investments.[1]

To explore prudent Social Security reform options that address the program's financial problems without imposing additional tax burdens on American workers or adding to the federal debt, we hosted the inaugural Social Security Symposium in May 2024. US experts shared a range of perspectives on how best to reform the nation's largest federal government program, while international experts—from Canada, Germany, New Zealand, and Sweden—offered their views on retirement reform and shared their countries' experiences in tackling common retirement challenges.

The experiences of Canada, Germany, New Zealand, and Sweden highlight that these countries have been far more proactive than the United States in addressing the demographic and economic pressures that posed challenges to their primary retirement programs. Each of these nations has enacted its latest reforms aimed at strengthening its pension finances well after 1983—the last time Congress made major changes to Social Security. This underscores a key lesson for US policymakers: the need for more active and timely retirement reform efforts.

Restoring the long-term sustainability of a retirement system inevitably involves some unpopular measures, leading to politically difficult decisions. This has been one of the primary factors that have been hindering meaningful Social Security reform in the United States. However, unless American lawmakers follow the examples of their Canadian, German, New Zealander, and Swedish counterparts and actively engage in pension system reform, the consequences will be severe. Importantly, if Congress postpones the reform until the eleventh hour, the eventual measures will have to be significantly more drastic than if we adopt more gradual measures earlier.

The international experiences with retirement security reforms offer several valuable insights for the United States as it confronts Social Security's challenges. In addition, these countries' retirement systems include features that, if adopted in the United States, could further improve the American retirement system while expanding individual liberty and boosting economic growth.

One crucial reform is raising the eligibility age for Social Security benefits. This would effectively mitigate the negative impacts of the aging population, distributing the burden across both workers and retirees, rather than placing the entire strain on workers. Germany and Sweden have recently raised the eligibility thresholds for their public pension programs. Germany began the process of increasing its statutory retirement age in 2012, with the transition set to be complete by 2031. Sweden started raising its pension eligibility ages in 2020, and from 2026 these thresholds will be linked to life expectancy. The United States last raised its Social Security eligibility age in 1983, with the changes phasing in over nearly 40 years. Congress should increase the early and full retirement ages of Social Security again and link further changes to rising life expectancy.

One major structural shift Congress should consider for Social Security is transforming it from an earnings-related program to a poverty-targeted, flat-benefit scheme. Social Security could provide prorated flat benefits to all seniors, based on the number of years worked. Eligibility might require a minimum of 10 years of qualifying earnings, with full benefits granted after 35 earning years, but not based on the amount of annual earnings. The New Zealand Superannuation (NZS), the sole public component of the New Zealand retirement system, offers a flat, predictable benefit based on residency requirements. The NZS effectively reduces old-age poverty while remaining relatively cost-efficient. Beyond NZS, which serves as a solid foundation for retirement security, New Zealand workers are encouraged to participate in voluntary savings schemes to build additional retirement savings.

US lawmakers should also think about strengthening the third pillar of the retirement system, which comprises voluntary savings. Specifically, the United States should introduce USAs, flexible savings vehicles that are particularly attractive to younger and lower-earner workers. Unlike traditional retirement accounts, access to USA funds would not be restricted until retirement, addressing a major deterrent factor for these groups of workers. Canada's experience with Tax-Free Savings Accounts—which have gained widespread popularity, including among younger and lower-income workers—demonstrates the potential success of such nonrestrictive savings tools.

If Congress is not prepared to shift to an entirely new benefit structure that provides predictable, flat benefits instead of replacing preretirement income based on earnings, there are other changes it can adopt to meaningfully improve Social Security's financing. For example, Congress should reconsider the method of calculating and adjusting Social Security benefits. Currently, initial benefits for new retirees are calculated by indexing their lifetime earnings to wage growth, which inflates lifetime earnings beyond what's needed to preserve purchasing power. Congress should instead index initial benefits to prices, which would maintain retirees' standard of living while avoiding the unsustainable growth in benefits tied to a rise in working wages. This adjustment could close about 80 percent of Social Security's long-term actuarial deficit. Moreover, the Social Security Administration uses a flawed measure to adjust ongoing benefits for inflation over time. Adopting a more accurate measure, such as the Chained Consumer Price Index, to protect current benefits from inflation would provide a more precise reflection of cost-of-living increases, helping further stabilize Social Security's finances.

As previously mentioned, political inaction has delayed Social Security reform and exacerbated the program's finances. However, as shown by Canada, Germany, and Sweden, maintaining the balance between the revenues and expenditures of an earnings-related system does not necessarily require legislative action. These countries have all implemented mechanisms that automatically adjust the benefits or tax rates of their schemes when demographic or financial conditions threaten the sustainability of their pension systems. By adopting a similar mechanism, Social Security's costs could automatically be aligned with revenues, avoiding program insolvency and the threat of indiscriminate benefit cuts. Moreover, such a mechanism could encourage political intervention, as its activation would involve unpopular benefit changes that might incentivize a replacement plan among voter-responsive politicians.

In summary, Congress has many options that could significantly strengthen Social Security without resorting to harmful tax increases or adding to the already unsustainable federal debt. However, delaying reforms reduces the number of options and worsens the program's challenges. By taking decisive action now, lawmakers can secure the long-term future of the program while protecting vulnerable retirees and ensuring fairness across generations.

Congress should move beyond temporary solutions and confront the program's structural flaws head-on by

- Raising the retirement age to reflect longer life expectancies
- Shifting toward a flat-benefit structure focused on poverty reduction or reducing program costs by adjusting how initial benefits are calculated and adopting a more accurate inflation index for cost-of-living changes
- Expanding savings options through USAs
- Introducing automatic balancing mechanisms to prevent future insolvency and prolonged periods of political inaction

The goal of Social Security reform should be to restore sustainability to public finances and empower workers to take greater control over their retirement futures. A system that emphasizes individual responsibility, with targeted government support for those most in need, offers a way to ensure that Amanda—and millions like her—can retire with dignity without burdening future generations with unsustainable debt.

Reform is never easy, and political challenges undoubtably exist. But the clock is ticking, and the financial challenges facing Social Security will only get worse. By adopting forward-looking reforms, the United States can create a system that reflects today's realities while protecting tomorrow's workers and retirees. Amanda's story, like that of so many others, need not end in broken promises—if policymakers are willing to act decisively.

ACKNOWLEDGMENTS

We are grateful to the many individuals who contributed to the creation of this book. Special thanks to the international panelists of the Social Security Symposium: A Global Perspective conference, held in Washington, D.C. on May 9, 2024: Philip Cross (Canada, Fraser Institute), Michael Littlewood (New Zealand, University of Auckland), Kristoffer Lundberg (Sweden, Swedish Ministry of Health and Social Affairs), and Martin Werding (Germany, Ruhr University Bochum), who generously shared the histories, challenges, and reform experiences of their countries' retirement systems, providing valuable insights that inspired this project. Beyond their Symposium discussions, they continued to support our work throughout the writing process by contributing research and reviewing relevant chapters. We are also thankful our American Symposium panelists: Andrew G. Biggs (American Enterprise Institute), Sen. Bill Cassidy (R-LA), Chris Edwards (Cato Institute), Jason Fichtner (Bipartisan Policy Center), Rachel Greszler (Heritage Foundation), Andrew Moylan (Arnold Ventures), and Veronique de Rugy (Mercatus Center)—for sharing their perspectives on Social Security and broader US retirement system reform. Their discussions enriched the insights featured in the book. We thank the Institute for Humane Studies for facilitating a peer review of the introduction and helping us to identify possible blind spots and critiques. We are further grateful to the readers of the *Debt Dispatch*, our Substack, where we regularly write about Social Security and broader fiscal policy issues. Your engagement and thoughtful feedback helped shape our thinking and strengthen this work. On the Cato team, we thank Ivan Osorio, Eleanor O'Connor, and Onur Yoruk, who supported the design and edits for this book, as well as Imani Harris, Kiana Graham, Jonathan Fields, and David Tassy, who organized conference logistics. Finally, we appreciate the continued support of Cato Institute Partners, whose generosity made this book and our work possible.

APPENDIX

The European Union's material and social deprivation index

The material and social deprivation index is measured as part of the European Union (EU) statistics on income and living conditions survey, which is conducted by Eurostat, the statistical office of the EU.

According to Eurostat: "Material and social deprivation refers to the inability to afford a set of specific goods, services, or social activities that are considered by most people as essential for an adequate quality of life. The material and social deprivation rate is defined as the share of the population unable to afford five or more of these thirteen items. The severe material and social deprivation rate applies to those unable to afford seven or more."*

Eurostat classifies the 13 items into two categories, household-related and individual-related.

At the household level:

- Capacity to face unexpected expenses
- Capacity to afford paying for one-week annual holiday away from home
- Capacity to being confronted with payment arrears (on mortgage or rental payments, utility bills, hire purchase installments, or other loan payments)

---

* "Living Conditions in Europe—Material Deprivation and Economic Strain," Eurostat.

- Capacity to afford a meal with meat, chicken, fish, or vegetarian equivalent every second day
- Ability to keep home adequately
- Capacity to access to a car/van for personal use
- Capacity to replace worn-out furniture

At the individual level:

- Having internet connection
- Replacing worn-out clothes with new ones
- Having two pairs of properly fitting shoes (including a pair of all-weather shoes)
- Spending a small amount of money each week on him/herself
- Having regular leisure activities
- Getting together with friends/family for a drink/meal at least once a month

TABLE A.1
Comparison of retirement systems in the United States, Canada, Germany, New Zealand, and Sweden

Category/metric	United States	Canada	Germany	New Zealand	Sweden
Zero pillar	Supplemental Security Income	Old Age Security (OAS), Guaranteed Income Supplement (GIS)	Basic Income Support in Old Age and in Case of Reduced Earning Capacity	New Zealand Superannuation (NZS)	Guarantee Pension
First pillar	Social Security	Canada Pension Plan (CPP)/Quebec Pension Plan (QPP)	Statutory Pension Insurance (GRV)	None	Income Pension
Second pillar	None	None	None	None	Premium Pension; occupational pensions
Third pillar	401(k)s, IRAs, Roth 401(k)s, Roth IRAs	RPPs, RRSPs, TFSAs (not exclusively retirement tool)	Occupational plans, personal (Riester) pensions	KiwiSaver	Voluntary pension plans that offer tax incentives for the self-employed
Eligibility[a,b]	Social Security: 66–67 years old, 10–40 years residency, early at 62, late at 70	OAS/GIS: 65 years old, 10–40 years residency; CPP/QPP: 65 years old, early at 60, late at 70	GRV: 66–67 years old, early at 63	NZS: 65 years old 10–20 years residency	Guarantee Pension: 66–67 years old, Income/Premium Pension: earliest at 63–64

(continued)

TABLE A.1 (*continued*)

Category/metric	United States	Canada	Germany	New Zealand	Sweden
Old-age dependency ratio[a]	29.4	31.7	38	27.7	35.9
Zero-pillar benefit amount (percent of gross average wage)[a]	15.60%	OAS: 9.80%, GIS: 14.6%	19.50%	39.70%	23.70%
Maximum taxable earnings for the first and second pillars (percent of annual average wage)[a]	227%	79%	154%	N/A	108%
Demographic impact ratio[a,b,c,d]	1.47	1.66	3.50	1.36	2.48
Total spending on public pensions per person, 2023 (US$)[b,c,d]	$4,020	$3,240	$6,545	$2,540	$4,625
Total spending on public pensions, 2023 (percent of GDP)[b,c,d]	5%	5.20%	9.20%	4.90%	6.90%
Total spending on public pensions, OECD, 2019 (percent of GDP)[a,e]	7.10% (data from 2019)	5%	10.40%	4.90%	7%

Replacement rate (public pensions)[a]	39.10%	36.80%	43.90%	39.70%	49%
Private retirement assets (percent of GDP)[a]	138%	153%	7%	32%	N/A*
Replacement rate (public and private)[a]	73%	57%	55%	57%	62.3%[†]
Private replacement share[a,c]	0.47	0.35	0.20	0.28	N/A*
Homeownership rate (percent of seniors)[b]	76.1% (aged 65–74) and 81% (75+), data from 2022	70% (aged 65+) (data from 2019)	60% (aged 65–74) and 49% (75+), data from 2021	74.5% (aged 65+), data from 2018	73.6% (aged 60–69), 74.3% (70–79), 64.7% (80+) (data from 2023)
Median net worth of seniors (US$)[b]	$410,000 (aged 65–74) and $335,000 (75+), data from 2022	$444,245 (aged 65+), data from 2019	$330,000 (aged 65–74) and $185,000 (75+) (data from 2021)	$290,000 (aged 65+) (data from 2021)	No data
Poverty rate (EU/national measure, percent of seniors)[b]	9.7% (data from 2023)[‡]	6% (data from 2022)	8.8% (data from 2023)	4% (data from 2018)	1.9% (data from 2023)

Note: CPP = Canada Pension Plan; EU = European Union; GDP = gross domestic product; IRAs = individual retirement accounts; N/A = not applicable; OECD = Organisation for Economic Co-operation and Development; QPP = Quebec Pension Plan; RPPs = Registered Pension Plans; RRSPs = Registered Retirement Savings Plans; TFSAs = Tax-Free Savings Accounts.

a. Data from OECD's *Pensions at a Glance 2023* report.
b. Data from a national/EU/US government source.
c. Authors' calculations.
d. Includes only the primary pension programs (e.g. Social Security for the United States).
e. Broader definition of public pensions; for example, includes Supplemental Security Income for the United States.
* OECD data on private retirement assets in Sweden include mandatory occupational schemes, but for this field, we focus exclusively on voluntary schemes.
[†] Includes occupational schemes, which are mandatory in Sweden, unlike the private schemes in the other countries listed in the table.
[‡] The US senior poverty rate is likely much lower because the official poverty measure does not account for most of the income seniors derive from private retirement accounts.

NOTES

Chapter 1

1. Saloni Dattani et al., "Life Expectancy," Our World in Data, 2023.
2. Max Roser, "Fertility Rate," Our World in Data.
3. "Ageing," United Nations.
4. "Ageing," United Nations.
5. "Ageing and Health," World Health Organization, October 1, 2024.
6. OECD, *Pensions at a Glance 2023: OECD and G20 Indicators,* chap. 6 (Paris: OECD Publishing, December 13, 2023).
7. OECD, *Pensions at a Glance 2023*, chap. 6.
8. "1984 Annual Report of the Board of Trustees of the Federal Old-Age and Survivors Insurance and Disability Insurance Trust Funds," Social Security Administration, April 5, 1984.
9. "Summary of P.L. 98-21, (H.R. 1900) Social Security Amendments of 1983—Signed on April 20, 1983," Social Security Administration.
10. "2024 Annual Report of the Board of Trustees of the Federal Old-Age and Survivors Insurance and Federal Disability Insurance Trust Funds," Social Security Administration.
11. "2024 Annual Report of the Board of Trustees," Social Security Administration.
12. Author's calculations; and "Annual Report of the Board of Trustees of the Federal Old-Age and Survivors Insurance and Federal Disability Insurance Trust Funds," 2010 to 2023, Social Security Administration.
13. Author's calculations; and *An Update to the Budget and Economic Outlook: 2024 to 2034* (Washington, Congressional Budget Office, June 18, 2024).
14. OECD, Members and Partners.
15. OECD, *Pensions at a Glance 2023*.
16. Eurostat, Glossary: Equivalised income. "Equivalised income is a measure of household income that takes account of the differences in a household's size and composition, and thus is equivalised or made equivalent for all household sizes and compositions. It is used for the calculation of poverty and social exclusion indicators."
17. Sylvester J. Schieber and Andrew G. Biggs, "Biggs and Schieber: Retirees Aren't Headed for the Poor House," *Wall Street Journal*, January 23, 2014.

18. Adam Bee et al., "National Experimental Well-Being Statistics," US Census Bureau, Working Paper no. SEHSD WP2023-02, February 14, 2023.

19. European Commission, *2024 Ageing Report: Economic and Budgetary Projections for the EU Member States (2022–2070)* (Luxembourg: Publications Office of the European Union, April 2024).

20. "The History of Canada's Public Pensions," Canadian Museum of History; and William McBride, "Canada's Tax-Free Savings Accounts Are a Huge Success. US Lawmakers Should Take Note," Tax Foundation, February 8, 2024.

21. Martin Werding, "One Pillar Crumbling, the Others Too Short: Old-Age Provision in Germany," CESifo Working Paper no. 5760, Center for Economic Studies and ifo Institute (CESifo), 2016.

22. "KiwiSaver," Inland Revenue.

23. Werding, "One Pillar Crumbling, the Others Too Short."

24. European Commission, *2024 Ageing Report*.

25. European Commission, *2024 Ageing Report*.

26. OECD, *Pensions at a Glance 2023*.

27. Elizabeth Arias et al., "Mortality in the United States, 2022," National Center for Health Statistics, NCHS Data Brief no. 492; and Elizabeth Arias, Jiaquan Xu, and Kenneth Kochanek, "United States Life Tables, 2021," National Center for Health Statistics, *National Vital Statistics Reports* 72, no. 12, November 7, 2023.

28. Larry DeWitt, "The Development of Social Security in America," *Social Security Bulletin* 70, no. 3, 2010; and Arias et al., "Mortality in the United States, 2022."

29. Brady E. Hamilton, Joyce A. Martin, and Michelle J. K. Osterman, "Births: Provisional Data for 2023," Centers for Disease Control and Prevention, Vital Statistics Rapid Release report no. 35, April 2024.

30. "Historical Background and Development of Social Security," Social Security Administration.

31. "2024 Annual Report of the Board of Trustees," Social Security Administration.

32. *Options for Reducing the Deficit: 2025 to 2034* (Washington: Congressional Budget Office, December 12, 2024).

33. Author's calculations; "Poverty Thresholds," US Census Bureau; and "What Is the Maximum Social Security Retirement Benefit Payable?," Social Security Administration, January 2, 2025.

34. OECD, *Pensions at a Glance 2023*, table 4.2.

35. Bryan Perry, "The Material Wellbeing of New Zealand Households: Trends and Relativities Using Non-Income Measures, with International Comparisons," Ministry of Social Development, November 2021.

36. Perry, "The Material Wellbeing of New Zealand Households."

37. OECD, *Pensions at a Glance 2023*, table 8.2.

38. "New Zealand Superannuation Fund Contribution Rate Model—HYEFU 2023," New Zealand Treasury, December 20, 2023; and *Update to the Budget and Economic Outlook*, Congressional Budget Office.

39. OECD, *Pensions at a Glance 2023*, table 6.2.

40. Author's calculations; "Revenue, Expenditure and Budgetary Balance—General Governments (x 1,000,000)," Statistics Canada, May 31, 2024; and "Gross Domestic Product, Expenditure-Based, Canada, Quarterly (x 1,000,000)," Statistics Canada, May 31, 2024; "PPP Conversion Factor, GDP (LCU per International $)," World Bank.

41. Bee et al., "National Experimental Well-Being Statistics."

42. "Low Income Statistics by Age, Sex and Economic Family Type," Statistics Canada, April 26, 2024.

43. "Material and Social Deprivation Rate by Age and Sex," Eurostat; author's calculations; "Tidsserier, statens budget m.m. 2023," Swedish National Financial Management Authority (in Swedish); and for GDP numbers, refer to "National Accounts, Quarterly and Annual Estimates," Statistics Sweden.

44. *Options for Reducing the Deficit: 2025 to 2034*, Congressional Budget Office.

45. OECD, *Pensions at a Glance 2021: OECD and G20 Indicators* (Paris: OECD Publishing, December 13, 2021).

46. Werding, "One Pillar Crumbling, the Others Too Short."

47. "Rentenversicherungsbericht/Alterssicherungsbericht," Federal Ministry of Labour and Social Affairs, November 22, 2023 (in German).

48. European Commission, *2024 Ageing Report*.

49. European Commission, *2024 Ageing Report*.

50. "Employee Benefits in the United States," US Bureau of Labor Statistics; and Mark J. Warshawsky, "Better Measurement of Income of the Elderly and Its Broader Implications," *AEIdeas* (blog), November 25, 2024.

51. McBride, "Canada's Tax-Free Savings Accounts Are a Huge Success."

52. McBride, "Canada's Tax-Free Savings Accounts Are a Huge Success."

53. "History of Canada's Public Pensions," Canadian Museum of History.

54. "CBO's 2024 Long-Term Projections for Social Security," Congressional Budget Office, August 28, 2024.

55. Author's calculations; "CBO's 2024 Long-Term Projections for Social Security," Congressional Budget Office; and Gloria Guzman and Melissa Kollar, "Income in the United States: 2023," US Census Bureau, September 10, 2024.

56. "2022 Survey of Consumer Finances (SCF), Internal Data, Estimates in Nominal Dollars," Federal Reserve, November 21, 2023.

57. "Canada Pension Plan Enhancement," Government of Canada.

58. "Canada Pension Plan Enhancement," Government of Canada.

59. Philip Cross, "Opinion: Canada's Mythical Retirement Income Crisis," *Vancouver Sun*, June 12, 2016; and Charles Lammam, Hugh MacIntyre, and Milagros Palacios, "Expanding the Canada Pension Plan Will Not Help Canada's Most Financially Vulnerable Seniors," Fraser Research Bulletin, Fraser Institute, June 2016.

60. Rachel Greszler, "Social Security Expansion Act: $33.8 Trillion Tax Would Destroy Jobs, Slash Incomes, and Increase Workers' Dependence on the State," Heritage Foundation Backgrounder no. 3758, March 31, 2023.

61. OECD, *Pensions at a Glance 2023*, table 8.1.

62. OECD, *Pensions at a Glance 2023*, figure 7.1.

63. *The 2024 Pension Adequacy Report: Current and Future Income Adequacy in Old Age in the EU* (Luxembourg: Social Protection Committee [SPC] and the European Commission [DG EMPL], the European Union, 2024).
64. OECD, *Pensions at a Glance 2023*, figure 7.1.
65. Romina Boccia, "Social Security Benefits Are Growing Too Fast," *Cato at Liberty* (blog), Cato Institute, September 21, 2023.
66. *Summary of Provisions That Would Change the Social Security Program*, Social Security Administration, September 25, 2024.
67. Romina Boccia, "Social Security's COLA Increase Is Based on an Outdated Inflation Measure," *Cato at Liberty*, (blog), Cato Institute, October 13, 2022.
68. US Bureau of Labor Statistics, News Room—Frequently Asked Questions. "The CPI-W places a slightly higher weight on food, apparel, transportation, and other goods and services. It places a slightly lower weight on housing, medical care, and recreation."
69. *Options for Reducing the Deficit: 2025 to 2034*, Congressional Budget Office.
70. Romina Boccia, "New Social Security Reform Bill Moves in the Right Direction," Daily Signal, December 15, 2016.
71. *Options for Reducing the Deficit: 2025 to 2034*, Congressional Budget Office.
72. Romina Boccia, "Social Security's $4.1 Trillion Hidden Government Deficit," *Cato at Liberty* (blog), Cato Institute, July 2, 2024.

Chapter 4

1. "Historical Background and Development of Social Security," Social Security Administration.
2. Elizabeth Arias, Jiaquan Xu, and Kenneth Kochanek, "United States Life Tables, 2021," National Center for Health Statistics; and "Historical Background and Development of Social Security," Social Security Administration.
3. "Presidential Statement Signing the Social Security Act—August 14, 1935," Social Security Administration.
4. "What Is the Maximum Social Security Retirement Benefit Payable?," Social Security Administration.
5. "Historical Background and Development of Social Security," Social Security Administration.
6. "1938 Advisory Council Report—The Social Security Board's Comments & Recommendations," Social Security Administration.
7. John R. Kearney, "Social Security and the 'D' in OASDI: The History of a Federal Program Insuring Earners against Disability," *Social Security Bulletin* 66, no. 3, August 2006.
8. Authors' calculations; *An Update to the Budget and Economic Outlook: 2024 to 2034* (Washington: Congressional Budget Office, June 18, 2024); and for population numbers, see US Bureau of Economic Analysis, "Population [B230RC0A052NBEA]," Federal Reserve Bank of St. Louis, accessed July 25, 2024.
9. Romina Boccia, "The Social Security Trust Fund Myth," Cato Institute Policy Analysis No. 984, November 13, 2024.

10. Romina Boccia, "Social Security's $4.1 Trillion Hidden Government Deficit," *Cato at Liberty* (blog), Cato Institute, July 2, 2024.

11. "The 2024 Annual Report of the Board of Trustees of the Federal Old-Age and Survivors Insurance and Federal Disability Insurance Trust Funds, Social Security Administration.

12. Elizabeth Arias et al., "United States Life Tables, 2021"; and "Historical Background and Development of Social Security," Social Security Administration.

13. Brady E. Hamilton, Joyce A. Martin, and Michelle J. K. Osterman, "Births: Provisional Data for 2023."

14. "2022 Survey of Consumer Finances (SCF), Internal Data, Estimates in Nominal Dollars," Federal Reserve, November 21, 2023.

15. Romina Boccia, "Social Security Benefits Are Growing Too Fast," *Cato at Liberty* (blog), September 21, 2023; and "Summary of Provisions That Would Change the Social Security Program," Social Security Administration.

16. Romina Boccia, "Social Security's COLA Increase Is Based on an Outdated Inflation Measure," *Cato at Liberty*, (blog), Cato Institute, October 13, 2022; and US Bureau of Labor Statistics, News Room—Frequently Asked Questions. "The CPI-W places a slightly higher weight on food, apparel, transportation, and other goods and services. It places a slightly lower weight on housing, medical care, and recreation."

17. *Options for Reducing the Deficit: 2025 to 2034* (Washington: Congressional Budget Office, December 12, 2024).

18. *Options for Reducing the Deficit: 2025 to 2034*, Congressional Budget Office.

19. "Worker Participation in Employer-Sponsored Pensions: Data in Brief and Recent Trends," Congressional Research Service, September 18, 2024; "Individual Retirement Account (IRA) Ownership: Data and Policy Issues," Congressional Research Service, December 9, 2020; and Mark J. Warshawsky, "Better Measurement of Income of the Elderly and Its Broader Implications," *AEIdeas* (blog) November 25, 2024.

20. William McBride, "Canada's Tax-Free Savings Accounts Are a Huge Success. US Lawmakers Should Take Note," Tax Foundation, February 8, 2024.

21. Authors' calculations; "Supplemental Security Income," Congressional Research Service, April 10, 2024; for GDP numbers, refer to *An Update to the Budget and Economic Outlook: 2024 to 2034*, Congressional Budget Office; "Supplemental Security Income," Congressional Research Service; and "U.S. and World Population Clock," US Census Bureau.

22. "Poverty Thresholds," United States Census Bureau.

23. "Primary Insurance Amount," Social Security Administration.

24. "Maximum Taxable Earnings," Social Security Administration.

25. "Starting Your Retirement Benefits Early," Social Security Administration.

26. *Update to the Budget and Economic Outlook*, Congressional Budget Office.

27. "Annual Report of the Board of Trustees of the Federal Old-Age and Survivors Insurance and Federal Disability Insurance Trust Funds," 2010 to 2023, Social Security Administration.

28. "2024 Annual Report of the Board of Trustees," Social Security Administration.

29. Authors' calculations; *Update to the Budget and Economic Outlook*, Congressional Budget Office; and "2024 Annual Report of the Board of Trustees," Social Security Administration.

30. OECD, *Pensions at a Glance 2023: OECD and G20 Indicators* (Paris: OECD Publishing, December 13, 2023, table 6.2).

31. Authors' calculations; "Poverty Thresholds," US Census Bureau; and "What Is the Maximum Social Security Retirement Benefit Payable?," Social Security Administration.

32. OECD, *Pensions at a Glance 2023*, table 9.2.

33. "Retirement Topics—401(k) and Profit-Sharing Plan Contribution Limits," Internal Revenue Service; "Traditional and Roth IRAs," Internal Revenue Service; and "401(k) Resource Guide—Plan Participants—General Distribution Rules," Internal Revenue Service.

34. "Worker Participation in Employer-Sponsored Pensions," Congressional Research Service; and "Individual Retirement Account (IRA) Ownership," Congressional Research Service.

35. OECD, *Pensions at a Glance 2023*, table 4.2.

36. "2022 Survey of Consumer Finances," Federal Reserve.

37. "Employee Benefits in the United States," US Bureau of Labor Statistics.

38. "Supplemental Security Income," Congressional Research Service.

39. Authors' calculations; "Supplemental Security Income," Congressional Research Service; for average wage numbers, refer to "Table B-3a. Average Hourly and Weekly Earnings of All Employees on Private Nonfarm Payrolls by Industry Sector, Seasonally Adjusted," US Bureau of Labor Statistics; and "Poverty Thresholds," US Census Bureau.

40. Authors' calculations; "Supplemental Security Income," Congressional Research Service; and for GDP numbers, refer to *An Update to the Budget and Economic Outlook*, Congressional Budget Office.

41. Authors' calculations; "Supplemental Security Income," Congressional Research Service; and "U.S. and World Population Clock," US Census Bureau.

42. "Maximum Taxable Earnings," Social Security Administration.

43. OECD, *Pensions at a Glance 2023*, table 3.4.

44. "Social Security Credits," Social Security Administration.

45. "Starting Your Retirement Benefits Early," Social Security Administration.

46. "Historical Background and Development of Social Security," Social Security Administration.

47. Elizabeth Arias et al., "United States Life Tables, 2021."

48. Elizabeth Arias, Jiaquan Xu, and Kenneth Kochanek, "Mortality in the United States, 2022," National Center for Health Statistics, NCHS Data Brief no. 492.

49. Hamilton et al., "Births: Provisional Data for 2023."

50. OECD, *Pensions at a Glance 2023*, table 6.2.

51. "Supreme Court Case: Flemming vs. Nestor," Social Security Administration.

52. "2022 Survey of Consumer Finances," Federal Reserve.

53. *Options for Reducing the Deficit: 2025 to 2034*, Congressional Budget Office.
54. "Primary Insurance Amount," Social Security Administration.
55. OECD, *Pensions at a Glance 2023*, table 4.2.
56. "Summary of Provisions," Social Security Administration.
57. Romina Boccia, "Social Security's COLA Increase Is Based on an Outdated Inflation Measure," *Cato at Liberty*, (blog), Cato Institute, October 13, 2022; and US Bureau of Labor Statistics, News Room—Frequently Asked Questions. "The CPI-W places a slightly higher weight on food, apparel, transportation, and other goods and services. It places a slightly lower weight on housing, medical care, and recreation."
58. *Options for Reducing the Deficit: 2025 to 2034*, Congressional Budget Office.
59. "What Is the Maximum Social Security Retirement Benefit Payable?," Social Security Administration.
60. "Poverty Thresholds," US Census Bureau.
61. Authors' calculations; *Update to the Budget and Economic Outlook*," Congressional Budget Office; and for population numbers, see US Bureau of Economic Analysis, "Population [B230RC0A052NBEA]," Federal Reserve Bank of St. Louis.
62. Authors' calculations; "2024 Annual Report of the Board of Trustees," Social Security Administration; and *Update to the Budget and Economic Outlook*, Congressional Budget Office.
63. "Income Taxes and Your Social Security Benefit," Social Security Administration. Individuals with incomes between $25,000 and $34,000 are subject to income tax on up to 50 percent of their Social Security benefits. For those with incomes exceeding $34,000, up to 85 percent of their benefits are taxable.
64. Boccia, "Social Security Trust Fund Myth."
65. "2024 Annual Report of the Board of Trustees," Social Security Administration.
66. Boccia, "Social Security's $4.1 Trillion Hidden Government Deficit."
67. "2024 Annual Report of the Board of Trustees," Social Security Administration.
68. Romina Boccia, "Medicare and Social Security Are Responsible for 100 Percent of US Unfunded Obligations," *Cato at Liberty* (blog), Cato Institute, March 20, 2024.
69. Authors' calculations; *CBO's 2024 Long-Term Projections for Social Security* (Washington: Congressional Budget Office, August 28, 2024); and Gloria Guzman and Melissa Kollar, *Income in the United States: 2023* (Washington: US Census Bureau, September 10, 2024).
70. Brian Riedl, "Don't Bust the Cap: Problems with Eliminating the Social Security Tax Cap," Manhattan Institute, April 11, 2024.
71. Ufuk Akcigit et al., "Taxation and Innovation in the 20th Century," National Bureau of Economic Research Working Paper no. 24982, September 2018.
72. *Options for Reducing the Deficit: 2025 to 2034*, Congressional Budget Office.
73. Romina Boccia, "New Social Security Reform Bill Moves in the Right Direction," Daily Signal, December 15, 2016; and "Summary of Provisions," Social Security Administration.

74. *Options for Reducing the Deficit: 2025 to 2034*, Congressional Budget Office.

75. Emily A. Shrider, "Poverty in the United States: 2023," US Census Bureau, September 10, 2024.

76. Sylvester J. Schieber and Andrew G. Biggs, "Biggs and Schieber: Retirees Aren't Headed for the Poor House," *Wall Street Journal*, January 23, 2014; and Andrew G. Biggs, "America's 'Retirement Crisis': The Emperor Has No Clothes," AEI Economic Perspectives, American Enterprise Institute, July 31, 2024

77. Adam Bee et al., "National Experimental Well-Being Statistics," US Census Bureau, Working Paper no. SEHSD-WP2025-01, January 29, 2025.

78. Bee et al., "National Experimental Well-Being Statistics."

79. "Never Beneficiaries, Aged 60 or Older, 2024," Social Security Administration, May 2024.

80. "PWBM Budget Contest: A Flat Benefit for Social Security," Penn Wharton Budget Model, January 26, 2021.

81. OECD, *Pensions at a Glance 2023*, table 9.2.

82. OECD, *Pensions at a Glance 2023*, table 9.2.

83. OECD, *Pensions at a Glance 2023*, table 4.2.

84. Authors' calculations; and OECD, *Pensions at a Glance 2023*, table 4.2.

85. "401(k) Plan Overview," Internal Revenue Service.

86. "Retirement Topics—401(k) and Profit-Sharing Plan Contribution Limits," Internal Revenue Service.

87. "401(k) Plan Overview," Internal Revenue Service.

88. "401(k) Resource Guide," Internal Revenue Service.

89. "Retirement Plan and IRA Required Minimum Distributions FAQs," Internal Revenue Service.

90. "Retirement Topics—Designated Roth Account," Internal Revenue Service.

91. "Traditional and Roth IRAs," Internal Revenue Service.

92. "Individual Retirement Account (IRA) Ownership," Congressional Research Service.

93. "Worker Participation in Employer-Sponsored Pensions," Congressional Research Service; and "Individual Retirement Account (IRA) Ownership," Congressional Research Service.

94. Authors' calculations; and OECD, *Pensions at a Glance 2023*, table 9.1.

95. McBride, "Canada's Tax-Free Savings Accounts."

96. Ryan Bourne and Chris Edwards, "Tax Reform and Savings: Lessons from Canada and the United Kingdom," Cato Institute, May 1, 2017; and Adam N. Michel, "Slashing Tax Rates and Cutting Loopholes," Cato Institute Policy Analysis no. 975, June 17, 2024.

97. "2022 Survey of Consumer Finances," Federal Reserve.

98. Kerry Farrell and Joana Allamani, "1974–2024: Celebrating 50 Years of Protected Retirement Plans," US Bureau of Labor Statistics, March 2024.

Chapter 7

1. OECD, *Pensions at a Glance 2023: OECD and G20 Indicators*, table 7.2 (Paris: OECD Publishing, December 13, 2023).

2. While both methods similarly compare incomes to national poverty thresholds, there are key differences in how these thresholds are constructed. The US thresholds are based on the cost of meeting basic necessities like food and other basic expenses, whereas Canada's Market Basket Measure considers the cost of a broader range of goods and services required for a modest standard of living.

3. For Canada, see "Table 11-10-0135-01: Low Income Statistics by Age, Sex and Economic Family Type," Statistics Canada, April 26, 2024; and for the United States, see Emily A. Shrider and John Creamer, *Poverty in the United States: 2022* (Washington: US Census Bureau, September 2023).

4. Sylvester J. Schieber and Andrew G. Biggs, "Biggs and Schieber: Retirees Aren't Headed for the Poor House," *Wall Street Journal*, January 23, 2014; and Andrew G. Biggs, "America's 'Retirement Crisis': The Emperor Has No Clothes," AEI Economic Perspectives, American Enterprise Institute, July 31, 2024

5. Adam Bee et al., "National Experimental Well-Being Statistics," US Census Bureau, Working Paper no. SEHSD-WP2025-01, January 29, 2025; and "Table 11-10-0135-01: Low Income Statistics," Statistics Canada.

6. Office of the Chief Actuary, *Actuarial Report (31st) on the Canada Pension Plan as at 31 December 2021*, (Ottawa, Ontario: Office of the Superintendent of Financial Institutions, December 14, 2022).

7. "The 2024 Annual Report of the Board of Trustees of the Federal Old-Age and Survivors Insurance and Federal Disability Insurance Trust Funds," Social Security Administration, May 6, 2024.

8. "Canada Pension Plan Enhancement," Government of Canada.

9. OECD, *Pensions at a Glance 2023*, table 8.2.

10. Authors' calculations; "Revenue, Expenditure and Budgetary Balance—General Governments (x 1,000,000)," Statistics Canada, May 31, 2024; "Gross Domestic Product, Expenditure-Based, Canada, Quarterly (x 1,000,000)," Statistics Canada, May 31, 2024; and *An Update to the Budget and Economic Outlook: 2024 to 2034* (Washington: Congressional Budget Office, June 18, 2024).

11. Adam Michel, "New Universal Savings Account Bill from Rep. Harshbarger," *Cato at Liberty* (blog), Cato Institute, July 15, 2024.

12. OECD, *Pensions at a Glance 2023*, table 9.2.

13. OECD, *Pensions at a Glance 2023*, table 4.2.

14. OECD, *Pensions at a Glance 2023*, figure 7.1. Note that the US data are for 2021 while the Canadian data are from 2020.

15. OECD, *Pensions at a Glance 2023*, table 3.2.

16. "Old Age Security Pension Recovery Tax," Canada Revenue Agency.

17. "Canada Pension Plan Enhancement.," Government of Canada.

18. "The History of Canada's Public Pensions," Canadian Museum of History.

19. "Canada Pension Plan: Fifteenth Actuarial Report as at 31 December 1993," Office of the Superintendent of Financial Institutions, 1995.

20. Sean Speer, *Getting out of a Fiscal Hole: Canada's Experience with Fiscal Reform* (Ottawa, Ontario: Macdonald-Laurier Institute, November 2017); and *Update to the Budget and Economic Outlook*, Congressional Budget Office.

21. Speer, *Getting out of a Fiscal Hole*.

22. OECD, *Pensions at a Glance 2023*, table 9.2.

23. William McBride, "Canada's Tax-Free Savings Accounts Are a Huge Success. US Lawmakers Should Take Note," Tax Foundation, February 8, 2024.

24. Ryan Bourne and Chris Edwards, "Tax Reform and Savings: Lessons from Canada and the United Kingdom," Cato Institute Tax and Budget Bulletin no. 77, May 1, 2017.

25. "Table 11-10-0016-01: Assets and Debts Held by Economic Family Type, by Age Group, Canada, Provinces and Selected Census Metropolitan Areas, Survey of Financial Security," Statistics Canada, December 22, 2020.

26. "Table 11-10-0053-01: Sources of Income of Senior Census Families by Family Type and Age of Older Partner, Parent or Individual," Statistics Canada, July 12, 2023.

27. OECD, *Pensions at a Glance: Country Profiles—Canada* (Paris: OECD Publishing, December 13, 2023).

28. "Old Age Security (OAS) Pension Amounts—April to June 2024," Government of Canada; unless otherwise specified, the following source is used throughout the book for PPP conversion: "Implied PPP Conversion Rate," International Monetary Fund (IMF), accessed June 2024.

29. OECD, *Pensions at a Glance 2023: OECD and G20 Indicators*, table 3.2.

30. "Old Age Security (OAS) Pension Amounts," Government of Canada.

31. "Old Age Security Pension Recovery Tax," Canada Revenue Agency, accessed June 2024.

32. OECD, *Pensions at a Glance 2023,* table 3.2.

33. "Guaranteed Income Supplement Amounts—April to June 2024," Government of Canada.

34. "Guaranteed Income Supplement Amounts," Government of Canada.

35. OECD, *Pensions at a Glance 2023,* table 3.2.

36. OECD, *Pensions at a Glance 2023,* tables 3.1 and 3.2.

37. Author's calculations; "Revenue, Expenditure and Budgetary Balance—General Governments (x 1,000,000)" Statistics Canada, May 31, 2024; "Gross Domestic Product, Expenditure-Based, Canada, Quarterly (x 1,000,000)," Statistics Canada, May 31, 2024; and "PPP Conversion Factor, GDP (LCU per international $)," World Bank.

38. OECD, *Pensions at a Glance 2023*, table 7.2. While the US data are from 2021 and the Canadian data are from 2020, such a notable difference is unlikely due to the timing of the data collection.

39. "Market Basket Measure (MBM)," Statistics Canada.

40. "Table 11-10-0135-01: Low Income Statistics," Statistics Canada.

41. Shrider and Creamer, *Poverty in the United States: 2022*; and "How the Census Bureau Measures Poverty," US Census Bureau.

42. Schieber and Biggs, "Retirees Aren't Headed for the Poor House;" and Biggs, "America's 'Retirement Crisis': The Emperor Has No Clothes."

43. Bee et al., "National Experimental Well-Being Statistics."

44. Bee et al., "National Experimental Well-Being Statistics"; and "Table 11-10-0135-01: Low Income Statistics," Statistics Canada.

45. "CPP Contribution Rates, Maximums and Exemptions," Government of Canada.

46. "Canada Pension Plan Enhancement," Government of Canada.

47. OECD, *Pensions at a Glance 2023*, table 8.1.
48. OECD, *Pensions at a Glance 2023*, table 8.1; and "Maximum Taxable Earnings," Social Security Administration.
49. "Canada Pension Plan Enhancement," Government of Canada.
50. "Primary Insurance Amount," Social Security Administration.
51. "What Is the Maximum Social Security Retirement Benefit Payable?" Social Security Administration; and "Canada Pension Plan: Pensions and Benefits Monthly Amounts," Government of Canada.
52. André Léonard, "Indexing of Canada Pension Plan and Old Age Security Benefits," Library of Parliament, August 2, 2011.
53. OECD, *Pensions at a Glance 2023*, table 6.2.
54. OECD, *Pensions at a Glance 2021: OECD and G20 Indicators* (Paris: OECD Publishing, 2021).
55. Social Security Administration, "1983 Annual Report—Federal Old-Age and Survivors Insurance and Disability Insurance Trust Fund," Social Security Administration, June 27, 1983; and "1984 Annual Report of the Board of Trustees of the Federal Old-Age and Survivors Insurance and Disability Insurance Trust Funds," Social Security Administration, April 5, 1984.
56. Romina Boccia, "US Workers Earning $60,070 Face $3,063 in Higher Taxes to Keep Social Security Solvent," Cato Institute, July 18, 2024.
57. Authors' calculations; "Revenue, Expenditure and Budgetary Balance—General Governments" Statistics Canada; "Gross Domestic Product, Expenditure-Based," Statistics Canada; and "PPP Conversion Factor, GDP," World Bank.
58. Authors' calculations; and for population data, "Population Estimates, Quarterly," Statistics Canada, June 19, 2024; "PPP Conversion Factor, GDP," World Bank.
59. Authors' calculations; *Update to the Budget and Economic Outlook*, Congressional Budget Office; and for population numbers, see US Bureau of Economic Analysis, "Population [B230RC0A052NBEA]," Federal Reserve Bank of St. Louis, accessed July 25, 2024.
60. OECD, *Pensions at a Glance 2023*, table 8.2.
61. Authors' calculations.
62. OECD, *Pensions at a Glance 2023*, table 4.1.
63. "Canada Pension Plan: Fifteenth Actuarial Report," Office of the Superintendent of Financial Institutions.
64. "History of Canada's Public Pensions," Canadian Museum of History.
65. Office of the Chief Actuary, *Actuarial Report (31st) on the Canada Pension Plan*. The total program income comprises taxes paid by workers and investment income.
66. Authors' calculations; Speer, *Getting out of a Fiscal Hole*.
67. Speer, *Getting out of a Fiscal Hole*, p. 10.
68. Speer, *Getting out of a Fiscal Hole*, p. 2.69.
69. François Vaillancourt et al., *Compulsory Government Pensions vs. Private Savings: The Effect of Previous Expansion to the Canada Pension Plan*, Fraser Institute, July 2015.
70. "CPP Contribution Rates, Maximums and Exemptions," Government of Canada.

71. "Canada Pension Plan Enhancement," Government of Canada.
72. "Canada Pension Plan Enhancement," Government of Canada.
73. Philip Cross, "Opinion: Canada's Mythical Retirement Income Crisis," *Vancouver Sun*, June 12, 2016.
74. Charles Lammam, Hugh MacIntyre, and Milagros Palacios, "Expanding the Canada Pension Plan Will Not Help Canada's Most Financially Vulnerable Seniors," Fraser Research Bulletin, Fraser Institute, June 2016.
75. Rachel Greszler, "Social Security Expansion Act: $33.8 Trillion Tax Would Destroy Jobs, Slash Incomes, and Increase Workers' Dependence on the State," Heritage Foundation Backgrounder no. 3758, March 31, 2023.
76. OECD, *Pensions at a Glance 2023*, table 4.2.
77. OECD, *Pensions at a Glance 2023*, table 9.2.
78. OECD, *Pensions at a Glance 2023*, table 9.1.
79. "Worker Participation in Employer-Sponsored Pensions: Data in Brief and Recent Trends," Congressional Research Service, September 18, 2024; and "Individual Retirement Account (IRA) Ownership: Data and Policy Issues," Congressional Research Service, December 9, 2020.
80. "Recent Trends in Families' Contributions to Three Registered Savings Accounts," Statistics Canada, October 17, 2023.
81. McBride, "Canada's Tax-Free Savings Accounts Are a Huge Success."
82. Adam N. Michel, "Slashing Tax Rates and Cutting Loopholes: Options for Tax Reform in the 119th Congress," Cato Institute Policy Analysis no. 975, June 17, 2024.
83. OECD, *Pensions at a Glance 2023*, figure 7.1.
84. "Table 11-10-0016-01: Assets and Debts Held," Statistics Canada.
85. Authors' calculations; and "Table 11-10-0016-01: Assets and Debts Held," Statistics Canada.
86. Authors' calculations; and "Table 11-10-0053-01: Sources of Income," Statistics Canada.
87. "2022 Survey of Consumer Finances (SCF), Internal Data, Estimates in Nominal Dollars," table 9, Federal Reserve, November 21, 2023.
88. "2022 Survey of Consumer Finances," table 6, Federal Reserve.
89. "2022 Survey of Consumer Finances," table 4, Federal Reserve.

Chapter 8

1. OECD, *Pensions at a Glance 2023: OECD and G20 Indicators*, table 4.2 (Paris: OECD Publishing, December 13, 2023).
2. Bryan Perry, "The Material Wellbeing of New Zealand Households: Trends and Relativities Using Non-Income Measures, with International Comparisons," Ministry of Social Development, November 2021.
3. OECD, *Pensions at a Glance 2023*, table 8.2. Note that the 2020 New Zealand figure is compared with the 2019 OECD average. Based on the limited data, New Zealand's pension expenditure remained below the OECD average in 2020.
4. "New Zealand Superannuation Fund Contribution Rate Model—HYEFU 2023," New Zealand Treasury, December 20, 2023; and "The 2024 Annual Report of the Board of Trustees of the Federal Old-Age and Survivors Insurance and Fed-

eral Disability Insurance Trust Funds," Social Security Administration, May 6, 2024.

5. Authors' calculations; Ben Trollip, *KiwiSaver Demographic Study* (Auckland: Melville Jessup Weaver, March 2022); and for GDP numbers, see "Budget Economic and Fiscal Update 2024," New Zealand Treasury, May 30, 2024.

6. OECD, *Pensions at a Glance 2023*, table 9.2.

7. OECD, *Pensions at a Glance 2023*, table 4.2.

8. OECD, *Pensions at a Glance 2023*, table 3.2.

9. OECD, *Pensions at a Glance 2023*, table 4.2.

10. Perry, "The Material Wellbeing of New Zealand Households."

11. "New Zealand Superannuation Fund," New Zealand Treasury; and *An Update to the Budget and Economic Outlook: 2024 to 2034* (Washington: Congressional Budget Office, June 18, 2024).

12. OECD, *Pensions at a Glance 2023*, table 8.2.

13. "Datasets for KiwiSaver Statistics," Inland Revenue, accessed July 9, 2024; and for population numbers, see "Budget Economic and Fiscal Update 2024," New Zealand Treasury.

14. Authors' calculations; "Census Update #3—Tenure of Households for People in Occupied Private Dwellings," Ministry of Housing and Urban Development, December 23, 2020; "Household Net Worth Statistics: Year Ended June 2021," Stats NZ Tatauranga Aotearoa, March 3, 2022; and "Population Estimates," Stats NZ Tatauranga Aotearoa, accessed July 10, 2024.

15. OECD, *Pensions at a Glance 2023*, table 3.1.

16. "New Zealand Superannuation and the Veteran's Pension," New Zealand Government, accessed July 3, 2024.

17. "An Introduction to New Zealand Superannuation," Te Ara Ahunga Ora Retirement Commission, 2021.

18. Author's calculations; "Implied PPP conversion rate," International Monetary Fund; and "How Much You Can Get for NZ Super," Work and Income, New Zealand Government, accessed July 3, 2024.

19. Author's calculations; "What Is the Maximum Social Security Retirement Benefit Payable?," Social Security Administration, accessed June, 2024.

20. OECD, *Pensions at a Glance 2023*, table 3.2.

21. OECD, *Pensions at a Glance 2023*, table 3.2.

22. "Introduction to New Zealand Superannuation," Te Ara Ahunga Ora Retirement Commission.

23. OECD, *Pensions at a Glance 2023*, table 3.2.

24. "Income After You Turn 65," New Zealand Government, accessed August 9, 2024.

25. OECD, *Pensions at a Glance 2023*, table 6.2.

26. "New Zealand Superannuation Fund," New Zealand Treasury; and for population numbers, see "Budget Economic and Fiscal Update 2024," New Zealand Treasury.

27. Author's calculations; "*Update to the Budget and Economic Outlook*," Congressional Budget Office; and for population numbers, see US Bureau of Economic Analysis, "Population," Federal Reserve Bank of St. Louis, accessed July 25, 2024.

28. OECD, *Pensions at a Glance 2023*, table 8.2.

29. OECD, *Pensions at a Glance 2023*, table 4.1.
30. Paul Bellamy, "Household Incomes, Inequality and Poverty," New Zealand Parliament, December 20, 2011.
31. OECD, *Pensions at a Glance 2023*, table 7.2.
32. OECD, "Annual GDP and Consumption per Capita, US $, Current Prices, Current PPPs," OECD Data Explorer, accessed July 9, 2024.
33. Perry, "The Material Wellbeing of New Zealand Households."
34. "Living Conditions in Europe—Material Deprivation and Economic Strain," Eurostat.
35. Perry, "The Material Wellbeing of New Zealand Households."
36. The United Kingdom was still an EU member at the time.
37. Perry, "The Material Wellbeing of New Zealand Households."
38. The seven items shared between DEP-17 and the EU-SILC index relate to essential aspects of material well-being, including the ability to afford a meal with meat every second day, own properly fitting shoes, and being able to cover unexpected expenses, avoid arrears on regular payments (e.g., housing or utilities), maintain a warm home, replace worn-out appliances, and replace worn-out clothing with new items. While the specific wording differs, these general concepts are included in both indexes.
39. OECD, *Pensions at a Glance 2023*, table 8.2.
40. Jessica Semega et al., *Income and Poverty in the United States: 2018*, US Census Bureau Report P60-266 (Washington: Government Printing Office, September 10, 2019).
41. Sylvester J. Schieber and Andrew G. Biggs, "Biggs and Schieber: Retirees Aren't Headed for the Poor House," *Wall Street Journal*, January 23, 2014; and Andrew G. Biggs, "America's 'Retirement Crisis': The Emperor Has No Clothes," AEI Economic Perspectives, American Enterprise Institute, July 31, 2024.
42. Adam Bee et al., "National Experimental Well-Being Statistics," US Census Bureau, Working Paper no. SEHSD-WP2025-01, January 29, 2025.
43. *Options for Reducing the Deficit: 2025 to 2034* (Washington: Congressional Budget Office, December 12, 2024).
44. For information on KiwiSaver details mentioned in this chapter, please refer to this dedicated page on the Inland Revenue website: https://www.ird.govt.nz/kiwisaver.
45. OECD, *Pensions at a Glance 2023*, figure 9.2.
46. Susan St. John, Michael Littlewood, and M. Claire Dale, "Now We Are Six: Lessons from New Zealand's KiwiSaver," University of Auckland Business School Retirement Policy and Research Centre, Working Paper no. 2014-1, February 2014.
47. "New Zealand Resident Individuals' Portfolio Investment Entity Income," Inland Revenue, accessed July 9, 2024.
48. "Tax Rates for Individuals," Inland Revenue, accessed July 9, 2024.
49. "Datasets for KiwiSaver Statistics," Inland Revenue, accessed July 9, 2024; and "Budget Economic and Fiscal Update 2024," New Zealand Treasury.
50. OECD, *Pensions at a Glance 2023*, chap. 9.
51. Author's calculations; Trollip, *KiwiSaver Demographic Study*; and for GDP numbers, see "Budget Economic and 2024," New Zealand Treasury.

52. OECD, *Pensions at a Glance 2023*, table 9.2; and for GDP numbers, see "Budget Economic and Fiscal Update 2024," New Zealand Treasury.

53. OECD, *Pensions at a Glance 2023*, table 4.2.

54. "Census Update #3," Ministry of Housing and Urban Development.

55. Author's calculations; "Household Net Worth Statistics," Stats NZ Tatauranga Aotearoa; and "Population Estimates," Stats NZ Tatauranga Aotearoa.

56. Author's calculations; "Household Net Worth Statistics," Stats NZ Tatauranga Aotearoa; and "Purchasing Power Parities (PPP)," OECD, accessed July 10, 2024.

57. "2022 Survey of Consumer Finances (SCF), Internal Data, Estimates in Nominal Dollars," table 9, Federal Reserve, November 21, 2023.

58. "2022 Survey of Consumer Finances (SCF)," table 4 and table 6, Federal Reserve.

59. Susan St. John, "New Zealand's Experiment in Tax Neutrality for Retirement Saving," Geneva Papers on Risk and Insurance: Issues and Practice, October 5, 2007.

60. OECD, *Financial Incentives for Funded Pension Plans* (Paris: OECD Publishing, 2021); and *How Is Super Taxed?* (Parliamentary Budget Office, April 27, 2023).

61. *Consultative Document on Superannuation and Life Insurance: Volume 1*, (Wellington: Inland Revenue, March 1988).

62. David Preston, *Retirement Income in New Zealand: the Historical Context* (Te Ara Ahunga Ora Retirement Commission, December 2008).

63. David Fergusson et al., *Living Standards of Older New Zealanders: A Technical Account* (Wellington: Ministry of Social Development, January 1, 2001); and *Private Provision for Retirement: The Way Forward—Final Report of the Task Force on Private Provision for Retirement* (Wellington: The Task Force, December 1992).

64. Preston, *Retirement Income in New Zealand*.

65. "Purpose and Mandate," NZ Super Fund.

66. "Reference Portfolio," NZ Super Fund.

67. OECD, *Pensions at a Glance 2023*, table 9.3.

68. "New Zealand Superannuation Fund: Contribution Rate Model—HYEFU 2023," New Zealand Treasury.

69. Author's calculations; *Annual Report 2023* (Auckland: Guardians of New Zealand Superannuation, 2023); and for GDP numbers, see "Budget Economic and Fiscal Update 2024," New Zealand Treasury.

70. Andrew G. Biggs, "Bill Cassidy's Well-Intentioned but Misguided Social-Security Reform," American Enterprise Institute, May 22, 2023.

Chapter 10

1. "Änderung bei den Hinzuverdienstgrenzen seit 1. Januar 2023," Deutsche Rentenversicherung (in German).

2. "Exempt Amounts under the Earnings Test," Social Security Administration.

3. OECD, *Pensions at a Glance 2023: OECD and G20 Indicators*, table 6.2 (Paris: OECD Publishing, December 13, 2023).

4. OECD, *Pensions at a Glance 2023*, table 8.2.

5. Martin Werding, "One Pillar Crumbling, the Others Too Short: Old-Age Provision in Germany," CESifo Working Paper no. 5760, Center for Economic Studies and ifo Institute (CESifo), 2016.

6. "Rentenversicherungsbericht/Alterssicherungsbericht," Federal Ministry of Labour and Social Affairs, November 22, 2023 (in German).

7. Werding, "One Pillar Crumbling, the Others Too Short."

8. "Rentenversicherungsbericht/Alterssicherungsbericht," Federal Ministry of Labour and Social Affairs.

9. OECD, *Pensions at a Glance 2023*, figure 7.1.

10. "Historical Background and Development of Social Security," "The Social Insurance Movement" section, Social Security Administration.

11. "Summary of P.L. 98-21, (H.R. 1900) Social Security Amendments of 1983—Signed on April 20, 1983," Social Security Administration; "1983 Annual Report—Federal Old-Age and Survivors Insurance and Disability Insurance Trust Fund," Social Security Administration, June 27, 1983; and "1984 Annual Report of the Board of Trustees of the Federal Old-Age and Survivors Insurance and Disability Insurance Trust Funds," Social Security Administration, April 5, 1984.

12. *Social Security at a Glance 2020* (Bonn: Federal Ministry of Labour and Social Affairs, January 2020), pp. 164–67.

13. Author's calculations; OECD, *Pensions at a Glance 2023*, table 3.2; "Sozialhilfeausgaben SGB XII im Jahr 2023 um 18 % gestiegen," Federal Statistical Office (in German); for PPP figures, see "PPP Conversion Factor, GDP (LCU per International $)," World Bank, accessed August 7, 2024; and for German GDP data, see "Monthly Report—July 2024," Deutsche Bundesbank, July 2024.

14. *Social Security at a Glance 2020*, Federal Ministry of Labour and Social Affairs.

15. "Rentenversicherungsbericht/Alterssicherungsbericht," Federal Ministry of Labour and Social Affairs.

16. OECD, *Pensions at a Glance 2023*, table 8.1.

17. "Monthly Report—July 2024," Deutsche Bundesbank.

18. Werding, "One Pillar Crumbling, the Others Too Short."

19. "Rentenversicherungsbericht/Alterssicherungsbericht," Federal Ministry of Labour and Social Affairs.

20. OECD, *Pensions at a Glance 2023*, table 9.1.

21. Werding, "One Pillar Crumbling, the Others Too Short."

22. Werding, "They Will Definitely Need Us, When We Are 64: Old-Age Provision in Germany," *Intereconomics* 55, no. 2 (April 2020): 88–91.

23. OECD, *Pensions at a Glance 2023*, chap. 9.

24. "Household Wealth and Finances in Germany: Results of the 2021 Household Wealth Survey," Deutsche Bundesbank, April 2023; and "2022 Survey of Consumer Finances (SCF), Internal Data, Estimates in Nominal Dollars," Federal Reserve, November 21, 2023.

25. "Residential Tenancy Law in Germany," Republikanischer Anwältinnen- und Anwälteverein e.V.

26. *Social Security at a Glance 2020*, Federal Ministry of Labour and Social Affairs, pp. 164–67.

27. Author's calculations; "Die Grundsicherung für Bedürftige," Deutsche Rentenversicherung (in German); for PPP figures refer to "Implied PPP Conversion Rate," International Monetary Fund; and for wage data, see "Average Gross Monthly Earnings," Federal Statistical Office.

28. Author's calculations; *Social Security at a Glance 2020*, Federal Ministry of Labour and Social Affairs, pp. 164–67; "Standard Requirement Levels According to § 28 in Euros," Federal Ministry of Justice and Consumer Protection (in German); and "Average Gross Monthly Earnings," Federal Statistical Office.

29. "Warum das Bürgergeld gestiegen ist," Federal Government, January 25 (in German).

30. *Social Security at a Glance 2020*, Federal Ministry of Labour and Social Affairs, pp. 164–67.

31. OECD, *Pensions at a Glance 2023*, table 3.2.

32. OECD, *Pensions at a Glance 2023*, table 3.2.

33. Author's calculations; "Sozialhilfeausgaben SGB XII im Jahr 2023 um 18 % gestiegen," Federal Statistical Office (in German); for PPP figures, refer to "PPP Conversion Factor, GDP (LCU per International $)," World Bank; and for German GDP data, see "Monthly Report—July 2024," Deutsche Bundesbank.

34. "Historical Background and Development of Social Security," "The Social Insurance Movement" section, Social Security Administration.

35. The description of the German retirement structure within this text is primarily sourced from the following document, unless otherwise specified: *Social Security at a Glance 2020*, Federal Ministry of Labour and Social Affairs.

36. "Änderung bei den Hinzuverdienstgrenzen seit 1. Januar 2023," Deutsche Rentenversicherung (in German).

37. Karolin Schaefer, "Rente: Was der Wegfall der Zuverdienstgrenze bedeutet," Frankfurter Rundschau. December 27, 2022 (in German).

38. "Exempt Amounts under the Earnings Test," Social Security Administration.

39. OECD, *Pensions at a Glance 2023*, table 8.1.

40. "Rentenniveau," Deutsche Rentenversicherung, accessed August 6, 2024. For more on how the replacement rate is calculated, see "Long-Term Outlook for the Statutory Pension Insurance Scheme," Deutsche Bundesbank monthly report, October 2019. A draft law (Rentenpaket II) proposes extending the 48 percent floor through 2039; see "Das Rentenpaket II," Bundesministerium für Arbeit und Soziales (in German).

41. OECD, *Pensions at a Glance 2023*, table 4.1.

42. OECD, *Pensions at a Glance 2023*, table 6.2.

43. Authors' calculations; for PPP figures, refer to "PPP Conversion Factor, GDP (LCU per International $)," World Bank; and for pension expenditure and German GDP data, see "Monthly Report—July 2024," Deutsche Bundesbank.

44. Authors' calculations; and for population numbers, refer to "Estimate of the 2023 Population Based on the 2022 Census," Federal Statistical Office, accessed August 7, 2024.

45. Authors' calculations; "An Update to the Budget and Economic Outlook: 2024 to 2034," Congressional Budget Office, June 18, 2024; and for population

numbers, see US Bureau of Economic Analysis, "Population [B230RC0A052N-BEA]," Federal Reserve Bank of St. Louis.

46. OECD, *Pensions at a Glance 2023*, table 8.2.

47. "Monthly Report—July 2024," Deutsche Bundesbank.

48. *Social Security at a Glance 2020*, Federal Ministry of Labour and Social Affairs, pp. 143–44.

49. "Rentenversicherungsbericht/Alterssicherungsbericht," Federal Ministry of Labour and Social Affairs.

50. "The 2024 Annual Report of the Board of Trustees of the Federal Old-Age and Survivors Insurance and Federal Disability Insurance Trust Funds," Social Security Administration, May 6, 2024.

51. Robert Holzmann, Richard Paul Hinz, and Mark Dorfman, "Pension Systems and Reform Conceptual Framework," SP Discussion Paper no. 0824, World Bank, June 2008.

52. OECD, *Pensions at a Glance 2023*, table 7.2.

53. "Living Conditions in Europe—Material Deprivation and Economic Strain," Eurostat, accessed August 8, 2024.

54. "Material and Social Deprivation Rate by Age and Sex," Eurostat, accessed August 8, 2024.

55. "The History of the Official Poverty Measure," US Census Bureau.

56. Emily A. Shrider, "Poverty in the United States: 2023," US Census Bureau, September 10, 2024.

57. Sylvester J. Schieber and Andrew G. Biggs, "Biggs and Schieber: Retirees Aren't Headed for the Poor House," *Wall Street Journal*, January 23, 2014; and Andrew G. Biggs, "America's 'Retirement Crisis': The Emperor Has No Clothes," AEI Economic Perspectives, American Enterprise Institute, July 31, 2024.

58. Adam Bee et al., "National Experimental Well-Being Statistics," Working Paper no. SEHSD-WP2025-01, January 29, 2025, US Census Bureau.

59. *Social Security at a Glance 2020*, Federal Ministry of Labour and Social Affairs.

60. "Rentenversicherungsbericht/Alterssicherungsbericht," Federal Ministry of Labour and Social Affairs.

61. "Rentenversicherungsbericht/Alterssicherungsbericht," Federal Ministry of Labour and Social Affairs.

62. "2024 Annual Report of the Board of Trustees," Social Security Administration.

63. "Rentenversicherungsbericht/Alterssicherungsbericht," Federal Ministry of Labour and Social Affairs.

64. 2 Martin Werding, "Is a Pension Reform Needed in Germany?," *CESifo Forum* 23, iss. 2, 58–62, 2022.

65. "Benefits," Deutsche Rentenversicherung.

66. Johannes Geyer and Peter Haan, "Bilanz der Grundrente: Weniger Menschen als erwartet profitieren davon," *DIW aktuell*, no. 91, Deutsches Institut für Wirtschaftsforschung (DIW), 2024 (in German).

67. For PPP figures, refer to "Purchasing Power Parities (PPP)," OECD.

68. Geyer and Haan, "Bilanz der Grundrente."

69. OECD, *Pensions at a Glance 2023*, chap. 9.
70. *Social Security at a Glance 2020*, Federal Ministry of Labour and Social Affairs.
71. "Betriebliche Altersversorgung," Deutsche Rentenversicherung, 2024 (in German); and for PPP figures, refer to "Implied PPP Conversion Rate," International Monetary Fund.
72. European Commission, *2024 Ageing Report. Economic and Budgetary Projections for the EU Member States (2022–2070)* (Luxembourg: Publications Office of the European Union, April 2024).
73. "Worker Participation in Employer-Sponsored Pensions: Data in Brief and Recent Trends," Congressional Research Service, September 18, 2024.
74. Werding, "One Pillar Crumbling, the Others Too Short."
75. "Alles zu Riester und zur Riester-Förderung," Deutsche Rentenversicherung (in German).
76. "Alles zu Riester und zur Riester-Förderung," Deutsche Rentenversicherung.
77. OECD, *Pensions at a Glance 2023*, table 9.1.
78. Werding, "They Will Definitely Need Us."
79. OECD, *Pensions at a Glance 2023*, table 9.2.
80. OECD, *Pensions at a Glance 2023*, table 4.2.
81. OECD, *Pensions at a Glance 2023*, figure 7.1.
82. "Residential Tenancy Law in Germany," Republikanischer Anwältinnen- und Anwälteverein e.V.
83. The information in this paragraph is sourced from "Household Wealth and Finances in Germany," Deutsche Bundesbank.
84. The information in this paragraph is sourced from "2022 Survey of Consumer Finances," Federal Reserve.
85. "Summary of P.L. 98-21," Social Security Administration; "1983 Annual Report—Federal Old-Age and Survivors Insurance and Disability Insurance Trust Fund," Social Security Administration; and "1984 Annual Report of the Board of Trustees," Social Security Administration.
86. Werding, "One Pillar Crumbling, the Others Too Short."
87. Werding, "Is a Pension Reform Needed in Germany?"
88. Werding, "One Pillar Crumbling, the Others Too Short."
89. Werding, "One Pillar Crumbling, the Others Too Short."

Chapter 11

1. "Material and Social Deprivation Rate by Age and Sex," Eurostat.
2. Authors' calculations; "Tidsserier, statens budget m.m. 2023," Swedish National Financial Management Authority; and for GDP numbers, refer to "National Accounts, Quarterly and Annual Estimates," Statistics Sweden.
3. Johan Norberg, "How Sweden Saved Social Security," *Wall Street Journal*, February 22, 2023.
4. European Commission, *2024 Ageing Report: Economic and Budgetary Projections for the EU Member States (2022–2070)* (Luxembourg: Publications Office of the European Union, April 2024).

5. "The 2024 Annual Report of the Board of Trustees of the Federal Old-Age and Survivors Insurance and Federal Disability Insurance Trust Funds," Social Security Administration, May 6, 2024.
6. Norberg, "How Sweden Saved Social Security."
7. European Commission, *2024 Ageing Report*.
8. *The 2024 Pension Adequacy Report: Current and Future Income Adequacy in Old Age in the EU* (Luxembourg, Social Protection Committee [SPC] and the European Commission [DG EMPL], the European Union, 2024).
9. OECD, *Pensions at a Glance 2023: OECD and G20 Indicators*, table 3.2 (Paris: OECD Publishing, December 13, 2023).
10. Authors' calculations; for coverage statistics presented in this section, see "Statistikdatabas, Pensionsstatistik," Pensionsmyndigheten (in Swedish); and for senior population numbers, see "Sweden's Population in Summary 1960–2024," Statistics Sweden.
11. "Material and Social Deprivation Rate by Age and Sex," Eurostat.
12. Authors' calculations; "Tidsserier, statens budget m.m. 2023," Swedish National Financial Management Authority; and for GDP numbers, refer to "National Accounts, Quarterly and Annual Estimates," Statistics Sweden.
13. OECD, *Pensions at a Glance*, "Retirement Age Reforms."
14. Malin Björkmo, "Fyra dyra fonder?," Expert Group for Studies in Public Finance, 2009 (in Swedish).
15. Norberg, "How Sweden Saved Social Security."
16. OECD, *Pensions at a Glance 2023*, table 4.2.
17. Authors' calculations; *Orange rapport 2023: Pensionssystemets årsredovisning*, Pensionsmyndigheten, 2023 (in Swedish); "Tidsserier, statens budget m.m. 2023," Swedish National Financial Management Authority; and *An Update to the Budget and Economic Outlook: 2024 to 2034* (Washington: Congressional Budget Office, June 18, 2024).
18. European Commission, *2024 Ageing Report*.
19. OECD, *Pensions at a Glance 2023*, table 8.1.
20. *2024 Pension Adequacy Report*, Social Protection Committee and the European Commission, the European Union.
21. "Boende i Sverige," Statistikmyndigheten (in Swedish).
22. "Garantipension," Pensionsmyndigheten, last updated January 9, 2025 (in Swedish); and unless otherwise specified, the following source is used for purchasing power parity (PPP) conversion throughout the chapter: "Implied PPP Conversion Rate," International Monetary Fund (IMF), accessed August 14, 2024.
23. OECD, *Pensions at a Glance 2023*, table 3.2; and European Commission, *2024 Ageing Report*.
24. Authors' calculations; for coverage statistics presented in this section, see "Statistikdatabas, Pensionsstatistik," Pensionsmyndigheten (in Swedish); and for senior population numbers, refer to "Sweden's Population in Summary 1960–2024," Statistics Sweden.
25. "Fakta om bostadstillägg," Pensionsmyndigheten (in Swedish).
26. *2024 Pension Adequacy Report*, Social Protection Committee and the European Commission, European Union.

27. OECD, *Pensions at a Glance 2023*, table 7.2.

28. "Living Conditions in Europe—Material Deprivation and Economic Strain," Eurostat.

29. "Material and Social Deprivation Rate by Age and Sex," Eurostat.

30. "The History of the Official Poverty Measure," United States Census Bureau, January 2014.

31. Sylvester J. Schieber and Andrew G. Biggs, "Biggs and Schieber: Retirees Aren't Headed for the Poor House," *Wall Street Journal*, January 23, 2014; and Andrew G. Biggs, "America's 'Retirement Crisis': The Emperor Has No Clothes," AEI Economic Perspectives, American Enterprise Institute, July 31, 2024.

32. Adam Bee et al., "National Experimental Well-Being Statistics," Working Paper no. SEHSD-WP2025-01, January 29, 2025, US Census Bureau.

33. Emily A. Shrider, "Poverty in the United States: 2023," US Census Bureau, September 10, 2024.

34. Authors' calculations; "Tidsserier, statens budget m.m. 2023," Swedish National Financial Management Authority (in Swedish); and for GDP numbers, refer to "National Accounts, Quarterly and Annual Estimates," Statistics Sweden.

35. OECD, *Pensions at a Glance 2023*, table 6.2.

36. OECD, *Pensions at a Glance 2023*, "Retirement Age Reforms."

37. European Commission, *2024 Ageing Report*.

38. OECD, *Pensions at a Glance 2023*, chap. 1.

39. Elizabeth Arias, Jiaquan Xu, and Kenneth Kochanek, "United States Life Tables, 2021," *National Vital Statistics Reports* 72, no. 12, November 7, 2023; and Kenneth D. Kochanek et al., "Mortality in the United States, 2022," NCHS Data Brief no. 492, March 2024; Martha A. McSteen, "Fifty Years of Social Security," Social Security Administration.

40. *Options for Reducing the Deficit: 2025 to 2034*, Congressional Budget Office, December 12, 2024.

41. OECD, *Pensions at a Glance 2023*, chap. 3, p. 134.

42. European Commission, *2024 Ageing Report*.

43. This example is a modified version of the example provided by the Swedish Pension Agency. See the original example here: *How the National Pension System Works* (Pensionsmyndigheten, 2020).

44. Authors' calculations; and OECD, *Pensions at a Glance 2023*, tables 7.5 and 8.1.

45. European Commission, *2024 Ageing Report*.

46. European Commission, *2024 Ageing Report*.

47. *Orange rapport 2023*, Pensionsmyndigheten (in Swedish).

48. Romina Boccia, "The Social Security Trust Fund Myth," Cato Institute Policy Analysis No. 984, November 13, 2024.

49. European Commission, *2024 Ageing Report*.

50. OECD, *Pensions at a Glance 2023*.

51. Malin Björkmo, "Fyra dyra fonder?," Expert Group for Studies in Public Finance, 2009 (in Swedish).

52. Rachel Fixsen, "Sweden Slims Pensions Buffer System to Three AP Funds from Five," IPE, January 31, 2025.

53. *Orange rapport 2023*, Pensionsmyndigheten (in Swedish).

54. Authors' calculations; *Orange rapport 2023*, Pensionsmyndigheten (in Swedish); and for GDP numbers, refer to "National Accounts, Quarterly and Annual Estimates," Statistics Sweden.

55. "2024 Annual Report of the Board of Trustees," Social Security Administration.

56. Andrew G. Biggs, "Bill Cassidy's Well-Intentioned but Misguided Social Security Reform," *National Review*, May 22, 2023.

57. Authors' calculations; *Orange rapport 2023*, Pensionsmyndigheten (in Swedish); and for GDP numbers, refer to "National Accounts, Quarterly and Annual Estimates," Statistics Sweden.

58. Kristoffer Lundberg, "Retirement: Lessons from the Swedish Reforms," Fondation pour l'innovation politique, April 2020.

59. Norberg, "How Sweden Saved Social Security."

60. European Commission, *2024 Ageing Report*; and *2024 Pension Adequacy Report*, Social Protection Committee and the European Commission, European Union.

61. "Premiepension—en del av den allmänna pensionen," Pensionsmyndigheten (in Swedish); and *2024 Pension Adequacy Report*, Social Protection Committee and the European Commission, the European Union.

62. Ann-Christine Meyerhöffer and Stefan Oscarson, *Fondförsäkring eller traditionellförsäkring?—Undersökning om valet av försäkringsform I premiepensionen*, Pensionsmyndigheten, May 24, 2024 (in Swedish).

63. European Commission, *2024 Ageing Report*.

64. OECD, *Pensions at a Glance 2023*, table 4.2.

65. Authors' calculations; *Orange rapport 2023*, Pensionsmyndigheten (in Swedish); "Tidsserier, statens budget m.m. 2023," Swedish National Financial Management Authority (in Swedish); and for population numbers, refer to "Sweden's Population in Summary 1960-2024," Statistics Sweden.

66. Authors' calculations; *Update to the Budget and Economic Outlook*, Congressional Budget Office; and for population numbers, see US Bureau of Economic Analysis, "Population [B230RC0A052NBEA]," Federal Reserve Bank of St. Louis, accessed July 25, 2024.

67. OECD, *Pensions at a Glance 2023*, table 8.2.

68. European Commission, *2024 Ageing Report*.

69. *2024 Pension Adequacy Report*, Social Protection Committee and the European Commission, the European Union.

70. European Commission, *2024 Ageing Report*.

71. Lundberg, "Retirement: Lessons from the Swedish Reforms."

72. "Räkna ut din tjänstepension," Pensionsmyndigheten (in Swedish).

73. European Commission, *2024 Ageing Report*.

74. "Det här är tjänstepension," Pensionsmyndigheten (in Swedish).

75. OECD, *Pensions at a Glance 2023*, table 4.2.

76. Authors' calculations; "Statistikdatabas, Pensionsstatistik," Pensionsmyndigheten (in Swedish); and for population numbers, refer to "Sweden's Population in Summary 1960-2024," Statistics Sweden.

77. Authors' calculations; *Update to the Budget and Economic Outlook*, Congressional Budget Office; and for population numbers, see US Bureau of Economic Analysis, "Population [B230RC0A052NBEA]."
78. OECD, *Pensions at a Glance 2023*, table 4.2.
79. European Commission, *2024 Ageing Report*.
80. European Commission, *2024 Ageing Report*; and "Price Base Amount for 2024," Statistics Sweden (in Swedish).
81. *2024 Pension Adequacy Report*, Social Protection Committee and the European Commission, the European Union.
82. OECD, *Pensions at a Glance 2023*, figure 7.1.
83. European Commission, *2024 Ageing Report*.
84. *En ny statistik över hushållens tillgångar och skulder* (Stockholm: Statens Offentliga Utredningar [SOU], 2022) (in Swedish).
85. "Boende i Sverige," Statistikmyndigheten (in Swedish).
86. "2022 Survey of Consumer Finances (SCF), Internal Data, Estimates in Nominal Dollars," Federal Reserve, November 21, 2023.
87. OECD, *Pensions at a Glance 2023*, figure 7.1.
88. European Commission, *2024 Ageing Report*.
89. Norberg, "How Sweden Saved Social Security."
90. *The Swedish Pension Agreement and Pension Reform* (Swedish Ministry of Health and Social Affairs).
91. Lundberg, "Retirement: Lessons from the Swedish Reforms."
92. *The Swedish Pension Agreement*, Swedish Ministry of Health and Social Affairs.
93. Lundberg, "Retirement: Lessons from the Swedish Reforms."
94. Norberg, "How Sweden Saved Social Security."
95. European Commission, *2024 Ageing Report*.
96. Norberg, "How Sweden Saved Social Security."

Chapter 13

1. Stephen C. Goss to Bernie Sanders, February 13, 2023, Office of the Chief Actuary, Social Security Administration, https://www.ssa.gov/oact/solvency/BSanders_20230213.pdf.

ABOUT THE AUTHORS

Romina Boccia is the director of budget and entitlement policy at the Cato Institute, where she focuses on stabilizing the growth of the US public debt, restraining federal government spending, and reforming the major entitlement programs: Social Security and Medicare. She has advised presidents and members of Congress on federal budget and Social Security policy and legislation for more than a decade. She testified before the Social Security Advisory Board and was a featured expert on AARP's 2016 Social Security Solutions Tour. She is an elected member of the US National Academy of Social Insurance. She writes a Substack called the Debt Dispatch. Before joining Cato, Boccia was the inaugural director of the Grover M. Hermann Center for the Federal Budget at the Heritage Foundation, where she led the production of the 2017 executive flagship budget proposal, Blueprint for Balance.

Ivane Nachkebia is a research consultant for budget and entitlement policy at the Cato Institute, with a primary focus on Social Security. Originally from the Republic of Georgia, Nachkebia completed his bachelor's degree in economics at the International School of Economics in Tbilisi. He is currently pursuing a master's degree in digital economy at the Vienna University of Economics and Business.

ABOUT THE CATO INSTITUTE

Founded in 1977, the Cato Institute is a public policy research foundation dedicated to broadening the parameters of policy debate to allow consideration of more options that are consistent with the principles of limited government, individual liberty, and peace. To that end, the Institute strives to achieve greater involvement of the intelligent, concerned lay public in questions of policy and the proper role of government.

The Institute is named for *Cato's Letters*, libertarian pamphlets that were widely read in the American Colonies in the early 18th century and played a major role in laying the philosophical foundation for the American Revolution.

Despite the achievement of the nation's Founders, today virtually no aspect of life is free from government encroachment. A pervasive intolerance for individual rights is shown by government's arbitrary intrusions into private economic transactions and its disregard for civil liberties. And while freedom around the globe has notably increased in the past several decades, many countries have moved in the opposite direction, and most governments still do not respect or safeguard the wide range of civil and economic liberties.

To address those issues, the Cato Institute undertakes an extensive publications program on the complete spectrum of policy issues. Books, monographs, and shorter studies are commissioned to examine the federal budget, Social Security, regulation, military spending, international trade, and myriad other issues.

In order to maintain its independence, the Cato Institute accepts no government funding. Contributions are received from foundations, corporations, and individuals, and other revenue is generated from the sale of publications. The Institute is a nonprofit, tax-exempt, educational foundation under Section 501(c)3 of the Internal Revenue Code.